Deleuze and Political Ac

Deleuze Studies Volume 4: 2010 (supplement)

Edited by Marcelo Svirsky

Edinburgh University Press

© Edinburgh University Press Ltd, 2010

Edinburgh University Press Ltd
22 George Square, Edinburgh EH8 9LF

Typeset in Sabon
by SR Nova Pvt Ltd, Bangalore, India, and
printed and bound in Great Britain by Page Bros, Norwich.

A CIP record for this book is available from the British Library

ISBN 978 0 7486 4052 2

The right of the contributors
to be identified as authors of this work
has been asserted in accordance with
the Copyright, Designs and Patents Act 1988.

Contents

Editor's Acknowledgments

I would like to express my profound gratitude to Ian Buchanan, first for encouraging and helping me to organise the international conference 'Deleuze and Activism', held at Cardiff University in November 2009, and for suggesting that I edit this Special Issue of *Deleuze Studies*, but also, and mainly, for always giving me reasons to believe in my work.

My appreciation also goes to all the anonymous reviewers of the articles published here – they definitely helped to improve each one of them. Finally I would like to thank the contributors themselves, for their patience and collaboration.

Deleuze Studies Volume 4: 2010 supplement: v
DOI: 10.3366/E175022411000108X
© Edinburgh University Press
www.eupjournals.com/dls

Introduction: Beyond the Royal Science of Politics

Marcelo Svirsky   Cardiff University

Anxieties over democracy in the post-war era, reinvigorated by philosophical nostalgia for the modern icons of civic engagement – including Jean-Jacques Rousseau, John Stuart Mill and James Madison – resulted in a flourishing industry of academic writing on political participation, especially in the English-speaking world and particularly in the field of political science. Almond and Verba's legendary *The Civic Culture* (1963) and Carole Pateman's *Participation and Democratic Theory* (1970), together with Robert Dahl's and Seymor Martin Lipset's works on democratic theory, are just a few of the most prominent names and different works that have become the pillars of a very influential clergy, which has helped circumscribe contemporary understandings of politics. The paradigm introduced by such thinkers (and supported more effervescently by republicans than by liberals) did not seek to replace or challenge the privileged political form that is 'representative democracy'; rather, it assumed that 'mass participation is the lifeblood of representative democracy' (Norris 2002: 5), and identified elitism as that which impedes the reinvigoration of democratic regimes (see Schumpeter 1950).

As a sequel to this colossal effort, researchers on political activism have anchored the concept firmly within official politics through the invention of a statistical science of voting fluctuations, participation in party politics and other formal indicators; only lately has this school of thought devoted any critical attention to the evident limits and barriers of formal political participation (see Norris 2002). Other trends in political theory have derided the efficacy of activism by forcing the concept into a reductive alignment with merely habitual social habits, thereby making the future of political life dependent on banalities such

Deleuze Studies Volume 4: 2010 supplement: 1–6
DOI: 10.3366/E1750224110001091
© Edinburgh University Press
www.eupjournals.com/dls

as 'bowling together' (cf. Putnam 2000). By default, such developments in political theory tend to categorise the informal protests of the citizenry as the most radical of activist practices. Ultimately, the tides and modes of civic engagement (or disengagement) are seen as symptomatic of either the flourishing or the declining state of an existent 'democratic spirit', which is invariably celebrated *per se*, leaving no room for significant criticism of the nature of the 'democracy' supposedly animating that 'spirit'.

As Deleuze and Guattari have explained, this characteristic 'royal' science of politics 'continually appropriates the contents of vague or nomad science' – those forms of political investigation looking 'to understand both the repression it encounters and the interaction ' "containing" it' (Deleuze and Guattari 1987: 367–8). One major task of new activist war machines is, then, to escape entrapment within the black hole of the majoritarian discourse on civil society, captured and defined by pervasive notions of 'representative participation'. Although the 'NGOisation' of the public sphere since the 1980s (see Yacobi 2007), together with other forms of political proliferation, have broadened the visible political field, the potential of non-institutional forms of action has been weakened ideologically by a whole state apparatus comprised of research centres and budgets, instrumental teaching, and a parliamentary politics that has incorporated the discourse of civil society – all of which have effected a *sectorisation* of society and political life. The epistemological aspirations of the three 'ideal circles' (Deleuze and Guattari 1987: 367) of the state, economy and civil society are commonly used to categorise political eruptions as forms of participation in the official, representative state politics. It is in this light that we must interpret the failure of academia to come to terms with the division of labour lately being imposed by the transversal relations between intellectual investigation and political situatedness embodied in *militant research*. As Deleuze and Guattari suggest, 'we know of the problems States have always had with journey-men's associations or *compagnonnages*, the nomadic or itinerant bodies . . .' (368).

It is clear that a Jamesonian 'strategy of containment' is at work in the narrative tradition of royal political science. It is in the notion of 'representative participation' that a function of formal unity or a strategy of containment has been founded, which, as Jameson puts it, 'allows what can be thought to seem internally coherent in its own terms, while repressing the unthinkable . . . which lies beyond its boundaries' (Jameson 1981: 38). By tying official politics together with every form of political participation it can ensnare, what royal political science does is 'radically impoverish... the data of one narrative line' – namely, that of the new activisms – 'by their rewriting according to the paradigm of another narrative...' – namely, that of representative participatory politics (Jameson 1981: 22). The subversive power of political *potentia* is thus contained by this reductive strategy; civil society becomes the main territory of this imprisonment, assisted by a false equation of official participation with challenging politics.

Rather than problematising the political, this royal understanding of activism uses its 'metric power' to axiomatise politics, while simultaneously repressing activist experiences that refuse simply to align with 'the given' of formal politics. An example of this can be seen in the hostility of western states towards organisations such as 'Wikileaks' or the 'Animal rights movement', each of which are immersed in creative acts of citizenship that actualise *ruptures*. Such new scenes and acts are constantly at risk of being appropriated by this royal science of politics, which imposes upon them a model that channels civic participation according to established rules and concepts. Activisms that seek *only* to guarantee the workings of representative democracy are essentially *slave activisms*; they dwell in safety and their impact and potential is expected to be absorbed without drawing the system into new structures of resonance.

The assumption that 'mass participation is the lifeblood of representative democracy' not only imposes a particular model of the political, it also reinforces a pejorative way to conceive activism. By positing representative democracy (or any other regime) as the reified model of political process, theory necessarily idealises certain forms of involvement over others. For example, classical participatory theory is often blind to the creative significance of the activist energies being unfolded in such events as critical teaching in schools, revolutionary philosophical writing, the deconstructive effect of a critical assemblage that confronts patriarchal power, or of civic homosexuality which disrupts heterosexism. In fact, the assumptions underlying 'representative' participation are troublesome for at least two reasons. Firstly, participation in the formal political process of 'representative democracy' does not in itself necessarily implicate a critical attitude or action, seeking a less repressive and more creative life. To evidence this, it is enough to keep in mind some fearful recent examples of mass political support for 'representative' state violence, as occurred last May when thousands of Israelis marched in Tel Aviv and the streets of Jerusalem to back the killing by the Israeli Defence Forces of nine activists from the Turkish Foundation for Human Rights and

Freedoms and Humanitarian Relief, as they boarded the *Mavi Marmara* ship sailing to Gaza as part of a humanitarian flotilla. Similarly, we might remain mindful of other, no less electrifying, cases of popular support for wars and genocides in South America, Asia, Eastern Europe and Africa, or of events such as the Holocaust. In these instances, mass participation more accurately falls within the Reichian analysis of a popular 'desire for fascism' – which lies worlds away from a participatory liberalism that idealises the commitment of the public to activist citizenship (see Isin 2009) and to the tolerant 'good life' that western democracy claims to represent. Secondly, passivity is not necessarily a sign of political anaemia, but may be a cultural expression that requires local explanation. Here, research at times confuses the visible with the political: absence of visible mass participation might be a sign of unconscious and pre-conscious compliance with ongoing forms of oppression, and can impact more energetically on the perpetuation of a regime than can tangible acts of the body – these modes of active abandonment produce the reign of daily microfascisms.

After Deleuze and Guattari, political activism may be approached in a fundamentally different way: without an image, without a form. As Deleuze and Guattari make clear, the interaction between royal and nomad science produces a 'constantly shifting borderline', meaning that there is always some element that escapes containment by the 'iron collars' of representation (Deleuze and Guattari 1987: 367; see also Deleuze 1994). This occurs when the plane of consistency is passionately thrown against the plane of organisation, when a nomad element inserts itself in political struggles in which, for instance, the boundaries of citizenship are challenged and reopened (as occurred in the struggle associated with the *sans-papiers* movement, see Isin 2009), or barriers of ethnic segregation are challenged by new forms of interculturalism (as occurs with bilingual forms of education). It is through these 'smallest deviations' that smooth types of political activity dwell within the striated forms of state politics (Deleuze and Guattari 1987: 371). Deleuze's and Deleuze and Guattari's political philosophies have created some of the conceptual tools which may be put to innovative use in activism that seeks to break with repressive traditions. Their alien relation to the standards set by the royal science of politics (see Patton 2000) – an alienation laid out in the philosophical resources they draw on, in the issues and concepts that characterise their work and, principally, in the incessant movement of their thought – points towards a richer philosophical weaponry with which to confront and possibly overcome political inhibitions, in both knowledge and practice.

In truth, Deleuze and Guattari do not provide ready-made blueprints for revolution – neither recipes nor rules – but they do certainly describe a minor art of thinking/doing, one which allows activists to target stable forms of life wherever they impede creation, wherever they are mystified by representation. Activists couldn't hope for more powerful tools to assist their diverse struggles to overcome oppression, where this is a phenomenon understood comprehensively as a reactive style of power manifested in techniques of conceptual and material capture. Indeed, the two volumes of *Capitalism and Schizophrenia* are slowly but surely beginning to share some of the glory that volume one of Karl Marx's *Capital* occupied for more than a century; henceforth, we are faced with the urgency of thinking anew the nature of social struggles, and how to engage them successfully.

Exchanging conservative for 'radical' ideologies, proving the guilt of the majoritarian group, celebrating recognition of identity, seeking political representation, instigating litigation and arousing strikes, marches and protests – all these conventionally privileged resources for transformative action are now seen as conforming to a certain model of activism. As Buchanan warns, 'from conformity it is but a short step to complicity' (Buchanan 2000: 75), because activism that treads established paths of dissent is always in danger of being besieged and contained by the organism of the State. A new horizon stretches out: by engaging more forcefully with the celerity of the 'itinerant' activist, a coextensive plane between the conceptual apparatus of politics and the more radical activist practices of rupture and creation may be constructed beyond the royal science of politics, while remaining prudent with respect to the 'gravitational field' of representative participation (Deleuze and Guattari 1987: 372). This is where a new science of activism is to be found:

> Whenever ambulant procedure and process are returned to their own model, the points regain their position as singularities that exclude all biunivocal relations, the flow regains its curvilinear and vertical motion that excludes any parallelism between vectors, and smooth space reconquers the properties of contact that prevent it from remaining homogeneous and striated. (Deleuze and Guattari 1987: 373)

The task undertaken by the contributors to this special issue is to launch a preliminary experimentation with the conceptual tools appropriate for a new science of activism, each exploring different dimensions of the 'Deleuzian horizon' outlined here. The issue is the result of a conference held at the Centre for Critical and Cultural Theory, Cardiff University, in November 2009. Here the participants gathered to discuss the idea that Deleuze offers activism a new kind of freedom from capture by the state-forms of representative politics; indeed, the speakers described how Deleuzian frameworks often engage with the smooth spaces that radical activism simultaneously practice and seek to create.

References

Almond, Gabriel and Sidney Verba (1963) *The Civic Culture: Political Attitudes and Democracy in Five Nations*, Princeton, NJ: Princeton University Press.

Buchanan, Ian (2000) *Deleuzism – A Metacommentary*, Edinburgh: Edinburgh University Press.

Deleuze, Gilles (1994) *Difference and Repetition*, trans. Paul Patton, New York: Columbia University Press.

Deleuze, Gilles and Félix Guattari (1987) *A Thousand Plateaus – Capitalism and Schizophrenia*, trans. Brian Massumi, Minneapolis: University of Minnesota Press.

Isin, Engin (2009) 'Citizenship in Flux: the Figure of the Activist Citizen', *Subjectivity*, 29, pp. 367–88.

Jameson, Fredric (1981) *The Political Unconscious: Narrative as a Social Symbolic Act*, London: Routledge.

Norris, Pipa (2002) *Democratic Phoenix: Reinventing Political Activism*, Cambridge: Cambridge University Press.

Pateman, Carol (1970) *Participation and Democratic Theory*, Cambridge: Cambridge University Press.

Patton, Paul (2000) *Deleuze and the Political*, London: Routledge.

Putnam, Robert (2000) *Bowling Alone: The Collapse and Revival of American Community*, New York: Simon & Schuster.

Schumpeter, Joseph (1950) *Capitalism, Socialism, and Democracy*, New York: Harper and Row.

Yacobi, Haim (2007) 'The NGOization of Space: Dilemmas of Social Change, Planning Policy and the Israeli Public Sphere', *Environment and Planning D*, 25:4, pp. 745–58.

Desire, Apathy and Activism

Simone Bignall   University of New South Wales

Abstract

This paper explores the themes of apathy and activism by contrasting the conventionally negative concept of motivational desire-lack with Deleuze and Guattari's positive concept of 'desiring-production'. I suggest that apathy and activism are both problematically tied to the same motivational force: the conventional negativity of desire, which results in a 'split subject' always already 'undone' by difference. The philosophy of positive desiring-production provides alternative concepts of motivation and selfhood, not characterised by generative lack or alienation. On the contrary, this alternative ontology describes an identity that is not primarily 'undone' by difference, but 'done' or 'made' through the complex and piecemeal relations it forges with various aspects of the bodies it encounters. Understood as a complex multiplicity, the self or community accordingly has a primary, immediate and active interest in the quality of its multifaceted relations with others. Finally, I argue that some contemporary forms of activism can be read as practices aimed at creating and safeguarding the social conditions that foster the complex relational composition of selves and communities.

Keywords: activism, apathy, identity, Deleuze, desire, ontology, negativity, politics

While global society flounders in economic crisis and political violence, middle-class white westerners comprise a political strata apparently characterised by 'motivational deficit' (Critchley 2007; Bernstein 2001). The rituals of liberal democracy produce a politics that palls with the immensity and complexity of global injustices and the tasks of redress

Deleuze Studies Volume 4: 2010 supplement: 7–27
DOI: 10.3366/E1750224110001108
© Edinburgh University Press
www.eupjournals.com/dls

that are called for. In modern thought, apathy is often associated with negativity – it signifies incapacity, immobility, absence of direction, or existential emptiness. In fact, the prevalence and constancy of apathy as an indicator of dissatisfaction in everyday life may correlate, at least in part, to the emphasis modern western philosophy places upon critical negativity and negation. I begin by arguing that this persistent emphasis on negativity is a residual effect of the negativity of desire which is conventionally understood to be the grounding condition of action. However, while this generative negativity is celebrated within modernism and many strains of 'postmodernism', neither style of thinking is capable of conceptualising a mode of transformative action that is not problematically fettered to the negativity that such action paradoxically aims to oppose. I then suggest that Deleuze and Guattari's absolutely positive concept of desire – and their corresponding ontology of the complex relational self – offers an alternative way of understanding political motivation, potentially enabling a path of flight from the pervasive problem of political disengagement.

I. Apathy

The amorphous phenomena of 'boredom' and 'apathy' define a characteristic modern negativity (Spacks 1995; Svendsen 2005). Modernism 'posits an isolated subject existing in a secularised, fragmented world marked by lost or precarious traditions: a paradigmatic situation for boredom' (Spacks 1995: 219). While alienation is associated with a sense of subjective disconnection and paralysis, modern apathy extends across the entire social field as an effect of 'profound' boredom that has no focus and no relief (Heidegger 1993: 99). Profound apathy is then socially indicated by a systemic loss of interest and attachment, a turning away and closing off from others, and an associated failure of responsibility and care in comportment towards others (Hammer 2004; Emad 1985). One ceases to be attentive to others when afflicted by apathy: 'boredom, unlike engagement, implies no respect for the identity of the other' (Spacks 1995: 231). The typically modern (and western) stance of foppish or cultivated disinterest in others may also serve a related socio-cultural function; in *contriving* to be bored, the subject rejects the possibility of intimacy and so 'repudiates attempts to establish a mode of equality' (199).

One's relation to oneself is also called into question by the experience of boredom. Conceptualised as a project of development, the modern self is constituted through reflexive acts of desire and by the recognition these acts solicit. The process of self-determination is effectively halted by boredom, since 'almost always it suggests disruptions of desire: the inability to desire or to have desire fulfilled' (Spacks 1995: x). For the self defined by desire, such disruption corresponds with a loss of motivation, direction and satisfaction. The negativity of profound boredom collapses the self into an existential crisis: one suffers a hiatus in one's project of self-directed desire and the material transformations associated with one's project.

However, negativity paradoxically plays a privileged role in modern critical philosophy and underlies modern conceptions of agency (see Coole 2000). Boredom is not simply disabling and disruptive, but is also understood as the putative ground for the emergence of reflexive selfhood: 'boredom reveals beings as a whole' (Heidegger 1993: 99). Boredom reveals an ontological void, an open emptiness which is a primary and defining negativity, but which is also constitutive and transformative because it defines one's fundamental attitude of being-in-the-world as unfinished and striving. In turn, this striving plays a causal role in projects of self-directed becoming. In this capacity, 'boredom aids the fulfilment of desire' (Spacks 1995: 242). On the one hand, then, boredom is an existential negativity that indicates an absence of desire or interest, a state of alienation and loss of affective capacity, and a moment of existential crisis experienced as a painful suspension of the passage of developmental time. In this sense, the primary cultural function of boredom is to serve as a critical indicator of subjective or social dissatisfaction. On the other hand, boredom is a generative negativity: a causal absence felt as alienation and emptiness, which prompts an active desire for alleviation of the uncomfortable experience of negativity. Such negativity constitutes a subject-in-process and causes the production and transformation of being. In this sense, a second overarching cultural function of boredom is the provocative role it plays as a causal or motivating force of constructive processes.

This ambivalence, I suggest, sits at the heart of the problem of apathy. While action seeks to 'negate the negative', negativity is always necessarily preserved because it is not only critical but also constitutive. This is often celebrated in terms of the resilience of 'difference' as the power of critical opposition or destabilisation within dialectical and deconstructive politics, but it also means that the causal or constitutive force of negativity has no final relief (see Coole 2000). Consequently, subjectivity is condemned to oscillate anxiously between tenuous existence and the void of subjective emptiness: 'every human life is thrown back and forth between pain and boredom' (Schopenhauer, cited in Svendsen 2005: 131). Apathy takes hold because negativity is always preserved as a necessary, constitutive force of subjective life. Critical theory thus often adopts an attitude of resignation towards the phenomenon of negativity. It seems 'there is no solution to the problem of boredom' (Svendsen 2005: 133), and with this resignation comes apathy. Alternatively, critical thought seizes upon the generative aspects of ontological negativity in order to reinvigorate a sense of democratic purpose and commitment to activity. Indeed, in grappling with the material reality of global conflict, post-imperialism, strife, terror, poverty, ecological devastation and global displacement, a significant strain of contemporary political philosophy takes ontological negativity as a given point of departure. Often drawing on Lacan's concept of the divided and self-alienated subject, this kind of project is exemplified by the post-Marxist political thought of Ernesto Laclau and Chantal Mouffe, or of Slavoj Žižek.

Another recent response, also starting from a Lacanian-influenced theory of split subjectivity (the 'dividual'), is given in Simon Critchley's work on ethics and commitment. Critchley begins with the idea that philosophy responds to the generative negativity that is the failure and disappointment thrown up by the 'present time defined by the state of war' in which global humanity finds itself (Critchley 2007: 8). In this morass of contemporary conflict, we suffer a 'motivational deficit' and a 'moral deficit', each connected to the 'felt inadequacy' that evidences 'the lack at the heart of democratic life'. Existing structures of liberal democracy have apparently failed to provide an alternative to the passive nihilism of apathy and the active nihilism of terrorism; they seem unable to stop us from plunging into 'violent injustice', and cannot alleviate the threatening suspicion that social participation is meaningless (6, 8). Critchley seeks a solution to this situation by reinvigorating the possibility of subjective conscience and commitment to ethical action. To this end, he connects Badiou's notion of 'fidelity' to Levinas' notion of the subjective 'trauma' prompted by the experience of the 'unfulfillable demand' of the alienated other in relation to the self. The unfulfillable demand is the source of splitting and felt inadequacy within the subject. Critchley argues that this experience of subjective trauma in the face of the other's demand – the experience of internal splitting and division – is itself the experience of 'conscience'. The affect of internalised trauma accordingly becomes the ground for ethical and political action. On Critchley's view, accepting the ontological negativity of the divided self as a ground for political action logically tends towards a deepening of democratic engagement.

Politics cannot be confined to order and consensus when the ethical subject is 'defined by commitment or fidelity to an unfulfillable demand'. Rather, politics involves the 'manifestation of dissensus, the cultivation of an anarchic multiplicity' that involves a 'continual questioning from below of any attempt to impose order from above' (13). While I am sympathetic to the 'responsible anarchism' and to the political outcome of reinvigorated democracy that Critchley arrives at, I worry that taking a starting point of given negativity – disappointment, strife, conflict, lack, inadequacy – maintains a problematic connection of negativity with motivation and action.

The key problem for activism is that both desire/action and apathy/inaction are prompted by constitutive negativity. Generative negativity has the potential to motivate action and transformation, but worldly evidence suggests that the response mostly tends towards apathy and inaction. In my view, this problem arises because apathy and activism are both tied to the same motivational force: the ambivalent negativity of desire. Desire/lack produces the model of the split self as the seat of motivation; the split subject is motivated to negate the negativity that divides it, but must paradoxically preserve this negativity that not only divides, but also constitutes its being. One way out of this difficulty is suggested by the alternative process of transformation or becoming described by Deleuze. This unconventional ontological process is not driven by lack or absence felt as emptiness, dissatisfaction or loss accompanied by a consequent longing for fulfilment. Nor does it rest upon an acknowledgement that the self is always already 'undone' by alterity and is moved to conscionable action for the other as a result. On the contrary, Deleuze's alternative theory of ontology describes an *unambiguously generative* process of association caused by a purely positive and productive force of desire. Desiring-production results in a process in which the self is not 'undone', but 'done' or 'made' through difference. The following section considers this alternative understanding of ontology, in order to re-assess the critical privilege currently attracted by the modern concept of negativity.

II. Desiring-Production and the Complex Self

The conceptualisation of desire as associational or 'machinic' appears as a persistent theme throughout Deleuze's work (Deleuze 1990, 1991, 1997; Deleuze and Guattari 1983, 1987). Unlike the conventionally negative concept of desire/lack, which undermines the unified self and results in the 'split' subject, desiring-production is a positive causal force that generates a 'complex' individual. Like the 'dividual', a 'complex' self is also decentred and uncertain, but not in the same way as the Lacanian subject is. Deleuze's alternative theory of ontology emerges from his quite particular and innovative reading of Spinoza (Deleuze 1990). As part of an assemblage also combining (and at times creatively transforming) aspects of Bergsonian, Humean and Nietzschean thought, Deleuze's Spinozism enables a model of selfhood that constantly flees or escapes its own limits by forging increasingly complex and active relations with other bodies.

According to Deleuze and Guattari, individuals are complex forms of order that develop consistency over time. Bodies are 'assemblages' that arise via the causal force of desire, which brings about the process of association and connection joining constituting elements (Deleuze and Guattari 1983: 1–9, 283–96). Desire results in emergent complex bodies when the elemental relations that compose the body take on enduring habits of association. The individual is thus a complex and shifting unity of 'movement and rest, speed and slowness grouping together an infinity of parts' into a set of resonating relations (Deleuze and Guattari 1987: 256). On this view, any consistent form of complex organisation constitutes an individual body, which therefore might not be material in a physical sense. Selves, communities, languages, philosophies: all are 'bodies' existing as relatively consistent forms of actual or ordered being, rather than formless virtual states of quickly morphing force relations that combine in transient unities and then fragment and dissolve.

Furthermore, as forms of enduring order comprised of semi-stable relationships between parts, bodies exist across varying levels of complexity. I am a body composed of elemental relations. Some of these are internal relations, for example between my biological cells or between the thoughts that lend order to my comprehension of things. Others are external relations I have forged with other bodies in my world, for example with colleagues, with locations, or with Deleuzian philosophy (Deleuze and Guattari 1987: 260, 254). These internal and external relations that engage me with varying kinds of consistency on various levels of order and in various circumstances of engagement collectively constitute and define me. Thus, bodies are complex forms of individuation defined by the stability or consistency of their internal and external relationships and the complex and multi-leveled affective capacities these produce.

However, while individuals are here constituted by their relations with others, these are not simply one-on-one encounters between entire entities. Revising Kleinian object-relations theory, Deleuze and

Guattari insist that an individual emerges with the forging of *part relations*, for example by incorporating 'a breast into his mouth, the sun into his asshole' (Deleuze and Guattari 1983: 4). Accordingly, individuation involves the establishment and perpetuation of the complex *part relationships* that collectively define a particular bodily entity. Our interrelationships, our desires, describe the complex 'piecemeal insertions' we make into each other's lives (Deleuze and Guattari 1987: 504). Complex bodies are thus affected *not wholly or in entirety*, but by a vast number of internal and external relations at any one time, which impact upon and transform them in partial and selective ways according to the nature of the elemental connections and disjunctions (261ff). Some of these partial affections are fairly constant forces in a life, giving individuals a certain consistency across time and environments; others are transient relations that affect bodies momentarily, though sometimes significantly enough to introduce a radical and lasting alteration to their character. Shifts in connective relations at the elemental level cause the kinds of continuity and change that simultaneously define the consistency of a character *and* evidence its transformation over time.

The rest of this paper will be devoted to expanding some rationale for argument about the superior affinity for activism of the complex relational subject. Deleuze's concept of causal desire as a generative positivity that produces and transforms complex bodies points to a way out of the difficulty described in the first half of this paper. Unlike 'split' subjectivity, the 'complex' subject is constructed through the creative force of desiring-production, which is unconnected with ontological lack, and thus neither depends upon nor multiplies negativity when it diversifies the desiring self. But it is not yet apparent how Deleuze's affirmative and relational bodily ontology and the causal positivity of desiring-production relates to the *activism* of the subject. It seems that bodies are complexly *constituted* by difference and desire – a body is a form that emerges or emanates via the force of desire, but apparently as a *passive* effect of the encounters and affective relations that define its character. In fact, for the Spinozist (and Nietzschean) Deleuze, there are active and passive forms of bodily constitution. The normative aim of a body is to increase its affective capacities by increasing its active powers of engagement and sociability (Deleuze 1988: 97–104). This idea, taken from Spinoza, is expressed in various places throughout Deleuze's own *oeuvre*. In the second chapter of *Difference and Repetition*, for example, he describes the becoming of being as a process involving an increasing activity of constitution, in terms of a kind of non-linear 'progression' through the moments described as the 'three syntheses of time' (Deleuze 1994: 70–91). This process is not so much a temporal progression of successive stages of bodily development occurring through time, as it is a description of the qualitative shifting of the nature of a body's constitution throughout its existence. A body takes shape with the initially passive or chance combination of simple elements into a complex order; but it may gradually develop a more active and directed process of self-formation, if it exercises a capacity to selectively choose the part-relations that will come to comprise the character of the emergent body.

The 'first synthesis' describes how the time of the present is constituted through the repetition of 'cases' across successive instants (Deleuze 1994: 70–2). For example, I am a materiality or a 'case' that 'repeats' from instant to instant in a form that is perceived to be consistent. In fact, with respect to my presence, the thing that is repeating from moment to moment is the perceived consistency of the internal and external relationships that define me. Of course, I am really undergoing constant transformation – as I write, millions of my cells are dying and being replaced; my brain waves are shifting in intricate patterns of excitation, and so forth – but I *imagine* myself to persist as a formal consistency in time, just as others similarly imagine me. Deleuze explains that this 'contractile power' of the imagination produces the lived experience of the actual present because the imagination fuses successive instances of actuality and the reality of bodily modifications into a continuity and consistency of perception (Deleuze 1994: 70; Deleuze and Guattari 1987: 281); but with this power of the imagination and the 'fusion of repetition' it produces comes a propensity for the contemplating mind to slip into habit (Deleuze 1994: 73–5). We habitually perceive the actual world of the present time consistently, as a repetition of the same from moment to moment.

The first synthesis of time is then a 'passive synthesis' in two respects: the actual present we inhabit from moment to moment takes form through a passive process of emergence, as chance relations between elements cohere into consistent relations to form actual bodies and worldly structures; furthermore, when imagination renders this actual present consistent we can slip into the passive acceptance of the 'givenness' of the actual world. Accordingly, Deleuze insists that the proper 'role of the imagination, or the mind which contemplates, is *to draw something new from repetition*, to draw difference from it' (Deleuze 1994: 76). With this 'drawing of difference' from the apparently repetitive relations that constitute the time of the present, the mind becomes capable of acting on and reconstituting the relations that comprise the present: 'underneath the self which acts are little selves which contemplate and which render possible both the action and the active subject' (75). The first synthesis of time is associated with the passive emergence of the actual present through the consolidation of constitutive relations; it accordingly tends towards the problem of habit. The second and third syntheses then describe the steps involved as the mind engages in 'becoming-active' and breaks with habit. With the passage from the first to the third syntheses of time, the contemplating mind develops active ways to modify the actual present. It does this by seeking virtual differences within and between actual repetitions in the present (76).

If the passive synthesis of habit constitutes the living present, the passive synthesis of memory involves the 'pure past' and this constitutes the second synthesis of time (81). The first synthesis comes 'first' since it provides the *foundation* of time; this is because we can only think of the process of time and of transformation on the basis of that which we have already become; we can only think at all in terms of the consistency the actual present allows us to experience. But the second synthesis that involves 'memory' *then* gives us awareness of the ground beneath or *prior to* this foundation. From the position of coherency described by our actual embodiment in a given circumstance, we can 'remember' the idea of this ground: we can become mindful of the virtual chaos that becomes actual order, 'the moving soil occupied by the passing present' (79). By 'memory', Deleuze does not mean simply the reminiscence of the former presents that we have previously lived, but rather the more profound memory of the virtual past which never was actually present. This is the 'unrepresentable' past in its pure form, which is the 'synthesis of all time in which the present and the future are only dimensions' (82). The memory of this 'pure past' involves the awareness that the relations comprising bodies – relations that repeat in the present to constitute actual lived experience – could always have been differently produced in different circumstances of emergence. It also reminds us that the 'cases' that repeat are comprised of differential relations between elements, and that these relations in fact constantly shift and recombine in complex associations. While the first synthesis concerns the habitual repetition of the same and the similar, the second synthesis concerns the retrospective repetition that is memory. With the second synthesis of time, the contemplating mind 'remembers' difference is the ground for the emergence of that actual consistency which repeats as the present. With this awareness of grounding difference comes the unsettling of the givenness of the actual, and the possibility of a 'third', active synthesis of time.

The third synthesis of time involves an *active* force of desire. The third, active synthesis is a rare event, which does not inevitably follow from the first two in a logical linear progression; it is the 'final' synthesis in the progression because it requires the groundwork of the first two to have already taken place. The third synthesis of time involves the thought of time as 'untimely'; it institutes a 'caesura' in the time of the present (Deleuze 1994: 88–9), with respect to the pure past that grounds it, in order to imagine a future which has not yet come to pass, and which imaginatively 'draws a difference' from the present. The mind engaged in contemplating the future-oriented third synthesis of time thinks the totality of all the actual presents (meaning not only 'the now', but also the history of the former presents that have been) – together with the virtuality of the 'pure past' which has never been (89). The third synthesis of time thereby involves thinking the actual lived present in terms of its repetitions and its habitual consistencies through time, and asking whether, if the part-relations that comprise actual complex bodies (the 'little selves' that exist 'underneath' the 'self that acts') were returned back to the virtual chaos from whence they came, they would be worthy of returning in the same form, reconstituting the same complex body (89). For example, I could ask of myself: is my habitual form partly comprised of some associations that I would be better off without (a draining colleague, an odious relative)? Are there certain elements within me (say, an interest in Deleuze scholarship) that could be differently combined with compatible others with the effect of producing a new and more complex body (say, a reading group) that joins all the participating bodies at their sites of affective involvement? Can this involvement add to my own existing level of complexity to produce a 'better' or more adequate self, one more complexly compatible or receptive to engagement with others? I might also ask which of the existing part associations I enjoy with others bring me particular satisfaction, and so might benefit from some reinforcement or development? For Deleuze, these decisions constitute the operations of the 'little selves' that comprise the complex and shifting subject:

> There is a self wherever a furtive contemplation has been established, whenever a contracting machine capable of drawing a difference from repetition functions somewhere. The self does not undergo modifications, it is itself a modification, the term designating precisely the difference drawn. (Deleuze 1994: 79)

While some bodies will only ever be the passive result of their formation through external forces, certain other bodies – those invested with the powers of imagination and reason – are capable of increasing their active powers of engagement, sociability and self-constitution. The three syntheses of time trace a 'progression' through passivity to activity: from habitual constitutions formed through passive associations, which can be transformed through the resource of 'pure memory', to result in active forces of desire. For Deleuze this active quality of desire is, properly speaking, the active force of material composition and transformation. The 'progression' is, however, non-linear because desiring-production is involved from 'the start' as the causal force that assembles complex bodies. But desire is initially passive and non-directed, and the passage towards active desire and the active synthesis of worldly being begins with the memory of virtual difference in the second synthesis of time, and emerges properly in the third (Deleuze 1994: 85, 90). Accordingly, it is possible to think that emergent complex bodies are not only produced through desire, but are also sometimes involved in *acts* of desire and directed assemblage.

But here arises a second problem: how is desiring-production invested with direction? With ontological negativity – the view that reality is produced and transformed by the compulsion to plug an original lack – the negative is the focus of desire's direction. Even while it seeks to preserve the negative (which is the condition of its existence as such), transformative desire actively opposes the negative. Desire transforms dissatisfaction into action, imperfection into ideal form, inequality into equity, alienation into unity. But what guides desire in the *absence* of negativity? *Why* might a body seek to desire in an active and self-transformative way, rather than a passive and habitual, safe and self-secure way?

A Deleuzian answer to this question is likely to be found in the Spinozist concepts of 'joy' and 'conatus', which together describe a normative principle of ethical association. Joy expresses the sensation a body experiences with the enhancement of its powers of affectivity and complexity. This is achieved when aspects of its own body are combined with those of another, to form a more complex emergent unity that is more affectively potential and expresses each individual in terms of those aspects they share in common (Deleuze 1988: 49–51). Properly conceived, joy is the basis for an ethical attitude of desire because it is *necessarily mutual* (Deleuze 1990: 281–2). Bodies sometimes experience a fortuitous, unplanned joy, but joy can be actively forged between bodies that understand they have something in common. This shared common element can form the basis of a more complex combination that can enhance them both. Joy is mutual because *both* bodies are enhanced by the emergent complexity that results from a compatible encounter. If bodies meet and only one body benefits or is enhanced, the resulting affect won't be joyful, it will be something else – pleasure or power – but not joy, which is strictly mutual.

'Conatus' refers to the desire of a body to persevere in its being, where being is defined in terms of affective capacity. Conatus entails that bodies will strive in 'an effort to augment the power of acting or to experience joyful passions' by actively organising their encounters. This allows them to form agreeable associations that enable them to mutually maximise their affective potentialities (Deleuze 1988: 101). However, bodily encounters do not involve the meeting of whole entities, but rather take place 'bit by bit' at the multifarious sites of elemental combination that bring individuals into part-relations (Deleuze 1990: 237). My striving for joy involves me in an effort to foster an adequate understanding of myself and others with respect to the ways in which we share *some* common constituting elements. This understanding provides me with the basis of an appropriate comportment towards another, assisting the better 'organising' of our encounter. Developing a *mutual* understanding of the elements we share helps us to actively and selectively build joyful combinations at suitable sites of affective compatibility and also to avoid disagreeable combinations that force incompatible associations between conflicting aspects of our personalities. Joy results from the active desire and the active forms of understanding that are necessarily involved when complex bodies engage in contrived acts of partial and selective relationship that produce preferred emergent forms (261). There will always be some elements of passive constitution involved in processes of individuation, since a body always partly results from passive encounters with other bodies it does not know and does not adequately understand. Indeed because of the complexity of material reality, one's knowledge of oneself, others and the world is never complete and transparent. However, equipped with a developing personal history of joyful encounters, an individual invested with the powers of imagination and understanding can strive to develop a more acute awareness of its constitution through multifaceted relations with others, informed by the experience of these part-connections as sympathetic or antipathetic. Such self–other awareness potentially enables a discerning and active desire to operate in the deliberate creation of new compatible associations: joining with another in ways that celebrate those aspects in which we agree while acknowledging that there are various ways in which aspects of our characters disagree and cannot happily combine. So, it is possible to think that emergent complex bodies are produced through desire, but that they are also involved in the laborious process of deliberately contriving some part-relations with other bodies. The 'bit by bit' partiality of bodily encounters transforms relational bodies in piecemeal and selective ways: some aspects of bodily constitution will always remain untouched by the engagement with the other. The promise of mutual joy potentially guides bodies in actively directing their affective relations. Active desire can discerningly develop certain elemental associations while avoiding others, thus providing scope for personal adaptation, mutual accommodation and complex relational development while simultaneously preserving the consistency or relative identity of the multiple subject.

I have argued that a complex subject is a 'producing/product identity' (Deleuze and Guattari 1983: 7), which may be simultaneously constituted by desire and actively involved in the constitution of relations through desire. The active desire of a complex subject will be guided by experience and the promise of joy. Complex bodies benefit from being actively involved in the constitutive process, even when this process transforms the self, because such activity leads to an increased affective potentiality and to finding joy with others. However, a third problem persists in Deleuze's positive ontology of desiring-production: how does a purely positive causal desire account for the existence of negativity? When desire is purely affirmative, how can one desire the refusal of the negativities that predominantly characterise the contemporary world?

One possible answer lies in Deleuze and Guattari's distinction between the different orders or qualities of desire that come to define the kinds of interactions a body is disposed to forming (Deleuze and Guattari 1983: 277–96). While everything emanates from the force of association that is desiring-production, the relations between elements comprising bodies may not develop into active organisations of desire, but alternatively may take form as reactive organisations. In *Anti-Oedipus*, this is discussed in terms of the difference between the 'subjected-group' and the 'group subject' – a distinction which recalls Sartre's critical comparison of the different styles of political organisation embodied by the 'serialised group' and the 'group-in-fusion' (Deleuze and Guattari 1983: 64, 256, 277ff; see also Sartre 1976; Guattari 1995; Genosko 2000: 123–33). The way desire is organised in a material form influences the subsequent openness of that body to forming new associations and increased levels of complexity. Bodies that welcome new part-associations with neighbouring bodies (because these are the key to self-transformation and increased joyful complexity) are defined by an active organisation of desire; such bodies enjoy a shifting consistency organised around a core set of characteristics, but are generally open to modification and brave the risks of instability. These bodies determine their constitution through immediate and open practices of relation (rather than by establishing rules concerning membership that limit and protect self consistency). They remain open to the primary creative force of desiring-production.

By contrast, a body that seeks to preserve its established identity will prevent its own transformation by resisting the formation of new associations with other bodies. This kind of body is a reactive body, which is restricted by the rules it enforces to protect its given identity. It 'wards off' the transformative force of desiring-production (Deleuze and Guattari 1983: 120). Reactive bodies are characterised by fixed constitutive relations and institutionalised habits of association. Reactive bodies resist the free flow of the primary force of desiring-production; this blockage can result in serial or systemic relations of inequality, when the associations comprising the body take on regular hierarchical forms. That is, a relation becomes unjust when it is cemented into a regular pattern of dominance and subordination; this fixture of relations introduces negativity into the positive flow of desiring-production. For Deleuze and Guattari, problems of injustice, alienation and other kinds of negativity are not already given. They are produced through concrete forms of reactive desire, for example an 'Oedipal' or 'imperial' coding which defines desire in relation to lack, longing and appropriative satisfaction (28; see also Bignall 2010). Constructed social negativities must accordingly be addressed and transformed at the level of desire. The distinction Deleuze and Guattari make between open/active and blocked/reactive organisations of desire suggest a basis for critique. Hierarchical and fixed relations that have become blocked and resistant to transformation, resulting in closed bodies that seek to preserve the givenness of their identities and their political relationships, can be criticised on the basis of the primary force of free-flowing desiring-production. The apparent givenness of entrenched orders is an illusion that is maintained by techniques of political coercion used by bodies with an interest in preserving such existing orders. Despotic bodies and the constructed negativity of economic scarcity or social alienation can each be criticised on this basis.

I have been arguing that desiring-production results in complex subjects formed through multifaceted relations with others; such subjects have an immediate interest in the quality of their social milieu and in making their relations ever more joyfully complex and actively directed. Accordingly, Deleuze's positive conceptualisation of desire offers a more appropriate ground for active subjectivity and political engagement than the conventional negativity that problematically grounds the 'split' subject. I have sketched three responses to the main criticisms of (Deleuze's) ontological positivism: that desiring-production produces subjects as passive effects of a constitutive process (the problem of agency); that desiring-production is not normatively directed towards the generation of preferred complex forms (the problem of intention or direction); and that desiring-production cannot account for the existence of negativity and does not allow for critical negation (the problem of critique). While more can be said about these problems, I hope to have gestured towards some possible bases for reply. The following section considers some of the political implications flowing from the idea that complex bodies emerge from an associative force of desiring-production.

III. Positive Politics and Activism

Deleuze's Spinozist ontology provides a conceptualisation of subjectivity entirely constituted by relations with others. This kind of reliance upon alterity is quite different from the sort of subject-constitution endured by the 'split' subject that is *'undone'* by alterity. Because they meet in *partial and selective* ways, complex individuals are not always already reduced or compromised by their one-on-one encounters with others and potentially moved to action on the basis of the conscionable trauma this provokes. Rather, complex individuals are intricate, shifting unities of the multipartite relations that immediately and qualitatively compose them. This means that the complex self has an *immediate* interest in activating and cultivating its relational being. More significantly, complex selves have a positive interest in forming increasingly complex interactions with the other – in fostering and not repudiating, managing or simply enduring their engagements with others. By developing multipart relations with multiple others, the individual develops an increasingly complex constitution that is more affectively potential and so is more joyful. This in turn implies that the 'complex' self has a direct interest in fostering a diverse and rich social milieu that ensures exposure to a wide variety of 'piecemeal encounters' with others, such that they may maximally find areas of mutual sympathy and enhanced affective capacity in their multifarious social relations.

While the activism of the 'split subject' is *mediated* by the experience of negativity which propels actions of redress, the rewarding experience of joyful mutuality means that the 'complex subject' has an *immediate* interest in the quality of associations and in making desire active. Such activism is not mediated by a negativity such as a 'disadvantage' that the activist community must simultaneously embody and struggle against; rather, it is motivated by the possibility of finding mutually beneficial relations with others, since these lead to the joy of increased complexity through community (see Bignall 2010). An important difference between the 'split' subject and the 'complex' subject thus concerns the different motivational starting points they figure. The split subject is motivated by the ontological negativity that it simultaneously embodies and struggles against, yet never finally overcomes; the complex relational subject is motivated by the principle of joyful mutuality, which corresponds with increased affective potentiality. The rewarding experience of joy means that the complex subject has an *immediate* and natural interest in desire and in making desire active. It is in the active selection of chosen affections that one forges compatible forms of relationship, increasing one's own powers of affectivity and capacity for affection and in turn finding increased possibilities for experiencing joy.

Deleuzian ontology encourages one to think of oneself as a 'complex' self, with a direct interest in activism that aims to create enabling social conditions of diversity, equity, liberty and radical democracy since these are the conditions that permit open exchange and interaction in communities of practice. As a 'complex' self, one also has an unmediated interest in activism that seeks to safeguard the wider ecological conditions that protect other forms of (non-human) diversity as part of a broad existential milieu. Part-connections with non-human others permit the privileged kinds of becoming (-animal, -molecular, and so forth) that Deleuze and Guattari associate with the radical diversification and enhanced complexity of established forms (Deleuze and Guattari 1987: 232–309). Arguably, a directed and constructive Deleuzian politics develops from a cultivated understanding that the complex social benefits of diversity and equality of opportunity act as the material scaffolding for the constitution of the complex self. A Deleuzian ethics develops from the notion that a conscientious effort must be made towards fostering the adequate understandings of self and other that could enable happy part-combinations, together with the practised commitment to refrain from imposing upon others in ways that diminish them. Both of these principles of ethical relationship are normatively guided by the promise of joy that flows from mutuality, where mutual compatibility leads bodies to join in more complex levels of community. The politically important thing about joy is therefore its function as a principle of *mutuality*. Active bodies will seek to maximise the mutual sympathy of their combinations; but this does not entail that they should strive to meet bodies they perceive as wholly similar, resulting in a politics of community based on identity and sameness. Rather, *conceptualised as complex*, bodies will strive to meet in active and joyful ways with sympathetic *elements or parts* of various other bodies they encounter. This means that quite radically different communities can combine successfully, when they seek to interact in ways in which they are compatible and do not force an unhappy combination at those sites of character where they conflict.

The activist tactics of some contemporary anarchist groups may be read as a subversive politics of joyful practice. Pink Bloc, Ya Basta!, Billionaires for Bush, and the Rebel Clown Army employ comic performance art, absurd costumes and high camp glamour in acts of non-violent disturbance against the world's macropolitical governing elite. In Simon Critchley's words, such activism works to

> exemplify the effective forging of horizontal chains of equivalence or collective will formation across diverse and otherwise conflicting protest groups... Deploying a politics of subversion, contemporary anarchist practice exercises a satirical pressure on the state in order to show that other forms of life are possible. (Critchley 2007: 124)

Like Critchley, I find this 'new language of civil disobedience' utterly compelling and often hilarious. However, 'it is the exposed, self-ridiculing and self-undermining character of these forms of protest' that Critchley 'finds most compelling', since he sees them as an exercise in political humour or 'tactical frivolity' expressing a 'powerless power that uses its position of weakness to expose those in power through forms of self-aware ridicule' (Critchley 2007: 124). By contrast, I think it is more useful to believe that something much more positive and constructive might be going on here than the critical deconstruction of the state through a conscientious political practice of ridiculous self-effacement.

In my view, the protesters *add* an extra dimension of complexity and potentiality, a virtual difference, into the mix of the protest situation. They perform difference by embodying it, clad in imaginative fancy-dress costume more 'appropriately' worn in festive situations or in fantastical other-worlds; they inject virtual difference into the actual-world space of civil and political engagement. Their bizarre presence compels the state forces to attend to the diversity they make manifestly visible, or else renders the guard ridiculous when it returns a blank stare of non-acknowledgement, and thereby implicitly critiques and destabilises the reactive body of the state that tries to ward off transformation as it denies and repels difference. This critique is, however, positive in conduct, designed not simply to destroy the self-composure of the state but also to evidence that 'other forms of life are possible' and, if possible, to seduce the state forces into a becoming-otherwise. Although their actions are underwritten by a serious political intent, the protesters engage playfully with the state forces, tickling them, affecting them with a sense of fun and hilarity, inventing new forms of 'combat' and 'weaponry': water balloons, feather dusters and wadding armour. They aim to combine opposing bodies in new assemblages of relation, not through violence and the polar separation of conflicting opposites, but more positively through the shared experience of fun, humour and festivity that potentially draws even the most disparate bodies together, allowing them to combine – not entirely, but at particular sites of affectivity – in micropolitical instances of joyful community. Beyond wry self-effacement and critical deconstruction, such acts might therefore best be thought of as positive and productive, aiming to create novel forms of engagement tactically invented through the manifestation of virtual differences in actual social relations. These potentially indicate ways of being-otherwise that broaden the habitual horizons of existing social and political conventions and encourage the becoming-minor of majoritarian forms. This positive ambition and achievement appears to me as the most significant aspect of these new forms of anarchist protest.

The principle of joyful interaction is clearly not an essentialist, stand-alone or cover-all principle for political society. *Starting* with the positive and abstract principle of mutuality does not mean that concrete institutions of common practice (such as those fostering democracy) and emergent principles of political protection (such as rights) are not needed to safeguard bodies from destruction by bodies who care less about cultivating mutual joy than they do about maximising their own pleasure or power. But *starting* with the notion of affirmative mutuality as a basis for thinking about active processes of self and social formation does avoid the problem that constitutive negativity leads to political inactivity as much as it does to activism. It also places a different *primary* emphasis on political society – away from a politics of restraint stemming from a subterranean ontological conflict, and towards a politics of complex recognition and sympathy. Here, mutuality is presented as a preferred (but not 'given') norm of political conduct and critical conflict becomes necessary when efforts to find mutual consensus fail, or when joyful practice is routinely crushed by forms of political domination. Similarly, the negativities of hostility, shame and boredom are not ontologically given, but more like errors of practice to be avoided and guarded against.

The notion that complex bodies can agree to meet 'bit by bit' in sympathetic ways and to avoid meeting in ways that diminish them suggests that Deleuzian philosophy offers some scope for a politics of consensus, supplementing the anarchic dissensus that Critchley privileges. However, consensus will never be final and complete, but is emergent, contextual and temporary, institutionally limited to recognised sites of part-commonality that enable complex bodies to form the sympathetic engagements leading to increased complexity and joy (cf. Tully 1995; Connolly 2008). Here, acknowledgement of dissent is intrinsic to the development of consensual group activity. Sympathetic disagreement involves understanding those aspects of complex bodily interaction that cannot currently combine well, and resisting the attempt to impose upon and homogenise disparate bodies under a coercive unity that betrays the differences between them. Formally identifying and recognising standard areas of disagreement is therefore also an important task of political society. Indeed, we might fruitfully rethink negative 'rights' in this way: not as eternal and inalienable principles of sovereign integrity flowing from fixed human characteristics, but as a meta-stable discourse about principles of political restraint that regulate human interaction. Such discourse would be constructed with respect to current understandings about the difference and dissensus that evidences the limits of consensual engagement. Even so, although limited and partial, finding productive consensus should be the *primary* aim of interacting orders, because (genuine) consensus is joyful and so is normatively preferred. Although this is an undeveloped aspect of his own work, Deleuze's philosophy arguably provides us with an attractive basis for rethinking rights and democratic engagement in a milieu of multicultural difference (see Patton 2010; Lefebvre 2008).

A starting point of given negativity – strife, conflict, lack – prompts the model of the divided self that has held such persuasive sway in modern critical thought and persists in many strains of postmodern thought, but which to me seems likely to compromise the quality of the social engagement that is possible. I have argued against the negative as a motivational force. A more effective starting point for activism is found by looking for examples of positive mutuality in encounters. This approach does not deny that most societies are predominantly characterised by conflict, inequality, war, trauma, alienation and exploitation. However, within this majoritarian state of violence and hostility, there also exist minor modes of positive social engagement, acts of respectful recognition, and exemplary practices of genuine care that join participating orders in the experience of mutual understanding and appreciation at particular sites of their relationship. *Starting with these moments of 'felt adequacy'* assists political communities in understanding how they can combine well in partial and selective ways; from the positive experience of mutual accord, they can start to identify new sites of combination that work well as the location of new forms of complex political union. This developing understanding is rewarded by the gradual emergence of an active understanding about 'good' forms of engagement, which may then guide the institutionalisation of preferred forms of complex national and international community. Starting with the experience of shared joy, rather than lack and division, provides selves with an unmediated interest in the quality of their relations with others, and, by extension, an interest in fostering the kinds of political community that are able to support diverse encounters, leading to forms of increased commonality and complexity. When desire is not mediated by negativity, we might even speculate that, severed from the conditions of its generation, profound apathy could cease to emerge and take hold as a systemic problem of political disenchantment.

Note

I am grateful to Marcelo Svirsky, Ian Buchanan and the participants in the 'Deleuze and Activism' conference held in Cardiff, November 2009. Paul Patton and others at UNSW also offered useful comments on an earlier version of this paper. I appreciate the thoughtful reading and criticism offered by reviewers. Thanks also to Tony Fletcher, Ben Sellar and Sam Sellar for helpful discussion of the 'three syntheses'.

References

Bernstein, Jay (2001) *Adorno: Disenchantment and Ethics*, Cambridge: Cambridge University Press.
Bignall, Simone (2010) *Postcolonial Agency: Critique and Constructivism*, Edinburgh: Edinburgh University Press.
Connolly, William (2008) *Democracy, Pluralism and Political Theory*, eds. Samuel Chambers and Terrell Carver, London: Routledge.
Coole, Diana (2000) *Negativity and Politics*, London and New York: Routledge.
Critchley, Simon (2007) *Infinitely Demanding: Ethics of Commitment, Politics of Resistance*, London and New York: Verso.
Deleuze, Gilles (1988) *Spinoza: Practical Philosophy*, trans. Robert Hurley, San Francisco: City Lights.
Deleuze, Gilles (1990) *Expressionism in Philosophy: Spinoza*, trans. Martin Joughin, New York: Zone Books.

Deleuze, Gilles (1991) *Empiricism and Subjectivity: An Essay on Hume's Theory of Human Nature*, trans. Constantin Boundas, New York: Columbia University Press.

Deleuze, Gilles (1994) *Difference and Repetition*, trans. Paul Patton, London: Athlone.

Deleuze, Gilles and Félix Guattari (1983) *Anti-Oedipus*, trans. Robert Hurley, Mark Seem and Helen Lane, Minneapolis: University of Minnesota Press.

Deleuze, Gilles and Félix Guattari (1987) *A Thousand Plateaus*, trans. Brian Massumi, Minneapolis: University of Minnesota Press.

Emad, Parvis (1985) 'Apathy as Limit and Disposition', *Heidegger Studies*, 1, pp. 63–78.

Genosko, Gary (2000) 'The Life and Work of Félix Guattari', in Félix Guattari, *The Three Ecologies*, trans. Ian Pindar and Paul Sutton, London: Athlone Press, pp. 106–61.

Guattari, Félix (1995) *Chaosmosis*, trans. Paul Bains and Julian Pefanis, Sydney: Power Publications.

Hammer, Espen (2004) 'Being Bored: Heidegger on Patience and Melancholy', *British Journal of the History of Philosophy*, 12:2, pp. 277–95.

Heidegger, Martin (1993) *Basic Writings*, ed. David Krell, New York: Harper Collins.

Lefebvre, Alexandre (2008) *The Image of Law: Deleuze, Bergson, Spinoza*, Stanford: Stanford University Press.

Patton, Paul (2010) *Deleuzian Concepts: Philosophy, Colonisation, Politics*, Stanford: Stanford University Press.

Sartre, Jean-Paul (1976) *Critique of Dialectical Reason: Volume 1*, trans. Alan Sheridan, New Jersey: Humanities Press.

Spacks, Patricia Meyer (1995) *Boredom: The Literary History of a State of Mind*, Chicago: Chicago University Press.

Svendsen, Lars (2005) *A Philosophy of Boredom*, trans. John Irons, London: Reaktion Books.

Tully, James (1995) *Strange Multiplicity: Constitutionalism in an Age of Diversity*, Cambridge: Cambridge University Press.

'To Believe In This World, As It Is': Immanence and the Quest for Political Activism

Kathrin Thiele   Utrecht University

Abstract

In *What is Philosophy?*, Deleuze and Guattari make the claim that '[i]t may be that believing in this world, in this life, becomes our most difficult task, or the task of a mode of existence still to be discovered on our plane of immanence today. This is the empiricist conversion.' What are we to make of such a calling? The paper explicates why and in what sense this statement is of exemplary significance both for an appropriate understanding of Deleuze's political thought and for a most timely conceptualisation of politics in a world so clearly defined by immanence, and nothing but immanence. I argue that Deleuze's rigorously constructive approach to the world is not beyond politics, as some recent readings have declared (e.g. those of Badiou and Hallward). Rather, we have to appreciate that in Deleuze and Guattari's demand for a 'belief in this world' the political intersects with the dimension of the ethical in such a way that our understanding of both is transformed. Only after this 'empiricist conversion' can we truly think of a Deleuzian politics that does justice to a plane of immanence 'immanent only to itself'.

Keywords: immanence, ethics, politics, transcendental empiricism, Badiou, Foucault, Spinoza

I. Deleuze and the Political

Writing on Deleuze and the question of politics does not really entail venturing into *terra incognita*. Given that so many founding thinkers

Deleuze Studies Volume 4: 2010 supplement: 28–45
DOI: 10.3366/E175022411000111X
© Edinburgh University Press
www.eupjournals.com/dls

in the Deleuzian legacy have already engaged with this theme, the indebtedness of one's argument and thought to others is inevitably unending.[1] However, looking at the many recent publications in what is called 'theory' in general, and in the vicinity of a Deleuzian philosophical horizon in particular, the question of politics stands out again and calls for renewed attention. Regarding Deleuzian scholarship in particular, the question is how things stand with Deleuze and politics now – after a first global round of philosophical reception of his philosophy. Can we really envision and concretise a Deleuzian political activism, a becoming-active so badly needed in relation to today's political state of affairs? Is there really a 'Deleuzian Politics', and if so, what does it look like?

When so many are calling for new political solutions, the question concerning the becoming-active of philosophical thought is not just one question amongst others. Rather, in times like these it becomes a question touching on the very legitimacy of a philosophical thought as such, that is, it becomes *the* criterion for measuring how and in what ways it relates to the world we are currently living in, and – most of all – to the world 'we are about to change'. So when, in 2006, Peter Hallward concluded his book on Deleuze, *Out of This World: Deleuze and the Philosophy of Creation*, with the statement that '[f]ew philosophers have been as inspiring as Deleuze. But those of us who still seek to change our world and to empower its inhabitants will need to look for our inspirations elsewhere' (Hallward 2006: 164), he was expressing only what our current situation seems so utterly determined by: change – at whatever cost.

This slightly ironical remark – which, I hope, will serve its purpose in this article – should, however, not give the impression that I disagree with Hallward's urge to relate thought and life. The times really are what they are, and Deleuzian trajectories are both needed and asked for.[2] In considering how to respond to the question as to what kind of politics the Deleuzian universe suggests, there is at least one answer that can be ruled out immediately: if what is meant by politics involves an axiomatic of categorical prescriptions, then no, there is no 'Deleuzian Politics'; there is in Deleuze's thought neither a set programme nor recourse to prescription. While this may not seem to be such big news given the well-known turn towards micropolitics in Deleuze and Guattari, one has to put emphasis on this moment of saying 'no'. Right at the beginning of the argument to be presented here it is important to stress that what is truly political in Deleuze and Guattari has less to do with what they stood up for than with how they managed to turn away from, and thus radically expose, the ways in which the question of politics itself is usually phrased.[3] In Deleuze and Guattari, politics is not discussed according to the kind of frameworks we are normally used to: neither normative or moral principles, nor a concern for justice, equality and freedom, nor any attempt to choose between or attempt to harmonise these conflicting categories, represents the frame in which they conceive of politics. Instead, in accordance with a very Spinozan *realism*,[4] the function of the term 'politics' in Deleuze and Guattari is, first of all, to stand in for the 'all there is' as such: politics – first of all – is nothing but the name of the force-relations, the milieu, and strata of everything that exists, the *always already yet never once and for all* territorialised regime,[5] the actualised plane of immanence which, however manifold in the virtual, only ever comes politically distributed. This is why Deleuze and Guattari, in *A Thousand Plateaus*, declare that 'politics precedes being', but also that, '[i]n short, everything is political, but every politics is simultaneously a *macropolitics* and a *micropolitics*' (Deleuze and Guattari 1987: 203, 213). From the affective structure of individual bodies to the structure of state-formations and beyond, everything is political in the sense that what 'there is' is a result of struggles between divergent forces, a result that shows greater or lesser stability and that can never definitively be fixed once and for all.[6]

This attitude towards politics comes very close to that of Michel Foucault, whose portrait as a political thinker likewise remains a contested one, and who also exemplifies this different approach, in particular in his lecture on 'Security, Territory, Population' at the *Collège de France* in 1978 (the famous course on biopolitics). There, Foucault explicitly presents his investigation as a philosophical inquiry, but that is an inquiry into 'the politics of truth', for, as he says, ' I do not see many other definitions of the word "philosophy" apart from this'. Since this is how he wants his undertaking to be understood, he rejects every sort of imperative discourse 'that consists in saying "love this, hate that, this is good, that is bad, be for this, beware for that"', and he most poignantly ends his enumeration with the following statement: 'So in all of this I will therefore propose only one imperative, but it will be categorical and unconditional: Never [do politics]' (Foucault 2009: 3–4).[7]

In framing my argument, however, with reference to this statement of Foucault's, am I not merely confirming Hallward's criticism of Deleuze, a criticism shared also by Alain Badiou who in his second opus magnum, *Logics of Worlds: Being and Event II*, states that 'Deleuze... came to tolerate the fact that most of his concepts were sucked up... by the *doxa* of the body, desire, affect, networks, the multitude, nomadism and enjoyment into which a whole contemporary "politics" sinks, as if into a poor man's Spinozism' (Badiou 2009: 35)? Is it not true then that Deleuze's *philosophical* gesture, rather than helping 'to change our world', simply leads 'out of this world'? Of course, this is not the conclusion to be drawn here, and what I hope to achieve in what follows will involve elaborating and unfolding the above mentioned alternative approach to political thinking in Deleuze: a becoming-active of philosophy which, in its concern for practice, requires a becoming-active in this world.

II. 'To Believe In This World, As It Is': Deleuze's Practical Philosophy of Immanence

In the face of heightened political expectations in many of today's philosophical discourses, it is important to take a step back and investigate the concepts themselves, to identify where they are located in the thought at stake, and how they function within this thought. In making use of one of Deleuze and Guattari's most central statements – the ethico-political demand for 'a belief in this world' – I would like to explicate how their thought intervenes into this world *beyond* any oppositional staging of the political concern that, as it seems right now, too many theoretical debates believe to be the only truthful one.[8] In developing such a reading of politics, it is important to operate on different levels: First, we have to adequately understand the rigorous philosophical demand for an immanence immanent only to itself that is so fundamental to Deleuze's thought. His strong commitment to immanence and nothing but immanence already turns every ontological endeavour into a practical one, and that is into an endeavour driven by an *ethico-political* impetus. It is only when we have reached this Spinozan cross-over of ontology and ethics that we can move further and inquire into more concrete *political* directions.

First Formula of Immanence: Ontology = Ethics

In *What is Philosophy?*, Deleuze and Guattari give us a first version of the statement of 'belief in this world': 'It may be that believing in this world, in this life, becomes our most difficult task, or the task of a mode of existence still to be discovered on our plane of immanence today. This is the empiricist conversion' (Deleuze and Guattari 1994: 75). If we take the demand for a 'belief in this world' as Deleuze's formula for addressing the question of immanence in its full ethico-political potential, then we have to understand that this thought is first of all announced as a 'task', even a 'most difficult task'. It is phrased as a radical shift, a turn away from what we are used to think, and think thought to be, and it is this that they call the 'empiricist conversion' – *conversio*, a turning, with a long philosophical heritage from St Augustine to the American philosopher Ralph Waldo Emerson.[9]

Earlier in *What is Philosophy?*, Deleuze and Guattari also say that 'the entire history of philosophy [can] be presented from the viewpoint of the instituting of a plane of immanence' (Deleuze and Guattari 1994: 44). Yet, they continue, even today '[i]mmanence can be said to be the burning issue of all philosophy' (45). And this is so because immanence 'takes on all the dangers that philosophy must confront, all the condemnations, persecutions, and repudiations that it undergoes' (45). This *difficult* heritage – we have to remember that Spinoza, their 'prince of philosophy' when it comes to immanence, was accused of the severest heresy – produces confusions, and instead of being thought in itself, i.e. as an immanence immanent only to itself, immanence in most of philosophy's history is related to something else that contains it: '[R]ather than this substance of Being or this image of thought being constituted by the plane of immanence itself, immanence will be related to something like a "dative," Matter or Mind' (44). Immanence is handed over to a *transcendent* frame, and the movement, the infinite movement that only a thought of pure immanence ('the empiricist conversion') enables the world to become, is stopped again. Movement and tendencies (to use a Bergsonian concept), or longitudes and latitudes (the Spinozan equivalent), in short 'the world' conceptualised immanently, is again brought to a halt and the dynamic plane of immanence is referred back to static verticality. Hence the claim: 'Whenever there is transcendence, vertical Being, imperial State in the sky or on earth, there is religion; and there is Philosophy whenever there is immanence' (43).

If immanence is the true business of philosophy – of a philosophy worthy of its name, finally 'mature enough' (Deleuze and Guattari 1994: 48) – and as such entails a truly *difficult* task, it would be wrong to assume that thinking immanence merely means substituting new terms, while the image of thought – that which thinking is believed to be – remains untouched. Most of the time, the transcendent – from its most commonsensical version as 'what everybody knows' to its most abstract a priori structure as universal law – is re-introduced into our ways of thinking. It is re-introduced both on the level of what is thought and on the level of what thought itself 'is'. What is not taken into account is that thinking immanence as immanent only to itself not only changes the linguistic registers of thought, but does something to the act of thinking such thought itself. This is the essential 'active' dimension of Deleuze's and Guattari's claim 'to create' and 'to invent' concepts. Everything is affected in this turn, because '[i]mmanence is immanent only to itself and consequently captures everything, absorbs All-One, and leaves nothing remaining to which it could be immanent' (45).

It is necessary to dwell a little further on this. In order to grasp this change of register for thought itself – a change in both its terminological and its practical dimensions – the notion of empiricism as linked to the Deleuzian concept of 'belief' needs further explication. Here it is fruitful to come back to the specific 'American' atmosphere of Deleuze's thinking and in particular to William James' early description of pragmatism as a radical empiricism in which, as Deleuze writes in his essay on 'Bartleby, or the Formula', it 'was also necessary for the knowing subject, the sole proprietor, to give way to a community of explorers, the brothers of the archipelago, who replace knowledge with belief' (Deleuze 1997: 87). It is via such superior empiricism – to read James alongside Bergson – that the demand for a 'belief in this world', as a 'most difficult task' that also implies a different *practice* of thinking itself, is best captured.[10] Thinking the world differently, when 'belief in' replaces 'knowledge of' the world, *turns* the world from something given into something to be explored, always to be constructed and created, and this again not according to the measure of 'what is' but according to the measure of 'what this world is capable of'.[11] What such a thought implies – at the very heart of it – is an *ethos*, an active and affirmative attitude towards the world (how to construct otherwise?); and Deleuze, in the context of discussing American pragmatism, also names its ingredients: truth *and* trust, hope *and* confidence – 'not belief in another world, but confidence in this one, in man as much as in God' (Deleuze 1997: 87). Relating the ethico-political dimension thus to the ontological undertaking is what a rigorous thought of immanence generates and where – one could say in a most Emersonian way – it truly turns away and averts itself from the conventions of thought, so that not only what is thought (the world) becomes something else, but thought itself becomes . . . *a* world.

Second Formula of Immanence: 'A Belief In This World, As It Is'

Let us turn to a second version of Deleuze's demand for a belief in this world. This time the expression is taken from Deleuze's *Cinema 2: The Time-Image*, and it is brought forth in the following way:

> The link between man and the world is broken. Henceforth, this link must become an object of belief . . . Whether we are Christians or atheists, in our

universal schizophrenia, *we need reasons to believe in this world*. It is a whole transformation of belief... to replace the model of knowledge with belief. But belief replaces knowledge only when it becomes belief in this world, as it is. (Deleuze 2000: 172)

In following my argument so far, a misunderstanding could sneak in that is important to avoid, and that – reading this version of the 'belief' statement closely – is addressed explicitly by Deleuze. While his notion of 'belief' can only ever be understood appropriately by linking it to a 'pragmatics'[12] such as I have shown above, Deleuze of course also sees the orienting framework of divine providence within this otherwise so *worldly* American tradition: a latent religiosity which, in the face of writers like Melville, Emerson and Thoreau, surely deserves an appropriate investigation in itself,[13] but which does not sufficiently transform the concept of belief in order to express what Deleuze is looking for, and thus cannot be taken as the endpoint of the discussion of belief.

Turning to the context of the discussion of 'belief in this world' in *Cinema 2*, we notice that Deleuze – although in a totally different thematic context – treats the problem of re-inscription of the transcendent into worldliness more thoroughly. The cited passage is taken from a discussion of the cinematographic significance of Roberto Rossellini and Jean-Luc Godard. Addressing again the turn from knowledge to belief, and in precisely the same manner as we saw in the first statement, Deleuze claims that Rossellini 'undoubtedly still retains the ideal of knowledge, he will never abandon this Socratic ideal'. For, '[w]hat made *Joan of Arc at the Stake* a misunderstood work? The fact that Joan of Arc needs to be in the sky to believe in the tatters of this world. It is from the height of eternity that she can believe in this world' (Deleuze 2000: 172). In contrast to any such transcendent height that safeguards the belief in this world, Godard's work stands alone in enduring an immanence immanent only to itself:

> In Godard the ideal of knowledge, the Socratic ideal which is still present in Rossellini, collapses: the 'good' discourse, of the militant, the revolutionary, the feminist, the philosopher, the film-maker, etc., gets no better treatment than the bad. Because the point is to discover and restore belief in the world, before or beyond words. (Deleuze 2000: 172)

The question of belief – of faith, hope and confidence – is, therefore, not as straightforward as it seems at first. We have already established that a rigorous thought of immanence captures everything and *leaves nothing* to which it could be immanent. Any undemanding belief in this world as harbinger of a better one – at which Deleuze hints with his reference to 'the "good" discourse, of the militant, revolutionary, feminist, philosopher', in which the divisions between good and evil, right or wrong, have already been decided on – is not at all what is required. His claim of restoring 'belief in the world, before and beyond words' indicates that this notion of belief precisely does not mean an already established 'belief in'. Belief in the Deleuzian sense must be understood as a continuing motor, an activity for keeping the movement which creates ... a world ... becoming-other: no freezing and blocking but endless transformation. Only in this way is the doubling of belief in this second version, according to which 'belief replaces knowledge only when it becomes belief in this world, as it is', fully understandable. The addition to the formula of belief in this version – the 'as it is' – thus makes all the difference. It is not an expression of resignation or an ultimate acceptance of the most visible limits that determine this world, but the paradoxical formulation of the only movement that might lead to real transformation: Active affirmation of 'what is' in order to become inscribed in a dynamic process and thus re-acquire the potential to create something new!

As if the demand for a belief in *this* world is not already a difficult and ambivalent enough task, Deleuze asks for more. What is needed is a practice that in a most Nietzschean sense 'wills everything all over again' – a belief in this world, *as it is*. There is to be no other sphere, no better world, providing this one with a saving horizon – such would only set limits to this world (in regard to what it is capable of) and allow for an escape from the bloody here and now. But also no conceptual movement that misunderstands the 'all over again' as 'every time a new beginning'.[14] Rather, in this kind of belief, what is fundamental is the endless task of repeating and thereby deepening the condition of immanence: We cannot turn back the wheel and will always have to carry on and work from what has already happened.

The task thus always gets more difficult, and Deleuze shows his heritage as a Spinozan *realist* nowhere better than here: 'To believe in this world, as it is', as a thought of pure immanence, does not mean producing an affirmation of the world according to the ideality of 'what should be' – measuring the possible via the criterion of 'what is', and thus *limiting* this world from the very start. No, what is truly required is to produce an active affirmation in the face of every single result the world ever takes. Only this way is the becoming-active in and for this world truly never ending; only this way is it an infinite task,[15] in which mere affirmation of chance becomes *active affirmation*, and belief in this world – still harbouring the comfort of the transcendent (divine providence, revolutionary axiomatic or a saving messianism) – becomes a 'belief in this world, as it is'. It is this most demanding *realist* undertaking that alone leaves open 'what the world is capable of'.[16]

However, given that this is such a difficult thought, and one so easily misread in political terms, it may be helpful to consider yet another context in which Deleuze emphasises the very same *realist* point. This is Foucault's *thought of the outside*, as it is treated in Deleuze's study *Foucault*, where, in reading the latter as a thinker of force-relations, not purely of the rigours of discourse analysis but most significantly of resistances too, Deleuze addresses the specific demand of immanence that concerns us here. When he discusses Foucault's early encounter with the Blanchotian 'thought from outside',[17] the seemingly all too *promising* notion of the outside is not to be understood as an outside beyond this world, a realm above or below which grounds it, thereby re-introducing transcendence. On the contrary, the outside is nothing but the other side, the literal outside of the formed strata: '[T]here is nothing lying beneath, above, or even outside the strata. The relations between forces, which are mobile, faint and diffuse, do not lie outside the strata but *form the outside of strata*' (Deleuze 1988: 84, my emphasis). Counter-intuitive at first but nonetheless most central, Deleuze and Foucault turn the thought of the outside from harbouring a promise of the *advent* of a better world – separated from the here and now – into the very *advent*urous process of the here and now itself, utterly *immanent* and *this-worldly*. No ticket to another world then, but only *negotiations* within this world, in the very middle of it, enable openings and niches which – at their best – escape and resist control.

Third Formula of Immanence: Negotiations

'The belief in this world, as it is' encapsulates the entirety of the complex thought of immanence which Deleuze pursues in all of his philosophical endeavours. His thought-universe is permeated structurally by this ethico-political dimension engaging with this world, and understanding itself as intervening therein. To demonstrate conceptually how the thought of an immanence immanent only to itself, rather than merely contemplating the world, *constructs* it in every move and gesture it makes, is to refute the argument according to which Deleuze's philosophy only leads us out of this world, with which it ultimately cannot be bothered. However, it would be a mistake to believe that this constitutes an effective response to those voices doubting the legitimacy of Deleuzian (and Foucauldian) thought for our world today. For much more is at stake – and here we have to return to our initial starting point and discuss the 'critical arrow' Alain Badiou has fired at Deleuze.

It could be argued that Badiou and Deleuze share extraordinary similarities in terms of their urge to practise philosophy as a form of intervention into this world. In what follows, however, a third version of the Deleuzian belief in this world will be introduced and juxtaposed to a statement by Badiou, in a way that reveals just how far such similarities ultimately turn out to mark deep differences. What will be argued here is that rather than there being a myriad of similarities between Badiou and 'Badiouians' on the one hand and Deleuze and 'Deleuzians' on the other, there is in fact – certain parallels notwithstanding – a major rift between the two thought-universes, a rift that concerns precisely the claim of immanence, which as a starting point for philosophy proper seems to be shared by both thinkers. Likewise, contrary to what is normally claimed on the Badiouian side – that it is Deleuze's thought of immanence which harbours a 'latent religiosity' (Badiou 2008: 387) because of its supposed misconception of the 'event' as 'the fate of the One' (385) – in my view precisely the opposite must be argued. It is Badiou's misconceiving of the thought of multiplicity as a thought of the One, and thus his reification of the virtual into a One, that leads to his opting for the supposedly pure immanence of the multiples, which in turn, however, instead of allowing for a thinking of immanence immanent only to itself, hands it over to a second order, to something that only ever contains immanence.[18]

But we have to move slowly and explain in detail what is at stake here. For the purposes of the present comparison with Badiou, it is best to consider at first only the beginning of Deleuze's third version of the demand for a 'belief in this world'. This is found at the end of a conversation with Antonio Negri in 1990, where Deleuze repeats again what he believes the modern relation to the world to be: 'What we most lack is a belief in the world, we've quite lost the world, it's been taken from us' (Deleuze 1995: 176). If we now turn to look at the epigraph to Badiou's *Logics of Worlds*, we encounter the exact same diagnosis in regard to the worldly state of affairs. The epigraph – taken from André Malraux's *Antimémoires* – reads as follows: 'France's agony was not born of the flagging reasons to believe in her – defeat, demography, industry, etc. – but of the incapacity to believe in anything at all.' (Badiou 2008: 1).

The same beginning, then – but what follows? Let us turn to Deleuze and see how he proceeds. After having stated that '[w]hat we most lack is a belief in the world, we've quite lost the world, it's been taken from us', he continues: 'If you believe in the world you precipitate events, however inconspicuous, that elude control, you engender new space-times, however small their surface or volume... Our ability to resist control, or our submission to it, has to be assessed at the level of our every move' (Deleuze 1995: 176). As we can see, in Deleuze's 'belief' there is no new collective imaginary (a One) from where and towards which our becoming-active is and ever will be legitimised; rather, the political impetus expressed here is no more, but also no less, than a most singular movement 'assessed at the level of our every move'. Only in this way is immanence not impeded, the world not blocked, such that everything becomes-transformed. Such active belief is apparently also nothing particularly grand. Most of the time – as the explications in this passage show – it is a very 'inconspicuous' and 'small' undertaking. It is thus to affirm and to become-active, but in a most moderate and indeed *negotiable* way. It is, as Gregg Lambert once described it:

> the affirmative principle... [that] can be understood as the most sobering response to this predicament: to believe in this world, as it is, neither in a transformed world, nor in another world, and to provide an image of thought that thoroughly belongs to this world which is ruled by the powers of the false; moreover to raise falsehood to a positive principle in the service of those who choose to live in this world and not in another... Restoring our connection to the world, but also assuming a constant vigilance over clichés and ready-made linkages. (Lambert 2002: 131)

A political horizon based on falsehood, negotiations and singular movements cannot but stand in opposition to Alain Badiou's rigid and truthful political vision. In Badiou's eyes it is precisely such 'contemporary *doxa*' (Badiou 2008: 2) that reduces the world to the political fallacies and lethargies of the majoritarian 'democratic materialism' in which 'the logic of the One' and, following from there, 'this sovereignty of the Two (bodies and languages)', rules, and to which he so strongly opposes a 'materialist dialectic' in whose formula the category of truth – although pluralised – reappears: '*There are only bodies and languages, except that there are truths*' (4).[19]

While it cannot but remain a matter of ongoing debate just how a Deleuzian point of view in regard to political action differs in kind from a Badiouian one,[20] one fact seems unambiguous: Badiou's claim to a renewed 'Politics of Truths', but also his harsh critique of all non-universal political formations from which he delimits a 'new universalism', underline the categorical differences at stake here.[21] While at first it seems to be a merely political dispute over the best or most appropriate strategy to adopt, what we are facing here is in fact more fundamental, revealing a *principal* difference in regard to the question of how thought and practice are interrelated. To unfold this categorical difference will form the last step of the present argument.

III. Spinoza's Heritage

What has been shown so far is that according to Deleuze's philosophy thought is always already thought as practice. It is a *practice of actual construction*, whose significance shows itself in every instance. The 'ability to resist control' (inasmuch as the 'submission to it') is to be 'assessed at the level of our every move'. The construction and practice of this world is everything, for the world 'is' nothing but politics. In staging the political problem thus, giving *practice* preference over *truths*, Deleuze, rather than weakening his thought into 'a poor man's Spinozism', rigorously continues what a thought of immanence immanent only to itself ever demands.

To envision politics again as 'knowing', as a *prescriptive* 'Politics of Truths' striving for axiomatic principles (and thereby clearly opposing what Foucault meant when he defined philosophy as a 'politics of truth'), is both *conceptually* undermining of the thought of immanence and *practically* counter-productive. What cannot be avoided in this rectification of politics is the re-introduction of transcendent principles (universals, truths) that pre-determine the political terrain and thus stop movement, freeze the world, and become yet another variation of the kind of politics of which Foucault was so weary, that (political) business as usual which he rejects by postulating: 'Never do Politics!'

Instead, in a truly immanent thought, one that pursues this demand also into practice, the political question itself must change. Rather than a *credo* that is to be 'followed' it must become first a *question* of analysis (of that which 'is' the world – in *A Thousand Plateaus* Deleuze and Guattari call this an a-signifying semiotics) and second, on a more affective level, a *carrying forward of the movement of immanence*, that is 'a belief in this world, as it is' as the only condition for a different future. A becoming-active as political activism cannot be based on the – however rigorous – renewal and restoration of categories such as universalism and truth, which are to be followed with the same categorical fidelity that any knowing 'believing in' has always prescribed. To the contrary, 'belief in the world, as it is', according to Deleuze, must remain a fully immanent process of experimentation – an open-ended process that only ever constitutes itself parallel to what it experiences; an experimentation, however, that is to be understood in a most sober sense, a *negotiating* from within. His epigraph to *Pourparlers* clarifies this:

> Philosophy isn't a Power. Religions, states, capitalism, science, the law, public opinion, and television are powers, but not philosophy. Philosophy may have its great internal battles (between idealism and realism, and so on), but they're mock battles. Not being a power, philosophy can't battle with the powers that be, but it fights a war without battles, a guerrilla campaign against them. And it can't converse with them, it's got nothing to tell them, nothing to communicate, and can only negotiate. Since the powers aren't just external things, but permeate each of us, philosophy throws us all into constant negotiations with, and a guerrilla campaign against, ourselves. (Deleuze 1995: epigraph)

If we let immanence capture everything, then every philosophical endeavour will be just as much entangled with politics in so far as the ethico-political is always already present in even the purest ontological undertaking. Rather than presupposing a descriptive ontological axiomatic from which a prescriptive politics follows, Deleuze claims that we have to *endure entanglements* if we are to claim to follow through a thought of immanence immanent only to itself. The political question today will not find an effective response without changing what it is that is being questioned. Foucault saw this in one of his interviews from 1984, when asked by Paul Rabinow what his own stand towards politics was:

> I have never tried to analyze anything whatsoever from the point of view of politics, but always to ask politics what it had to say about the problems with which it was confronted. I question it about the positions it takes and the reasons it gives for this; I don't ask it to determine the theory of what I do. I am neither an adversary nor a partisan of Marxism; I question it about what it has to say about experiences that ask questions of it. (Foucault 1997a: 115)

While Deleuze's thought puts more emphasis on potential resistances, the openings of lines of flight and of *escapes*,[22] he nonetheless follows this cautious Foucauldian line whenever he speaks of politics in the concrete, that is, in its *actuality*. The non-unifiable concept of the 'body without organs' illustrates this just as much as the deterritorialising series of 'becomings' developed in *A Thousand Plateaus*. Rather than judging such caution as revealing a weak approach to political actuality, it is up to us finally to learn that this indirect approach is precisely not an escape from the world but a rigorous transformation of the question of politics according to the practice of a thought that affirms its absolute immanence. Whoever we are, we need reasons to believe in this world. It is, however, important to realise fully the inexistence of any dative whatsoever that could contain this immanence. Instead of again referring to nameable truths, we have to learn to *turn* the question, and with it the apparent political vacuum, into a practice that – at its best – confirms a belief in this world, as it is, wherein our ability to resist will be assessed on the level of our every move.

It is here that one last time we come up against the significant heritage of Spinoza. The Spinoza who not only is the prince of philosophy when it comes to the question of immanence but who is also the principal point of reference when it comes to both entangling and disentangling the questions of ontology, ethics and politics. And while both Badiou and Deleuze share this heritage, Spinoza at the same time represents the line of delimitation that must be drawn between them. For, whereas Deleuze values Spinoza's *affective realism* as fundamental to an understanding of the latter's metaphysical and political system, it is Spinoza's rigour in the *mathematisation of the world* that Badiou clearly favours (and where he ultimately also sees his limits). While it is much too early to jump to the conclusion that it is precisely because of these two different Spinozas that we find such different political agendas in the two philosophers – one prescriptive and the other, as I have called it, realistic – what can definitely be concluded at this moment is that it is because of Badiou's negligence of Spinoza's theory of affects that he must ultimately criticise and reject Spinoza as a metaphysical thinker who forecloses 'the void' – which, according to Badiou, alone represents the possibility 'of thinking multiplicity, on the one hand, and novelty, on the other' (Gillespie 2001: 63). The debate over the relation between the philosophical claim of immanence and the quest for political activism here reaches another level of sophistication that will require further analysis. My aim in this article was to reach this point. Right now, the quest to link immanence and politics unfolds in two diverging directions: either formalisation (Badiou) or actualisation (Deleuze); that is, radical fidelity to the axioms of truths and universality on the one hand and active experimentation with resistances and negotiations on the other.

Notes

1. I am especially indebted to Deleuzian scholars such as Braidotti, Grosz, Marrati and Patton who in regard to the question of politics not only illuminate Deleuze's thought but also push his thinking in fruitful new directions.
2. I have also developed this demand of philosophical thought as 'active thought' in my book *The Thought of Becoming: Gilles Deleuze's Poetics of Life* (Thiele 2008).
3. Interview with Catherine Clément, 'Entretien 1980', *L'Arc*, 49, cited in Patton 1984.
4. The reference to a 'Spinozan realism' will recur in this article. It is most clearly articulated in the famous beginning of Spinoza's *Tractatus Politicus*

(1677) in which the philosophical temptation to approach the subject matter in question (in Spinoza's case 'men') 'not as they are, but as they [the philosophers] themselves would like them to be' is rejected and a realist approach to 'what is' – 'not what is new and unheard of, but only such things as agree best with practice' – is taken as the only valid method for an effective conceptual investigation (Spinoza 1956: Introduction).

5. While the formula 'always already yet never once and for all' cannot rid itself completely from the Heideggerian 'always already' as it determines Heidegger's definition of *Dasein* as 'always already ahead of itself', here it rather stands for the attempt to bring to language the logic of repetition in difference that is the beginning (without beginning) of Deleuze's thought-practice as such: 'the repetition of an internal difference which it incorporates in each of its moments, and carries from one distinctive point to another' (Deleuze 1994: 20).

6. Cf. also Paul Patton: 'Nomadology certainly does not offer any political program, any more than did schizoanalysis. Nor does it offer any straightforward political morality, in the sense of imperatives addressed to subjects... the question is never simply one of good or bad, but of the specificity of each case... It is a matter of assessing the qualities present in a given situation or the true nature of a given process: is it a creative or a destructive line?' (Patton 1984: 79–80).

7. The French version says: 'Je ne proposerai donc en tout ceci qu'un seul impératif, mais celui-là sera catégorique et inconditionnel: ne faire jamais de politique' (Foucault 2004: 6). In the English edition of the lectures, the expression 'ne faire jamais de politique' is, however, translated as 'never engage in polemics' (cf. Foucault 2009: 4). While, considering the actual context, the translation seems possible, Foucault's having meant 'politics' is, of course, much more provocative than if he had merely stated – in a real philosophical manner – that one should not engage in polemics. Since for my purposes it is important to push Deleuze and Foucault as far as possible on this, I take the French 'politique' to translate as 'politics', no matter that, for example, in the interview 'Polemics, Politics, and Problematization' from 1984, the first question Paul Rabinow asks is the following: 'Why is it that you don't engage in polemics?' – an apparent repetition of Foucault's 1978 'categorical imperative'. See Foucault 1997a.

8. This 'beyond' must of course not be read in a Levinasian sense, in which it signifies a gesture towards (necessary) transcendence – absolute Otherness.

9. 'The virtue in most request is conformity. Self-reliance is its aversion', says Emerson in one of his most important essays (Emerson 1983: 261). Given Deleuze's many references to the Anglo-American tradition, its 'superiority' in what concerns literature (cf. Deleuze and Parnet 2002: 36–76), and the pervasive re-turn to an empiricist line of thought originating in William James' radical empiricism (cf. e.g. Deleuze 1997: 68–90, esp. pp. 88ff), reading the 'empiricist conversion' in such an 'American way' is not too far fetched.

10. For both the central notion of belief in James and his radical empiricism, cf. his famous essay 'The Will to Believe' (James 1956: 1–31), and his *Essays in Radical Empiricism* (James 2003).

11. 'What the world is capable of' is not merely another phrasing of the usual moral of 'what should be', as it can be found in most (post-Kantian) practical philosophy. The latter refers the 'what is' to something else – 'a dative' as Deleuze and Guattari say – and thus reintroduces the transcendent, while 'what the world is capable of' enacts the Spinozan credo of a logic of pure force-relations.

12. Deleuze and Guattari use this term to name their politico-philosophical undertaking in *A Thousand Plateaus*.

13. Cf. Branka Arsić's work on the American literary and philosophical tradition (Arsić 2007, 2010).
14. Such as, for example, Hannah Arendt would have it in a Augustinian heritage. Cf. her dissertation on St Augustine from 1929 (Arendt 1998).
15. For the characterisation of philosophical thought as an 'infinite task', cf. Gasché 2007, in which he also discusses Deleuze as 'Thinking Within Thought'. Cf. also his most recent study on *Europe, or The Infinite Task* (Gasché 2009).
16. Again, it is important to refer here directly to Spinoza's *Tractatus Politicus* which, read in conjunction with his *Ethics*, effectuates precisely such a construction: a most rigorous affirmation of 'what is', based on the premise that 'what is' is a measure of power and not essence, for 'no one has so far determined what the body can do'. For Spinoza's discussion of natural right in the *Political Treatise* cf. Spinoza 1956: ch. II; and with regard to his central statement from *The Ethics* see Spinoza 2000: EIIIP2 S.
17. On the thought of the outside, cf. Foucault 1997b.
18. For a more detailed discussion of the diverging lines of thought of Badiou and Deleuze in regard to 'immanence' and 'ontology', leading into a discussion of how to understand the different/ciation of virtual/actual in Deleuze, cf. Thiele 2008: especially part V, 164ff.
19. While in the argument developed here the categorical concept of 'truths' – reintroduced into the domain of both philosophy and politics by Badiou – is contested because of its conceptual shortcomings in the face of a political thought based on immanence, Badiou's extrapolation of the problem alongside Descartes' early 'intuition of the same order regarding the ontological status of truths' (Badiou 2008: 5) is a most fruitful discussion of how the concept of truth/s could be torn away from a far too reductive positivist category, to be thought as 'generic multiplicities' (6).
20. One of the clearest discussions of the differences between Badiou and Deleuze can be found in Sam Gillespie's *Mathematics of Novelty: Badiou's Minimalist Metaphysics* (Gillespie 2008). For the same cluster of questions, this time also in respect to their readings of Spinoza, cf. Gillespie 2001.
21. For Badiou's well-elaborated political thought in which the categories of truth(s) and universality play a most significant role, see especially Badiou 2003 and 2005.
22. This is what especially the feminist legacy in Deleuzian scholarship (Braidotti, David-Ménard, Grosz, Marrati, to name just a few) has most poignantly shown by engaging with the Deleuzian concepts of difference, immanence, nomadology and bodies. Instead of painting yet another grand picture of thought *beyond* different/ciation, theirs is the task of furthering and carrying forward this condition for a different future. To give just one example (from Elizabeth Grosz): '[F]eminist politics should, I believe, now consider the affirmation of a politics of *imperceptibility*, leaving its traces and effects everywhere but never being able to be identified with a person, group, or organization. It is not a politics of visibility, or recognition and of self-validation, but a process of self-marking that constitutes oneself in the very model of that which oppresses and opposes the subject' (Grosz 2005: 194).

References

Arendt, Hannah (1998) *Love and Saint Augustine*, ed. Joanna Vecchiarelli Scott and Judith Chelius Stark, Chicago: University of Chicago Press.
Arsić, Branka (2007) *Passive Consititutions; or 7½ times Bartleby*, Stanford, CA: Stanford University Press.

Arsić, Branka (2010) *On Leaving: A Reading in Emerson*, Cambridge, MA: Harvard University Press.

Badiou, Alain (2005) *Metapolitics*, trans. Jason Barker, London and New York: Verso.

Badiou, Alain (2007) *Saint Paul: The Foundation of Universalism*, trans. Ray Brassier, Stanford, CA: Stanford University Press.

Badiou, Alain (2009) *Logic of Worlds: Being and Event II*, trans. Alberto Toscano, New York and London: Continuum.

Deleuze, Gilles (1994) *Difference and Repetition*, trans. Paul Patton, New York: Columbia University Press.

Deleuze, Gilles (1995) *Negotiations: 1972–1990*, trans. Martin Joughin, New York: Columbia University Press.

Deleuze, Gilles (1997) *Essays Critical and Clinical*, trans. Daniel Smith and Michael Greco, Minneapolis: University of Minnesota Press.

Deleuze, Gilles (1988) *Foucault*, trans. Sean Hand, Minneapolis: University of Minnesota Press.

Deleuze, Gilles (2000) *Cinema 2: The Time-Image*, trans. Hugh Tomlinson and Robert Galeta, London: Athlone Press.

Deleuze, Gilles and Félix Guattari (1994) *What is Philosophy?*, trans. Hugh Tomlinson and Graham Burchell, Minneapolis: University of Minnesota Press.

Deleuze, Gilles and Félix Guattari (2000) *A Thousand Plateaus*, trans. Brian Massumi, Minneapolis: University of Minnesota Press.

Deleuze, Gilles and Claire Parnet (2006) 'On the Superiority of Anglo-American Literature', in *Dialogues II*, trans. Hugh Tomlinson and Barbara Habberjam, New York and London: Continuum, pp. 27–56.

Emerson, Ralph Waldo (1983) 'Self-Reliance', in *Essays and Lectures: First and Second Series*, New York: The Library of America, pp. 259–82.

Foucault, Michel (1997a) 'Polemics, Politics and Problematization', in *Ethics: Subjectivity and Truth: Essential Works of Foucault*, vol. 1, New York: The New Press, pp. 111–20.

Foucault, Michel and Maurice Blanchot (1997b) *Foucault/Blanchot: Maurice Blanchot: The Thought from Outside and Michel Foucault As I Imagine Him*, New York: Zone Books.

Foucault, Michel (2004) *Sécurité, Territoire, Population. Cours au Collège de France, 1977–1978*, Paris: Gallimard/Seuil.

Foucault, Michel (2009) *Security, Territory, Population. Lectures at the Collège de France 1977–1978*, trans. Graham Burchell, New York: Palgrave Macmillan.

Gasché, Rodolphe (2007) *The Honor of Thinking: Criticism, Theory, Philosophy*, Stanford, CA: Stanford University Press.

Gasché, Rodolphe (2009) *Europe, or the Infinite Task*, Stanford, CA: Stanford University Press.

Gillespie, Sam (2001) 'Placing the Void. Badiou on Spinoza', *Angelaki*, 6:3, pp. 63–77.

Gillespie, Sam (2008) *Mathematics of Novelty: Badiou's Minimalist Metaphysics*, Melbourne: re.press.

Grosz, Elizabeth (2005) *Time Travels: Feminism, Nature, Power*, Durham and London: Duke University Press.

Hallward, Peter (2006) *Out of This World: Deleuze and the Philosophy of Creation*, London and New York: Verso.

James, William (1956) *The Will to Believe and Other Essays in Popular Philosophy*, New York: Dover Press.

James, William (2003) *Essays in Radical Empiricism*, New York: Dover Press.

Lambert, Gregg (2002) *The Non-Philosophy of Gilles Deleuze*, New York and London: Continuum.

Patton, Paul (1984) 'Conceptual Politics and the War-Machine in *Mille Plateaux*', *SubStance*, 13:44–5, pp. 60–81.

Spinoza, Baruch de (1956) *A Theologico-Political Treatise and A Political Treatise*, ed. and trans. R.H.M. Elwes, New York: Dover Press.

Spinoza, Baruch de (2000) *The Ethics*, ed. and trans. G.H.R. Parkinson, Oxford: Oxford University Press.

Thiele, Kathrin (2008) *The Thought of Becoming: Gilles Deleuze's Poetics of Life*, Berlin/Zürich: Diaphanes Verlag.

The Common as Body Without Organs

Vidar Thorsteinsson   Ohio State University

Abstract

The paper explores the relation of Michael Hardt and Antonio Negri's work to that of Deleuze and Guattari. The main focus is on Hardt and Negri's concept of 'the common' as developed in their most recent book *Commonwealth*. It is argued that the common can complement what Nicholas Thoburn terms the 'minor' characteristics of Deleuze's political thinking while also surpassing certain limitations posed by Hardt and Negri's own previous emphasis on 'autonomy-in-production'. With reference to Marx's notion of real subsumption and early workerism's social-factory thesis, the discussion circles around showing how a distinction between capital and the common can provide a basis for what Alberto Toscano calls 'antagonistic separation' from capital in a more effective way than can the classical capital–labour distinction. To this end, it is demonstrated how the common might benefit from being understood in light of Deleuze and Guattari's conceptual apparatus, with reference primarily to the 'body without organs' of *Anti-Oedipus*. It is argued that the common as body without organs, now understood as constituting its own 'social production' separate from the BwO of capital, can provide a new basis for antagonistic separation from capital. Of fundamental importance is how the common potentially invents a novel regime of qualitative valorisation, distinct from capital's limitation to quantity and scarcity.

Keywords: the common, body without organs, biopolitical production, Marxism, communism, value theory

It is well known that Michael Hardt and Antonio Negri's work owes much to the thought of Gilles Deleuze. Negri co-operated with Deleuze and Guattari during his exile in Paris; he wrote texts with Guattari and

Deleuze Studies Volume 4: 2010 supplement: 46–63
DOI: 10.3366/E1750224110001121
© Edinburgh University Press
www.eupjournals.com/dls

he shares with Deleuze a passion for Spinoza. Furthermore, Michael Hardt is the author of an introductory book on Deleuze's philosophical writings from the 1960s (Hardt 1993), and Hardt and Negri mention *A Thousand Plateaus* as one of the two 'models' for their book *Empire* (the other being Marx's *Capital*) (Hardt and Negri 2000: 415). While it is necessary to understand the relationship between these authors through their shared appreciation of philosophies of materialism and immanence, for example those of Marx and Spinoza, they also share to a large degree an understanding of certain developments in contemporary capitalism. Interesting comparisons can be made between Deleuze and Guattari's later, more explicitly social theory, as put forth in the *Capitalism and Schizophrenia* volumes, and Hardt and Negri's trilogy *Empire*, *Multitude* and *Commonwealth*. Here we will explore how Hardt and Negri's relatively newly developed concept of *the common* complements Deleuze and Guattari's political thought, while also demonstrating how it might benefit from being understood in light of Deleuze and Guattari's terminology, and in particular their concept of the 'body without organs' (BwO), as it appears in *Anti-Oedipus*.[1]

Hardt and Negri claim to rely heavily on 'the excellent commentaries of Gilles Deleuze' on the passage from disciplinary society to the society of control in Foucault's work (cf. Hardt and Negri 2000: 22–3, 419). Deleuze interpreted Foucault as having implicitly analysed the arrival of post-industrial *societies of control*, where the disciplinary capitalism of the factory is replaced by more fluid forms of control characterised by a regulation of space that is open, and dependent on internally motivated cooperation of its subjects (Deleuze 1992). This corresponds in many ways to Hardt and Negri's description of advanced capitalistic societies where older, Fordist modes of production have been replaced by more flexible, immaterial and 'feminised' ones (Hardt and Negri 2009: 131–5). Hardt and Negri maintain that since the 1970s a new technical composition of labour has begun to dominate in what they term 'biopolitical production'. Simultaneously, Foucauldian biopower completes a process in which the inner, subjective life of the worker has been fully subsumed under capital, turning the worker into both the subject and object of work.

Michael Hardt, however, 'both adopts and inverts Michel Foucault's usage' of the term biopower, in a manner that emphasises not only its oppressive aspect but also its liberating potentials (see Hardt 1999: 90, 98–9). In this, Hardt and Negri build upon similar approaches already developed to some extent by the Italian workerists' thesis of the 'social factory'. This thesis is based on passages in Marx's *Grundrisse* and *Capital* relating to 'real subsumption' and the 'general intellect'.[2] Marx's notion of the general intellect indicates 'to what degree general social knowledge has become a direct force of production' (Marx 1973: 706), general social knowledge here referring to, for example, the level of education, technical skills and other immaterial assets that are required for workers and machines to fulfil their function. Real subsumption refers to the stage in capitalist development when capital has increased 'the value of its operations to the point where it assumes social dimensions', in which 'the immediate purpose of production is to produce *as much surplus value as possible*' (Marx 1976: 1035, 1037). That is, all of society's productive powers have in actuality been directed towards maximisation of surplus value and capitalist social relations entirely subsume and transform the labour process.

The social-factory thesis, of which Negri was one of the main proponents in 1970s Italy, consequently argues that class composition has to be understood not solely in terms of factory-workers versus capital owners, but as a more extensive system containing also unwaged labour, women's work inside the household, students, the unemployed, etc. Surplus-producing labour, then, comes to be seen as not confined to the interior of the factory, but as dispersed throughout society as a whole.[3]

I. Dilemmas of Autonomy

What these descriptions of the developments of contemporary capitalism have in common – regardless of whether we call them societies of control, the social factory, biopolitical production, or the capitalism of real subsumption – is a notion of the *immanence* of capitalist productive relations to all of social life. Capitalism is no longer an objective structure to which subjects can oppose themselves, because even subjectivity is already moulded and produced by capital: labour and capital – defined by Marx as 'variable' and 'fixed' capital (Marx 1976: 317) – tend to become one. The emphasis on this aspect of Marxism in workerist thought is well explained by Nicholas Thoburn in his discussion of Raniero Panzieri. Panzieri argued that capitalistic productive *relations* (that is, the social structure of capitalism) could not be distinguished from capitalistic productive *forces* (that is, labour and its subjective and social composition): 'The *forces* of production thus had capitalist *relations* immanent to them in a "unity of 'technical' and 'despotic' moments"' (Thoburn 2003: 77, quoting Panzieri). This resonates perfectly with Foucault and Deleuze's poststructuralist account of power as immanently constitutive of social structures rather than as neutral to them, and even more so with Deleuze and Guattari's schizoanalysis where there is no distinction in nature between desiring-production and social-production but only in regime (Deleuze and Guattari 1983: 31). Hence, it is difficult to imagine an 'outside' to productive relations, and it becomes hard to see what physical or mental activity is not already social or immaterial labour. Hardt and Negri phrase it thus:

> the capitalist market is one machine that has always run counter to any division between inside and outside. It is thwarted by barriers and exclusions; it thrives instead by including always more within its sphere. ... In its ideal form there is no outside to the world market: the entire globe is its domain. (Hardt and Negri 2000: 190, see also 413)

In real subsumption, there is no outside to neither capital nor market; 'work is always already capital' (Thoburn 2003: 109), and labour loses its autonomy as it emerges structured by capital. Despite the problematic created by labour and capital becoming increasingly indistinguishable, Hardt and Negri have remained remarkably faithful to Italian workerism's 'reversal of perspective'. Mindful of how the *operaismo* and *autonomia* movements of the Italian 1960s and '70s were able to reverse the dominant perspective on labour towards viewing it as the site of political energy and resistance, Hardt and Negri see biopolitical production as not only exploitative and oppressive. In work, there remains the potential for autonomous productive organisation that could serve the needs of workers in a supposedly communist manner – even if work has undergone significant transformations with the decline of Fordism. Simultaneously, they have continued to emphasise resistance as ontologically prior to the powers of state and capital (Hardt and Negri 2005: 64). In fact, they maintain that the global emergence of Empire is not only the result of capital's own dynamics of expansion but a reaction to working-class struggles in the occident, national liberation struggles in the global south, and state socialism (Negri and Dufourmantelle 2004: 60). Hardt and Negri emphasise that any separation from or refusal of capital must – paradoxically, as it were – be socially and economically grounded in capitalistic productive relations and in fact they state that *any* 'theoretical effort in this context to pose the autonomy of the political, separate from the social and the economic, no longer makes any sense' (Hardt and Negri 2005: 78).

The major theme of Hardt and Negri's research, at least since the publication of *Empire*, has been to grapple with the challenge of how it would be possible to radically oppose capital while not introducing any ideological separation from it that would entail betraying the tenets of a materialist philosophy of immanence; an opposition that would make sense despite the pervasiveness of social and biopolitical production. This attempt can be traced further back to the workerist notion of the *operaio sociale* or 'socialised worker', originally developed by Negri (Wright 2002: 171–5). An attempt to formulate the socialised worker's opposition to capital is contained in the notion of 'autonomy-in-production', which tries to formulate an antagonistic autonomy from capital.[4] This autonomy is not gained by negating an increasingly cognitive and subjectively internalised labour-process, but by affirmation of workers' power and productivity along the militant lines of a workerist reversal of perspective.

Some critics, however, have argued that Hardt and Negri's notion of autonomy-in-production is untenable. Thoburn is one such critic, agreeing in his book *Deleuze, Marx and Politics* that certain '[n]ew aspects of social productivity might escape for a little while' (Thoburn 2003: 98) and could indeed become the 'driving force of production', but nevertheless insisting that such a situation could really only develop in 'disciplinary space', not in contemporary spaces of biopolitical control. Thoburn phrases his argument thus:

> Indeed the capitalist socius has many little lines of flight, even autonomous zones where creation is allowed to operate outside of capitalist relations of productivity ... before they are generalized as a new productive activity; but such spaces (or lines of flight) enrich rather than contradict capital. (Thoburn 2003: 98)

Thoburn goes on to point out that Negri's image of the autonomous, socialised worker of the Italian 1970s – which later mutates into the *multitude* of Hardt and Negri's eponymous book – has a tendency to exceed Deleuze and Guattari's political horizon, especially in terms of what Thoburn calls the latter's 'minor' characteristics. Thoburn quotes Guattari as claiming that even though there are interesting ways in which new productive forces contain liberating potentials, 'capital still operates as the universal plane' of these forces (Thoburn 2003: 98). And Deleuze, we should recall, gives a similar kind of warning in his 'Postscript on the Societies of Control', speaking of how the new and seemingly more flexible spaces of late capitalism 'could at first express new freedom, but ... could participate as well in mechanisms of control that are equal to the harshest of confinements' (Deleuze 1992: 4). For Deleuze and Guattari, this position will only offer modest opportunities for resistance, which Thoburn designates with the terms 'cramped' and 'minor', implying that radical politics must be 'premised on cramped, impossible, minority positions where social forces constrain movements' (Thoburn 2003: 90). If this is the case, then it seems indeed like Hardt and Negri's notion of autonomy-in-production as an effective strategy against and beyond capital is mistaken, or worse, a self-delusion. This dilemma is well put by Alberto Toscano in a recent essay:

> The challenge today is to think an antagonism that would not be entirely detached from the conditions of production and reproduction of contemporary capitalism. The mere positing of duality, say between Empire and multitude, without the conflictual *composition* that can provide this duality with a certain degree of determinateness, can arguably be seen to generate a seemingly heroic, but ultimately ineffectual horizon for theoretical analysis and political militancy. (Toscano 2009: 127)

What a truly radical autonomy from capital requires, again in Toscano's words, is the 'twin affirmation of an integral *immanence* of capitalist relations to the social (of a thoroughgoing *socialisation* of production) and of the radicalisation of the antagonism between capital and labour' (Toscano 2009: 111). Such an antagonism would amount to perceiving 'communism as separation' (110) from the social fabric that simultaneously sustains its immanent foundation.

II. Bodies of Disjunction

Taking the cue from Toscano's twofold challenge, I think it may be convincingly argued that Hardt and Negri's notion of autonomy-in-production already fulfils the demand of being sufficiently rooted in the production and reproduction of capital – in fact, most of Hardt and Negri's critics maintain that their theory is *too* immersed in these; too immanent, as it were.[5] Therefore, it seems like the question of whether 'autonomy-in-production' entails sufficient antagonism between capital and labour is the more pertinent one.

Hardt and Negri's latest work, *Commonwealth*, is perhaps their most innovative attempt at the formulation of just such an immanent antagonism. However, it does not consist of an antagonism between *capital and labour* in the classical sense. What Hardt and Negri are proposing is an antagonism of a new kind: the antagonism between *capital and the common*. This juxtaposition, I argue, is Hardt and Negri's attempt at giving autonomy-in-production the necessary foundations to overcome a 'seemingly heroic' posture eventually generalised by the plane of capital, but also at resolving the dilemmas that the social-factory thesis inevitably creates by its fusing of labour and capital. This could, then, also allow Hardt and Negri to exceed the cramped and impossible space of Deleuze and Guattari's minor politics in a more successful way than before, when simple autonomy-in-production was lacking the notion of the common. In fact, Negri has stated that the common is his main point of divergence from Deleuze and Guattari. In a recent volume, Negri puts it clearly: '*the common* constitutes indeed the crucial element differentiating my theorization... from Deleuze and Guattari's theorization' (Negri and Casarino 2008: 118).

What is the common then, and how does it attain antagonistic autonomy while being at the same time grounded in the productive relations of actually existing capitalism? How does it remain faithful to Deleuze and Guattari's philosophy of immanence while also subverting capital in an antagonistic manner? What kind of phenomenon is it? In answering these questions I take advantage of the fact that the exact ontological status of the common still remains fairly fluid and open in Hardt and Negri's writings. Even though Negri grants that 'the common in the end is that which differentiates most [his] thought from Deleuze and Guattari's thought' (Negri and Casarino 2008: 120), I would like to suggest an interpretation of the common which relies heavily on a key concept from Deleuze and Guattari's work. I will try to demonstrate that the common is in fact a 'body without organs', albeit of a kind that is not anticipated in concrete terms in the two volumes of *Capitalism and Schizophrenia* where the concept is developed. This will demonstrate that while Hardt and Negri develop a 'major' politics as opposed to Deleuze and Guattari's minor politics, their thinking continues to be lucidly interpretable in light of a Deleuzo-Guattarian conceptual apparatus.

In Deleuze and Guattari's presentation, different bodies without organs (BwOs) pertain to different regimes or relations of production, different 'abstract machines' corresponding to the productive machinery and organisation characterising a particular mode of production. This applies to production in the universal sense developed in *Anti-Oedipus*, regardless of the split between desiring-production and social-production characteristic of capitalism. In *Anti-Oedipus*, the BwO is most prominent in Deleuze and Guattari's discussion of psychoanalysis and desiring-production, and less so in their treatment of capitalism and social-production, where the 'full body' of the socius comes to the fore. Hence it might seem more appropriate to discuss a given social regime – despotism, capitalism or, as I will attempt, the common – as a socius or full body. The benefit of sticking with the conceptual tool of the BwO, however, is that it provides us with a level of abstraction that is suitable for the discussion of an as-yet unrealised social formation. This is in no way an illegitimate use of the concept, for the difference between social-production and desiring-production is not a difference in nature but only in regime, as already noted (Deleuze and Guattari 1983: 31).

According to the description in *Anti-Oedipus*, the BwO is linked to 'a full body that functions as a socius' but is distinct from the historically separate social formations designated by different sociuses as its more general, universal condition. This socius may be the 'body of the earth' (savagery), the body of the tyrant (despotism), or the body of capital (Deleuze and Guattari 1983: 10). Deleuze and Guattari claim that the 'body without organs belongs to the realm of antiproduction' and that it 'couples production with ... an element of antiproduction' (8). This antiproductive element of organisation and selection is required for a specific desiring-machine to sustain its production; this is its BwO. Its function is, specifically, to add the *disjunctive synthesis* of recording, selection and differentiation to what would otherwise remain a directionless and accumulative desiring-production invested through the *connective synthesis*.[6] With some degree of simplification, we can say that the disjunctive synthesis of selection and recording performed by the BwO corresponds to Marx's *relations of production*, while the more primal connective synthesis of undifferentiated accumulation is characteristic of the *forces of production*.

Despite the abstractness of the concept of the BwO, we can now see how it underlies the relations that define actual social regimes. The BwO of capital has certain characteristics that serve to distinguish the socius of capital from the other social bodies. Speaking of older social forms, Deleuze and Guattari write that '[t]he prime function incumbent upon the socius has always been to codify the flows of desire, to inscribe them, to record them, to see to it that no flow exists that is not properly dammed up, channelled, regulated' (Deleuze and Guattari 1983: 33). This description would, presumably, apply to rigid social structures such as despotism. But 'the *capitalist machine* ... finds itself in a totally new situation: it is faced with the task of decoding and deterritorializing the flows' (33). Capitalist relations of production, then, rely on a particular kind of BwO that manages or subsumes desiring-production without directly controlling it, that is, it functions by decoding and releasing flows on its surface rather than restraining them. The encounter of decoded flows of money-capital and the decoded flows of labour, according to Deleuze and Guattari, is essentially what gives rise to capitalism, meaning that the task of the capitalist BwO is not to code or recode but to decode: 'Capitalism is in fact born of the encounter of two sorts of flows: the decoded flows of production in the form of money-capital, and the decoded flows of labor in the form of the "free worker" ' (33). This decoding is the essential, defining feature of capital – its 'very fabric of existence'– and the role of the surface of its BwO is primarily to 'register' these flows by the means of axiomatisation. And in the case of capital, this axiomatisation takes the simple form of money rather than the semiotic code characteristic of savagery and despotism: 'unlike previous social machines, the capitalist machine is incapable of providing a code that will apply to the whole of the social field. By substituting money for the very notion of a code, it has created an axiomatic of abstract quantities' (33). Money, according to Marx, is the 'universal or social equivalent' forming an 'independent presence of exchange value' (Marx 1976: 183, 235) which under real subsumption is capable of investing the whole social field.

This axiomatic, of course, is Marx's general formula for capital of M-C-M' (Marx 1976: 247–57). One important consequence of this axiomatic of the capitalist BwO is that it moves 'further and further in the direction of the deterritorialization of the socius' (Deleuze and Guattari 1983: 33) – that is, to be able to create surplus value (the difference between M and M'), the axiomatic demands a constant cycle of investment and reinvestment which knows no limits and will for that reason ultimately pose problems for capital. 'Value therefore now becomes value in process, money in process, and, as such, capital' (Marx 1976: 256), capital which is bound to an everlasting search for surplus value and will stop at nothing. Deleuze and Guattari phrase it thus: 'Capitalism tends toward a threshold of decoding that will destroy the socius in order to make it a body without organs and unleash the flows of desire on this body as a deterritorialized field' (Deleuze and Guattari 1983: 33).

Deleuze and Guattari go on to describe how the BwO of capital serves to continuously repress and destroy the socius, while simultaneously injecting it with its vast productive energies. In this manner, capitalism is always acting against limits that are its own creation: 'capitalism constantly counteracts, constantly inhibits this inherent tendency while at the same time allowing it free rein; it continually seeks to avoid reaching its limit while simultaneously tending toward that limit' (Deleuze and Guattari 1983: 34, see also 303, 320). So, on the one hand, there is an abstract socius which serves as capital's 'fundamental raw material' which capital 'does not confront... from the outside' (33) but immanently, and on the other hand, the BwO of capital which is in charge of registering the flows on its surface, that is, the exchange of commodities and labour – thereby forming the basis of the quantitative axiomatic of value that expresses the ultimate productive relation of capital, Marx's M-C-M'. Hence the BwO of capital expresses the characteristics of capital in a twofold way as a *relation of production* and also as a corresponding *mode of valorisation*, requiring a special kind of value-theory as will be discussed in more detail below.

III. Social-production of the Common

Let us briefly observe how Hardt and Negri define the common in *Commonwealth*:

> By 'the common' we mean, first of all, the common wealth of the material world – the air, the water, the fruits of the soil, and all nature's bounty... *We consider the common also and more significantly those results of social production that are necessary for social interaction and further production, such as knowledges, languages, codes, information, affects, and so forth.* (Hardt and Negri 2009: viii; emphasis added)

This emphasis on the common as social production and reproduction suggests that for Hardt and Negri the common indeed designates a social relation, a relation of production. Hardt and Negri – even before *Commonwealth* – have repeatedly emphasised the *social* nature of what is produced in biopolitical production, making frequent use of the term *social production*. In *Commonwealth*, Hardt and Negri claim that the arrival of biopolitical production poses 'significant challenges to traditional concepts and methods of political economy in large part because biopolitical production shifts the economic center of gravity from the production of material commodities to that of social relations, confusing, as we said, the division between production and reproduction' (Hardt and Negri 2009: 135). They thus echo Deleuze and Guattari's use of the term 'social production', which is a major constitutive element in how Deleuze and Guattari see productive and social relations as being immanently 'produced' themselves, that is, the BwO of a certain socius is a *product* of a particular kind. The BwO, in other words, is the product of social production whereas the flows it registers are the products of desiring-production. Hardt and Negri speak of the 'biopolitical economic growth' of the common as 'a process of social composition' (284), that is, as a production of the socius.

The fundamental difference between Hardt and Negri's social production in relation to the BwO of capital, and Deleuze and Guattari's, is that for the latter this social production is not pictured otherwise than as the social production of that same body of capital. Desiring-production on the BwO of capital may seek and create lines of flights, but social production is always exclusively an extension of capital's BwO.[7] Hence, even though Deleuze and Guattari picture BwOs as corresponding to modes of production (savagery, despotism and capitalism, respectively), they articulate neither how one such BwO comes to succeed another nor how the BwO of capital could be transformed.

For Hardt and Negri, conversely, the social production taking place in capitalism does not exclusively contribute to the perpetuation of capital's own BwO: it is producing a new social body, the body of the common. The common, as Hardt and Negri state clearly, is a new mode of production, socially produced by the existing body of capital: 'Every mode of production, capital included, at first powerfully expands productive forces but eventually holds them back, thereby generating the foundations of the next mode of production' (Hardt and Negri 2009: 298), that 'next mode' clearly involving the common. Hence, the 'counteracted tendencies' of contemporary biopolitical capital are not merely internal to it, but are constituted by the presence of two heterogeneous and conflicting social elements: capital and the common.

A useful way of distinguishing between the biopolitical production of capital and the biopolitical production of the common, then, is to view capital and the common as separate bodies, even though the latter emerges from the former by means of immanent social production. '[T]he biopolitical process', Hardt and Negri write, 'is not limited to the reproduction of capital as a social relation' – that is, it is not entirely limited to the social production or reproduction of the BwO of capital as it seems to be on Deleuze and Guattari's account – 'but also presents the potential for an autonomous process that could destroy capital and create something entirely new' (Hardt and Negri 2009: 136). Biopolitical, social (re)production begins to introduce its own, separate, BwO, the BwO of the common.

The common thus attempts to give new foundations to 'autonomy' under real subsumption: it is an economic regime that radically subverts and distinguishes itself from capital's BwO while simultaneously remaining 'immanent' to it. Capital is increasingly dependent on the common as its source of wealth, and hence the common is 'immanent' to biopolitical production in capital even as these are two distinct bodies.

IV. Opposed Regimes of Value

There are many ways to picture the juxtaposition of the common with capital and how it might successfully replace the conceptually and practically untenable distinction between capital and labour. I argue that its most explosive aspect, however, is contained in the incompatible modes of valorisation intrinsic to the respective bodies of the common and capital. The *actual relationship* between the two bodies as they currently exist, in Hardt and Negri's description, is such that while the common forms the body of autonomously organised biopolitical production, capital forms the exploitative body which hovers over it – having to invent novel ways of extracting surplus value from it. These ways of exploitation are part new and part old. They are old in the sense that they involve a recourse to what Marx termed 'primitive accumulation': 'And insofar as today's neoliberal economy increasingly favors accumulation through expropriation of the common, the concept of primitive accumulation becomes an even more central analytical tool' (Hardt and Negri 2000: 138). But they are new in the sense that they account for the growing hegemony of the most advanced form of capital, finance capital: 'The key for finance is that it remains external to the production process. It does not attempt to organize social labor-power or dictate how it is to cooperate. It grants biopolitical production its autonomy and manages nonetheless to extract wealth from it at a distance' (289). Postmodern, financialised capital, then, depends on and exploits the common in a way that is different from Fordist capitalist management. We have already seen how the exploiter (capital) and the exploited (the common) have acquired two distinct BwOs, which form essentially different productive regimes. This means that exploitation – the extraction of surplus value – has to adapt itself to this reality with a fitting mode of valorisation. The BwO of capital that Deleuze and Guattari describe in *Anti-Oedipus* involves some characteristics that can be directly related to the new mode of valorisation that is a fundamental and novel part of Hardt and Negri's theory of the common. Deleuze and Guattari write that the BwO of capital

> will give to the sterility of money the form whereby money produces money. It produces surplus value ... It makes the machine responsible for producing a relative surplus value, while embodying itself in the machine as fixed capital [i.e. machinery]. Machines and agents cling so closely to capital that their very functioning appears to be miraculated by it. (Deleuze and Guattari 1983: 10–11)

Here, Deleuze and Guattari are of course dealing with the riddle of how money seems able to generate more money – a capacity for limitless multiplication that the common and finance capital actually seem to share. Interestingly, Deleuze and Guattari seem inclined to solve this riddle by referring to the classical Marxist distinction between labour and capital, quoting Marx's discussion in the third volume of *Capital* of how the 'productive powers and the social interrelations of labour time ... seem transferred from labour to capital' (Deleuze and Guattari 1983: 11). Deleuze and Guattari seem content to describe capitalist valorisation as completely explainable by the labour–capital distinction, speaking of the 'apparent objective moment' (11) of money begetting more money as 'fetishistic' and 'miraculated' – always requiring the input of abstract labour, the cornerstone of Marx's theory of value.

At other points, however – and much more in line with the real subsumption thesis, whereby labour becomes increasingly indistinguishable from capital and hence unable to account on its own for the creation of value – Deleuze and Guattari seem to be advancing a more complex theory of how surplus value would actually be created on the BwO of capital. Indeed, as Thoburn points out, Deleuze and Guattari maintain that capitalism depends less on the quantitative extraction of surplus value via exploitation of labour and more on a 'complex *qualitative* process' (Deleuze and Guattari 2004: 543), although this process remains largely unexplained. This kind of surplus value cannot be accounted for by hypothetical allocation of socially necessary labour time and would require a whole new theory of value. Such a theory, Thoburn argues with reference to Guattari's work, would have to conceptualise what Guattari calls *machinic surplus value* as 'based on qualitative intensity and variation of work' (Thoburn 2003: 97). However, Deleuze and Guattari's emergent value-theory of qualities remains ambiguous as to how machinic surplus value is really created, and does not detach itself fully from the classical Marxist notion that such an 'abstract-machinic' or 'social' surplus value would have to be understood as somehow untenable, fetishistic or miraculated.

A theory of qualitative value, however, is unequivocally demanded by Hardt and Negri in *Commonwealth*. They seem to argue that such a new theory of value could not truthfully apply to capital, which on their thesis is always and inevitably 'constrained by the logic of scarcity' (Hardt and Negri 2009: 283). The biopolitical cycle, on the other hand, has 'to be understood now in relation to the *qualities* of the common' (284). These qualities are not translatable onto the surface of the BwO of capital and this incommensurability is demonstrated by the fact that 'when capital accumulates the common and makes it private, its productivity is blocked or lessened' (288). Here we see an emerging juxtaposition of two modes of valorisation, corresponding to the two different modes of production: the quantitative logic of scarcity that is a by-product of capital, and the qualitative logic of excess and growth that belongs to the common.

On the body without organs of the common, the apparatuses of capture of the capitalist BwO appear as fetters and limitations to productivity, perhaps akin to the elements that 'botch' the BwO as described in *A Thousand Plateaus* (Deleuze and Guattari 2004: 166). Hardt and Negri give an outline of a new theory of value that could account for these problems:

> The critique of political economy, too, including the Marxist tradition, has generally focused on measurement and quantitative methods to understand surplus value and exploitation. Biopolitical products, however, tend to *exceed* all quantitative measurement and take *common form*, which are easily shared and difficult to corral as private property. (Hardt and Negri 2009: 135–6)

Subsequently, Hardt and Negri draw a comparison with the standard numerical columns of debit and credit in conventional quantitative economy, and move on to pose the question thus: 'How can one create an economic table filled with qualities?' (Hardt and Negri 2009: 287). Although this question remains an open one in *Commonwealth*, I suggest that we interpret it as opening towards a solution of Deleuze and Guattari's problematic notion of machinic surplus value. It seems that the BwO of capital is actually not capable of any valorisation other than of the quantitative kind. This, then, would be a description commensurable with both Marx's *and* Deleuze and Guattari's analysis of capital as a quantitative axiomatic in which exchange value (quantitative by nature) fully dominates. The features that seem to contradict this – that is, abstract-machinic surplus value, qualitative social production, the production of subjectivities and so forth–can now be understood as part of biopolitical production, not properly belonging to the BwO of capital, but to the BwO of the common. This machinic surplus value might of course still *appear* as 'miraculated' on the BwO of capital, but only if we fail to perceive that it is in fact created (*not* miraculated) on another BwO: the BwO of the common.

V. A Common Program

Let us now readdress Toscano's challenge: to 'think an antagonism' closely related to 'the conditions of production and reproduction of

contemporary capitalism' while holding 'a certain degree of deter-
minateness' (Toscano 2009: 127). What the common brings together
and clarifies are two aspects of biopolitical production: First, social
production, which is now understood as the social production of the
common as a new relation of production, or a new BwO. Thus, social
forces do not necessarily constrain the movements of the multitude, as
Thoburn argues with reference to Deleuze and Guattari (Thoburn 2003:
90); rather, the multitude produces its own socius because the 'surplus'
of social production under biopolitical capitalism is, of course, also
social in nature: it is the common. Second, the common seems to provide
us with a new kind of BwO on which it would be possible to theoretically
account for the creation of qualitative machinic surplus value – social in
nature, which could be called 'abstract-machinic surplus value'. On the
BwO of the common, such a social surplus value would neither have
to be seen as 'miraculated' or fetishised as Deleuze and Guattari would
have it, nor as requiring a recourse to a pre-biopolitical labour-theory of
value which makes an untenable distinction between labour and capital.[8]

Eugene W. Holland writes that considerations of the 'different
relations of production' that could potentially free difference (meaning
surplus value) from capitalist axiomatisation – such as the productive
relations here ascribed to the common – 'already point well beyond any
capitalist horizons, about which Deleuze and Guattari are not inclined
to say very much at all' (Holland 1997: 531). The common certainly
points beyond these horizons, and, primarily because of the novel ways
in which value can be created by and within the common, arguably
does so better than Hardt and Negri's previous concept of autonomy-
in-production. The merit, hence, of introducing what I am here calling
the BwO of the common is that it links the notion of the common
to Deleuze and Guattari's insightful analysis of capitalist valorisation
and social production, while also transcending their silent or 'minor'
horizon. It articulates a dimension of conflict with capital that reaches a
truly 'social' level; immanent to the social field, yet extending beyond the
cramped and minor position Deleuze and Guattari limit themselves to.

It falls outside the scope of this essay to describe what concrete
forms the antagonism between capital and the common might take
in future social struggles. Let it suffice to mention two practical
advantages offered by insisting on the capital–common distinction:
First, the common is a very apt tool for analysis of the evolving and
complex dynamics of post-Fordist capitalism, especially as they relate to
immaterial labour and production, direct exploitation, financialisation,
and debates over intellectual property. Thus, the common contributes

significantly to a Jamesonian 'cognitive mapping' of the apparent mysteries of postmodern capitalism. Second, the common offers a framework for political activism that is grounded in the economic contradictions of the current social order. Such a framework does not limit itself to, say, minor lines of flight, voluntarism, racial and gender identity politics, communicative action or antagonism within social discourse, to name only a few examples of the modest terrains marked out by leftist theory over the last decades. The common offers an opportunity to revisit the old Marxist insistence on the social embeddedness of any radical ideology; communism not only as an idea but also as a movement springing from within the social body.

Perhaps unexpectedly for a consistent critic of Hardt, Negri and poststructuralist tendencies within Marxism in general, Slavoj Žižek has in fact emphasised the importance of Hardt and Negri's concept of the common for the first three of what he calls the four 'possible antagonisms' contained in contemporary capitalism: ecological catastrophe, intellectual property, biogenetics and social exclusion (Žižek 2009: 53). Even though Žižek implies mistakenly that the fourth antagonism does not fall within the domain of the common, his acceptance of the common as a designator for the revolutionary challenges of the near future indicates that the common–capital distinction could become the basis of a communist programme extending well beyond the scope of Hardt and Negri's current readership.[9]

Notes

1. It falls outside the scope of this paper to fully examine the variations of the concept of the BwO through Deleuze's *The Logic of Sense* and his and Guattari's *A Thousand Plateaus*. See, however, note 7.
2. Marx discusses real subsumption (as opposed to formal subsumption) in his appendix to *Capital Volume I* (Marx 1976: 1034–38). A helpful analysis of the social-factory thesis and its relation to readings of Marx can be found in Thoburn 2003, especially Chapters 4 and 5, 'The Social Factory' and 'The Refusal of Work', as well as in Chapter 6 of Wright 2002. See also Read 2004, Chapter 3, for a thorough discussion of formal and real subsumption.
3. Mariarosa Dalla Costa was 'the first of the workerists to advance a coherent case for the claim that the extraction of surplus value could occur outside the sphere Marx had designated as the direct process of production' (Wright 2002: 134–5).
4. I imitate Thoburn's use of the phrase 'autonomy-in-production'. Negri and Hardt more often use the phrase 'autonomous production' (see e.g. Hardt and Negri 2000: 276; 2009: 334, 364).
5. To name one example of such a critique, Slavoj Žižek equates Hardt and Negri's socio-political analysis with a 'fascination' for contemporary capitalism (Žižek 2007: 47). This is paralleled in Žižek's critique of Deleuze, whom he views as

'the ideologist of late capitalism' given the aptness of his and Guattari's analysis in the *Capitalism and Schizophrenia* volumes (Žižek 2004: 293).

6. For a concise analysis of the three syntheses (connective, disjunctive and conjunctive) developed in *Anti-Oedipus* see Holland 1999: 26–35.

7. It should be noted, importantly, that in *A Thousand Plateaus*, Deleuze and Guattari begin to develop their understanding of the body without organs in a direction that is somewhat more inimical to capitalist social production than in *Anti-Oedipus*. However, it can be concluded that the productive capacities of the BwO of *A Thousand Plateaus* are either directed solely towards desiring-production (i.e. not social production), or towards extremely 'cautious' modes of social assemblage that would certainly conform to Thoburn's 'minor' interpretation of Deleuzian politics. The BwO of *A Thousand Plateaus* is described in terms of 'disarticulation', 'experimentation' and 'nomadism' and stands opposed to 'organisms' of any kind. However, its separation from existing structures – the organism, the sign and the subject – demands '[c]aution' and skilful negotiations with 'the dominant reality' so as not to bring it 'back down on us heavier than ever' (Deleuze and Guattari 2004: 176–8).

8. It is important to keep in mind that Hardt and Negri are not offering a full-fledged value-theory of common qualities and their surplus. Cesare Casarino indicates the extent of ontological research required for such a theory, which would account for the 'two radically different modalities of surplus' constituted by capital and by the common (Negri and Casarino 2008: 30). Perhaps the most exciting challenge for a new theory of value would be to address the question of money, thus posed by Hardt and Negri: 'Might the power of money (and the finance world in general) to represent the social field of production be, in the hands of the multitude, an instrument of freedom, with the capacity to overthrow misery and poverty? ... We cannot answer these questions satisfactorily yet, but it seems to us that efforts to reappropriate money in this way point in the direction of revolutionary activity today' (Hardt and Negri 2009: 295).

9. This essay is based on a paper of the same name delivered at the conference 'Deleuze and Activism' at the University of Cardiff on 13 November 2009.

References

Deleuze, Gilles (1992) 'Postscript on the Societies of Control', trans. Martin Joughin, *October*, 59 (Winter), pp. 3–7.

Deleuze, Gilles and Félix Guattari (1983) *Anti-Oedipus*, trans. Helen R. Lane, Robert Hurley and Robert Seem, Minneapolis: University of Minnesota Press.

Deleuze, Gilles and Félix Guattari (2004) *A Thousand Plateaus*, trans. Brian Massumi, London: Continuum.

Hardt, Michael (1993) *Gilles Deleuze: An Apprenticeship in Philosophy*, Minneapolis: University of Minnesota Press.

Hardt, Michael (1999) 'Affective Labor', *boundary 2*, 26:2, pp. 89–100.

Hardt, Michael and Antonio Negri (2000) *Empire*, Cambridge, MA: Harvard University Press.

Hardt, Michael and Antonio Negri (2005) *Multitude*, London: Penguin Books.

Hardt, Michael and Antonio Negri (2009) *Commonwealth*, Cambridge, MA: Harvard University Press.

Holland, Eugene W. (1997) 'Marx and Poststructuralist Philosophies of Difference', *South Atlantic Quarterly*, 96:3, pp. 525–42.

Holland, Eugene W. (1999) *Deleuze and Guattari's Anti-Oedipus*, London and New York: Routledge.

Marx, Karl (1973) *Grundrisse. Foundations of the Critique of Political Economy*, trans. Martin Nicolaus, New York: Vintage Books.

Marx, Karl (1976) *Capital Volume I*, trans. Ben Fowkes, London: Penguin Books.

Negri, Antonio and Anne Dufourmantelle (2004) *Negri on Negri: Antonio Negri in Conversation with Anne Dufourmantelle*, trans. M. B. DeBevoise, New York: Routledge.

Negri, Antonio and Cesare Casarino (2008) *In Praise of the Common: A Conversation on Philosophy and Politics*, Minneapolis: University of Minnesota Press.

Read, Jason (2004) *The Micro-Politics of Capital: Marx and the Prehistory of the Present*, Albany: State University of New York Press.

Thoburn, Nicholas (2003) *Deleuze, Marx and Politics*, London: Routledge.

Toscano, Alberto (2009) 'Chronicles of Insurrection: Tronti, Negri and the Subject of Antagonism', in A. Toscano and L. Chiesa (eds.), *The Italian Difference: Between Nihilism and Biopolitics*, Melbourne, re.press, pp. 109–28.

Wright, Steve (2002) *Storming Heaven: Class Composition and Struggle in Italian Autonomist Marxism*, London: Pluto Press.

Žižek, Slavoj (2004) 'The Ongoing 'Soft Revolution', *Critical Inquiry*, 75 (Winter), pp. 292–323.

Žižek, Slavoj (2007) 'Multitude, Surplus, and Envy', *Rethinking Marxism*, 19:1, pp. 46–58.

Žižek, Slavoj (2009) 'How to Begin From the Beginning', *New Left Review*, 57 (May–June), pp. 43–55.

Activist Materialism

Dimitris Papadopoulos   University of Leicester

Abstract

This paper explores a form of activism that operates with and within matter. For more than 150 years materialism has informed activist practice through materialist conceptions of history and modes of production. The paper discusses the ambivalences of these previous configurations of activism and materialism and explores possibilities for enacting activist interventions in conditions where politics is not only performed as a politics of history but as the fundamental capacity to remake and transform processes of matter and life. What is activism when politics is increasingly performed as a politics of matter? What is activism when it comes to a materialist understanding of matter itself?

Keywords: activism, materialism, matter, Marx, minor science, technoscience

I. 1844

> The real unity of the world consists in its materiality...
> (Engels 1987 [1878])

The recent resurgence of materialism poses questions about its implications and relevance for politics. Rather than addressing institutional or representational politics I am interested here in tracing the connections of materialism to the transformative politics of social movements: collective direct activism on the immediate level of social and material life. In each particular historical chronotope there is a distinctive set of social movements which become capable of initiating social change. How is materialism related to these transformative

Deleuze Studies Volume 4: 2010 supplement: 64–83
DOI: 10.3366/E1750224110001133
© Edinburgh University Press
www.eupjournals.com/dls

forces? And what kind of political activism do today's novel forms of materialism promote?

The articulation between materialism and activism is unstable, full of discontinuities and breaks. It is in Marx and the early rebellions that took place in the 'New World', and in the Communes and uprisings across Europe, that materialism first becomes directly linked to political activism: activist materialism. Since then materialism has been the target of interrogation not only from idealist positions and various dualist ontologies but also more recently from within the very political forces of the western post-1960s Left which were embracing materialism in one form or another. Critiques from the Left did not position themselves outside the materialist movement, they were not first and foremost an opposition; rather, it was an immanent movement enunciated from the very core of materialism itself that lasted up until the 1980s and 1990s and finally ushered a new version of materialism to the fore. Deleuze and Guattari's work exercised an important influence on the movements that attempted to rework materialism. During the long history of the encounter between materialism and activism both of them changed meanings, and each new formation of the one influenced the meaning of the other, producing new configurations of social practice.

Marx's work is probably the first attempt to connect activism and materialism on the level of everyday political practice. The *Theses on Feuerbach* exemplifies the articulation between materialism and activism in a remarkable and equally unexpected way. Thought objects and abstract contemplation are what Marx tries to defy, that is, idealism. The movement which changes society is the movement which opposes idealism. It is real, objective, that is, material, says Marx. Marx's materialism is conceived as sensuous everyday practical activity which has the capacity to change the material conditions of existence. The moment of transformation is the moment when, to use Marx's term, civil society collapses and a new social material order emerges. This very modern understanding of materialism was epitomised in *The German Ideology*: here communism is not 'an ideal to which reality have to adjust itself'; it is 'the real movement which abolishes the present state of things' (Marx and Engels 1846: 48).

It is in the *Economic and Philosophical Manuscripts* (1844) that Marx introduces a new definition of materialism grounded on inserting political activism into the understanding of materiality. Here he uses the concept of 'species-being' to describe human activity as the process of the self-making of the human species in a direct practical and organic relation to other species and the whole of the natural world. Despite its essentialist connotations, 'species-being' is as close as one can get to a radical understanding of a form of self-instituted collective emancipation in which cooperation and interaction among humans as well as between humans and the material world is crucial (Dyer-Witheford 2006). For Marx the question is to uncover both what impedes this process, i.e. how capitalist labour alienates 'species-being', and how collective material self-transformation is possible. Who controls the process of material transformation, who participates and in which position, are questions which drive Marx's activist reading of materialism. This materialism is activist because it is a 'life activity', in the literal sense: 'life engendering life'. There is no social transformation outside of the material realm.

Marx's early materialism avoids the pitfall of epistemology: the attempt to distinguish between a strong materialist perspective which gives absolute primacy to matter (all that exists is matter) and a weak materialist perspective that puts the emphasis on how we conceive matter (all that exists is dependent on matter). Such an epistemological definition of materialism wouldn't be sufficient to distinguish it from idealism because at the end what we define as matter would involve an idealist move. From an epistemological viewpoint both positions, the materialist as well as the idealist one, are in principle tenable. But Marx's early materialism is ontological through and through: there is no transformative activity which is non-material. Since activity is inherently material, matter itself cannot be conceived as an outside or as an object of human practice: matter is humanity's body. 'Species-being' is the collective metabolic transformation of matter: activist materialism. There is a monist understanding of matter here that resonates with today's neo-materialism (for a superb example of the new materialism see Bennett 2010), so much influenced by Deleuze and Guattari's work which will be discussed extensively later in the paper. For now we can say that both Marx's early materialism and today's neo-materialism share a strong emphasis on matter as a vital force: inorganic matter as well as biological and social life are movements of matter itself. Nevertheless, in terms of Marx's early definition of materialism, merely highlighting the importance of materiality as an assemblage of heterogeneous forces is not enough to account for the kind of transformative political engagement that was his main concern. Marx's monist ontological materialism is infused with an activist dimension which takes place on the actual everyday life of 'species-being': the collective capacity to affect material change. Marx's ontological reading of materialism is one that focuses on practice, but a form of practice which is not solely in the hands of people but also depends on non-human forces ('nature'). Practice and matter cannot be thought independently. And the reason for this is not epistemological but political: activist materialism is a response to capital's breaking up of the 'species-being' into classes and races. Materialism without activism is not transformative, in fact it is impossible. This is the quintessence of Marx's early account of a practical ontology and an activist materialism. What happens to this configuration of materialism 34 years before the bicentenary anniversary of the *Economic and Philosophical Manuscripts*?

Marx's and in particular Engels' late work contains a second reading of the activist materialism developed in their early writings: dialectical materialism. 'Diamat' consolidated the absolute emphasis on matter but introduced a different conception of its role which had tremendous impact on theorists of the Second International and the emerging Marxist social movements. 'Diamat' foregrounded activist materialism as a rather dogmatic epistemological doctrine that gradually removed the practical ontological concern with matter and subsequently transformed the meaning of activism. Already in the early writings there are numerous instances where, instead of the practical ontology described in the previous paragraphs, we find a relation to nature dominated by the ideal of progressivism and the total human mastery of nature's laws. This understanding also changed the meaning of activism. In *Anti-Dühring* (1878) and *Ludwig Feuerbach* (1886) Engels set out a materialist cosmology that served to define activism as a political practice which is mono-causally determined by a set of laws extracted from nature: historical materialism. This is characterised by both a bifurcated dualist ontology – with objective material reality and its inherent laws on the one hand and social practice on the other – and also by a reduction of materiality to human social institutions and structures. Activism was reduced to the efficacy of changing social structures. Historical materialism announces the erasure of the activist materialism to be found in the early works of Marx and Engels.

II. 1908

> Moscow! Moscow! Moscow! (Irina in Chekhov 1900)

In *Materialism and Empirio-Criticism* Lenin follows this line and conceives materialism exclusively as a theory of knowledge. He writes: 'For the sole "property" of matter with whose recognition philosophical materialism is bound up is the property of being an objective reality, of existing outside our mind' (Lenin 1908: 260). Materialism here starts from the assumption of an ontological duality, two separate entities: matter on the one hand, mind on the other. Lenin reduces materialism to gnosiological realism, while the activist materialism of the early Marx was one which asserted a monist ontology: mind is matter, the unity of the world is sustained by its materiality and the immanent action of matter and mind alike. Lenin's approach is a radical departure from a position which is concerned with bringing together practice and matter. Rather, his concern was to develop a conceptual instrument which splits ideas in two opposite camps. While Marx and Engels' early activist materialism was concerned with how matter is changing and can be changed, Lenin's materialism was developed as a strategic tool for the selection of the social and political forces of his time which might potentially transform into a revolutionary historical subject.

Lenin was building a war machine. He was trying to develop a philosophical conception of materialism which had no other target than to reveal the functioning of a deep social dichotomy between the working class and capital (for an extended analysis of these issues see Jordan 1967). His only goal was to submit theory to the everyday requirements of his revolutionary practice. This was truly phenomenal and unparalleled (albeit fatal). With his philosophical work Lenin developed a tool to extend the social division as far it could go, to the far end of mind and the history of ideas. In the unsurpassable *What Is To Be Done?* (1902) Lenin claims that social conflict penetrates every corner of society, every social relation, every idea. Nothing is untouchable by class antagonism, it takes a partisan organisation and a revolution to change it. This is partisan philosophy and partisan practice. And it is a truly activist move; however this particular move enacts a different materialism. It is carried out in the name of materialism but it is not an activist monist materialism. It is one which subsumes matter and dominates nature in the name of historical progress. If Marx's early materialism was of a kind which proclaimed the irresistibility of revolution on the grounds of a unified monist movement of matter and activism, Lenin's materialism is dualist, elevating irresistibility to something completely different: the will for action.

'Materialism must be a form of idealism, since it's wrong – too' (Sahlins 2002: 6). Marshall Sahlins' aphorism concentrates the post-Second World War predicament with the configuration of an activist materialism à la Lenin. Lenin's reduction of monist materialism to gnosiological realism had far-reaching consequences for the philosophical scaffolding of the social forces which found themselves entangled in the Marxist enterprise and in the emerging working-class movements from the beginning of the twentieth century up to the 1970s and 1980s. The most important consequence was that gradually materialism failed to contribute to an ethical and political programme for the everyday enactment of activist practice. Activist materialism became everything but activist, quickly turning into an ideology of state socialism and an abstract philosophical system. In the post-Second World War period, materialism gradually lost its strength as an ethical project for revolutionising everyday practice.

III. 1977

Always historicize! (Jameson 1981)

The end of the 1970s probably saw a peak in the process of an immanent critique of materialism which rendered visible its contradictions as inherited from the Leninist period. The following quote from Raymond Williams displays the state of thought and mood among politically committed left intellectuals at the time:

> It took me thirty years, in a very complex process, to move from that received Marxist theory (which in its most general form I began by accepting) through various transitional forms of theory and inquiry, to the position I now hold, which I define as 'cultural materialism'. The emphases of the transition – on the production (rather than only the reproduction) of meanings and values by specific social formations, on the centrality of language and communication as formative social forces, and on the complex interaction both of institutions and forms and of social relationships and formal conventions – may be defined, if any one wishes, as 'culturalism', and even the crude old (positivist) idealism/materialism dichotomy may be applied if it helps anyone. What I would now claim to have reached, but necessarily by this route, is a theory of culture as a (social and material) productive process and of specific practices, of 'arts', as social uses of material means of production. (Williams 1980: 243)

During the period of the crisis of materialism which unfolded in the decades between 1950 and 1990 the notion of culture reordered the existing meanings of materialism and fuelled the development of a new constellation of concepts and activities into the heart of the social conflict of the post-war period. Of course, not all of the various movements and critiques of materialism embraced the notion of culture. The point here is not to unify these extremely diverse movements and traditions under one overarching rubric. Rather, what is of importance is that the insurgency against the previous materialism evolved in proximity to new everyday activities whose many faces and actions pertain to changing cultural power (see Gilbert 2008; Papadopoulos, Stephenson and Tsianos 2008).

This turn to culture thoroughly changed the way political activism is performed, moving the target away from the state itself towards power's pervasive materialisation in the whole societal nexus: in terms of gender relations, racialisation processes, social institutions, social and civil rights, the political representation of excluded groups, and so on. Many societies, many cultures, many socialisms, Raymond Williams would have said. This remaking of materialism corresponds with the practices of new social forces that found themselves outside the traditional organisational forms of the working-class movement which appeared as the inheritor of the materialist politics of the previous periods. The new politics of cultural counterinsurgency, not least as exemplified in the new youth cultures of the 1960s and the variously globalised events of 1968, spread across the globe with a velocity far beyond the wildest utopian dreams that Soviet propaganda bureaucrats and western communist parties ever imagined for their own materialist politics (see Connery 2005).

But where exactly was the materialism in this activism which propelled itself through cultural politics? The most likely answer is that there was very little materialism in this 'cultural materialist' politics, at least not in the sense of an activist and practical ontology concerned with a monist understanding of matter (as in Marx's early version). Nor was there much of the materialism of the late Marx/Lenin period with its strong focus on gnosiological dualism and the efficacy of social structures. Cultural politics questioned both versions of materialism and developed along many disparate and diverse paths: all of which were, however, occupied with the centrality of representation and its critiques. 'Discourse' seems to have been one of the paths that helped this move. Ironically, the discursive turn and the turn to language set in motion an activist politics which followed the activist materialism of the previous decades. Umberto Eco's *The Open Work* (Eco 1989) and James Clifford's collection *Writing Culture* (Clifford and Marcus 1986), as well as the broader linguistic turn (Rorty 1967) and the interest in hermeneutics (Gadamer 1989), are just some examples of intellectual engagements that marked the path to the undiscovered continent of representation. It was through the changing of meanings and the challenging of representations that the very process of social activism was now being performed.

Another important path for the revision of materialism that developed during this period came from an interest in social space as a key battlefield for social antagonisms. How is space regulated, appropriated and re-appropriated by marginalised social groups? Marxist inspired readings of everyday space (Lefebvre 1991), the situationist movement (Debord 1981), and cultural geographers (Harvey 1990) all turned to kaleidoscopic remakings of space in order to articulate an everyday, mainly urban, activism that made radical interventions in the politics of post-war Europe and North America possible. The attention to space as lived experience is closely related to body politics. The body becomes an open substratum for the inscription and re-inscription of social signification. In this sense signification moves from the mind itself to the body and emerges in a process of subjective embodiment through a social context (cf. Csordas 1994; Harré 1996; Overton 1998) or through cultural-political constellations (cf. Bourdieu 1987; Braidotti 2002; Fausto-Sterling 2000).

But actually what the activism of the post-war period was mainly preoccupied with was subjectivity and difference (Blackman et al. 2008). As cultural studies has so vividly shown, subjectivity is always in the making because it entails a non-expressed otherness, a non-discursified and imagined possibility of social relations (Hall 1990; Papadopoulos 2006). Such a theoretical move was particularly important in a period where identity politics occupied a central place in the political life of the societies of the Global North (Clifford 2000). Already in the 1970s and 1980s, cultural studies, feminist politics, anti-racism and gender studies identified the limitations of an activist materialism qua Lenin which saw social consciousness either as committed to working-class change or as wrong and ideological. In resonance with Althusser's take on ideology (Althusser 2001), new social movements focused on the emergence of multiple political subjectivities that defy straightforward classification as wrong (false consciousness) or right (revolutionary) according to previous conceptions of activist materialism. Crucial for this attempt was the process of articulation (Clifford 2001; Hall 1986a; Slack 1996). Activism here is conceived as a movement of articulation which by rethinking Gramscian hegemony attempts to contest domination through 'rendering the symbolic increasingly dynamic, that is, by considering the conditions and limits of representation and representability as open to significant rearticulations and transformations under the pressure of social practices of various kinds' (Butler 1997: 23; see also: Hall 1986b; Laclau and Mouffe 1985). This understanding of political subjectivity as subjectification and the result of articulation is what essentially captured activist practices in this period, positioning subjectivity in the tension between coercion by institutional mechanisms and articulation through them.

Cultural politics challenged previous versions of materialism on the grounds of an increasing diversification of social strata and classes. It is this diversification that brought a new form of activism which, rather than focusing on materialism was concerned with the fight for representation. In this struggle, discourse, space, body and subjectivity are approached as constitutive of an oppositional politics of difference. Cultural studies, women's studies, postcolonial studies and queer politics have all participated in and critiqued this fight for representation (see Hall and Jefferson 1976; Clifford 1986; Sedgwick 1990; Spivak 1999; Warner 1999; Butler, Laclau and Žižek 2000; Mouffe 2000). The importance of representation comes from the dissolution of social class as the central actor and political force in society. The political order of transnational neoliberal societies is an order which is supposed to be occupied by multiple players working to foster alliances between themselves and to establish new relations of power. And it is precisely this form of relationality which triggers the imperative for representation (Stephenson and Papadopoulos 2006). Representation enters the realm of politics as the attempt to give voice and operative agency to social groups who have been excluded by the politics of the traditional versions of activist materialism. We can trace the singular trajectories of these emergent oppositional subjectivities of new diverse social groups in civil rights movements, in the events of 1968, in feminist movements, anti-work movements and new forms of social cooperation, in the 1960s cultural rebellions and in the fight against colonialism and racism.

IV. 1987

> The only enemy is two. (Deleuze 2001)

However deep the break between Leninist activist materialism and the cultural materialism of the post-war period might be, there remains nevertheless a peculiar form of continuity. Lenin's materialism reduced activism to the radical intentionality of a subject determined to reflect the antagonistic conditions of existence. Cultural materialism retained this reduction but introduced a differentiation with respect to the subject itself. Instead of a unified self-identical subject we now have a plethora of subjectivities and of possible contexts in which they are constituted. This break implied a deep change in the way political activism was conceived: Leninist activism subsumed every activity under a single social conflict between labour and capital, while the activism of cultural politics multiplies the fronts on which social antagonisms are encountered and fought. Nevertheless, despite this radical break, both positions retain a strange commitment to epistemological dualism. Representation and ideas are the battleground on which the conceptualisation of activism thrives. It is about negotiating and transforming the conditions of thinking and feeling that make activism possible. In a peculiar way cultural materialism followed Lenin's path in focusing on how we represent reality. What cultural materialism introduced was a new conceptualisation of the main determinants of representation. It is no longer the class structure of society but rather the endless variability of social contexts that allows different configurations of representation. In this sense the question for cultural activism becomes one of how reality is constructed in the subject itself, or 'social constructionism'. In both positions, however, practice and matter are subsequent to ideas; and despite their pervasive critiques of dualism, both retained a dualist ontology. Here is Deleuze and Guattari's well-known diagnosis of this situation:

> We invoke one dualism only in order to challenge another. We employ a dualism of models only in order to arrive at a process that challenges all models. Each time, mental correctives are necessary to undo the dualisms we had no wish to construct but through which we pass. Arrive at the magic formula we all seek – PLURALISM = MONISM – via all the dualisms that are the enemy, an entirely necessary enemy, the furniture we are forever rearranging. (Deleuze and Guattari 1987: 20)

In much of their work, and most centrally in *A Thousand Plateaus*, Deleuze and Guattari introduce a monist materialism which attempts to rehabilitate matter from its enslavement in representation. Their move is co-extensive with the (re-)appearance of a form of materialism that puts the primacy of matter on the agenda of political practice and theory after the 1990s and creates the possibility for the emergence of a novel configuration of activist materialism. Strangely enough it was the poststructuralist faction of the cultural activism of the previous decades that prepared the way for this move – in particular feminist materialism, the attention to the body, as described earlier, and the persistent but evasive attempts to put materialism back on the agenda (one need only recall Althusser's (2006) subterranean movements). But even more crucial to the reinvigoration of activist materialism is the increasing impact of scientific knowledge on everyday life and on the structures of production in the Global North that posit matter as an active, self-ordering, emergent player in a radically post-human world (see Papadopoulos 2010). Matter is before thinking, matter is in thinking, matter is everywhere. For Deleuze and Guattari there is no empty space, there is always matter and matter is always differentiated. Representations are a particular form of differentiation in their own right, they do not exist prior to or *vis-à-vis* matter. Representations are movements of matter as much as genetic mutations or geological movements are. Deleuze and Guattari's point is not to eliminate the distinctive importance of representations and ideas, rather, their claim is that when representations are considered as separated from matter they become strategic tools for ordering material reality. Representations are closures and reterritorialisations that are used as powers to organise matter in a particular way.

The materialism emerging gradually after the 1990s focuses on the question of monism instead of concentrating on the binary opposition between materialism and idealism. It is this very dichotomy that undermines monist materialism. It is not about which position you take in this thinking, it is about the very act of taking a position. For Deleuze and Guattari the real enemy of materialist thinking is not idealism, it is dualism. 'The only enemy is two' (Deleuze 2001: 95). Materialism after the 1990s is an anti-dualism that gradually transforms the relation between activism and materialism that informed most of social movements during the Leninist period and after: matter and mind, activism and materialism start to fuse again into one process. The practice itself, the site of action and its thinking, gradually became equally important for the activism of the 1990s. It is not a coincidence that many of the social movements of this period and since focus on the question of reclaiming. The activism of reclaiming attempts to re-appropriate the immediate spaces of existence by simultaneously transforming them through everyday actions: reclaim the streets, reclaim the city, earth activism and the permaculture movement, the remaking of transnational spaces through migration movements, radical queer activism and the building of new social relationalities and communities, cyberactivism, the alter-globalisation movement, the production of the commons. In all of them we encounter an emphasis on reclaiming material spaces and relations vital for developing new alternative social and material projects (for an extended discussion see Papadopoulos et al. 2008; Chesters and Welsh 2006). This was, of course, also a central characteristic of previous forms of political activism, in particular of feminism. But the primary difference here is that either the question of reclaiming social and material spaces was not conceptualised as such or else was considered secondary with regards to the 'real' and 'primary' struggle, which was supposed to focus on radical demands addressed to the state and its institutions in respect of recognition and representation. In contrast, the activism emerging after the 1990s, and in particular since the Zapatista movement, is less concerned with the state's mediation; instead it *consciously* attempts to force existing institutions to change by creating alternative materialities and forms of life.

Deleuze and Guattari's monist materialism captures a key moment of this form of activism that reconnects us with the activist materialism of the early Marx described at the beginning of this paper. It is the question of how to change matter and create new forms through collective practices. Deleuze and Guattari's materialism questions how the very moment of morphing matter comes into being. The emergence of form is neither the transcendent imposition of a preconceived plan on matter – forget the architect and the bee – nor is it simply a movement of self-organised matter that becomes represented in the mind of the subject – forget autopoietic systems. Neither external plan, nor internal self-organisation. In this sense, it is neither idealism nor materialism (as conceived until now). The position Deleuze and Guattari try to develop is that it is the movement of matter itself that makes both a materialist as well as an idealist stance possible. Both the capacity to create form and the capacity to understand the emergence of form are immanent to existence. There is no monism if there *is* a dualist option; 'there is nothing that is one, there is nothing that is multiple' (Deleuze 2001: 99). Deleuze and Guattari tried to avoid thinking along the either-or of materialism and idealism/dualism. The very possibility of thought is immanent to matter's movements.

Morphogenesis in Deleuze and Guattari is neither a property of self-ordering material systems nor the result of a vitalist force that initiates material change; nor of course is it the ability of the subject's mind to form matter according to a preconceived plan. There is something not immediately present in the actuality of material flows – something virtual – that makes matter congeal into stratified stable forms. In each particular setting there is a virtual ordering principle (an abstract machine in Deleuze and Guattari's words) that links and connects flows and properties of matter. An often utilised example in *A Thousand Plateaus* is the organism. When does an aggregate of various bodily processes and functions become a thing which can be called an organism? An organism is ordered matter – the moment when matter in flux, in movement, in variation becomes a discernible thing amenable to intervention, management, manipulation (through medical practice for example, or in the course of ontogenetic development). Embryology and biology, medicine and psychology, play an equal role with ontogenetic change, gene activity, epigenetic interactions and the environment to produce a coherent story of what an organism is in a particular historical chronotope. Out of the movement of unformed matter and non-formalised processes of the body without organs (BwO), as Deleuze and Guattari call the non-organismic body, we encounter the formed and stratified form of the organism:

> The organism is not at all the body, the BwO; rather, it is a stratum on the BwO, in other words, a phenomenon of accumulation, coagulation, and sedimentation that, in order to extract useful labor from the BwO, imposes upon it forms, functions, bonds, dominant and hierarchized organizations, organized transcendences. The strata are bonds, pincers. 'Tie me up if you wish.' We are continually stratified. But who is this we that is not me, for the subject no less than the organism belongs to and depends on a stratum? (Deleuze and Guattari 1987: 159)

In this understanding of monist materialism, matter becomes the horizon and the substratum on which an alternative to the previous versions of materialism can emerge. Matter becomes (once more) the way to reconnect activism and materialism. The crucial move for materialism since the 1990s is to seek in matter an escape from a situation where the demise of the everyday transformative activist aspect of materialism became so pervasive. Deleuze and Guattari's move to a monist materialism is not a theoretical choice; it is the result of a political diagnosis according to which any desire for change has been vampirised by the institutions of the state. Even more than that, in the previous decades desire itself has been transformed into a capitalist institution (cf. Holland 2005). Every social struggle is reinserted as a rejuvenating feature of capitalist production, every social innovation is made productive. The story of the twentieth century is not a history of revolutions; it is rather a history of counter-revolutions (Müller 2000) where every desire has been appropriated, regurgitated and effaced by capitalism. The bottom line for Deleuze and Guattari's take on materialism, as a monist materialism based on a renewed attention to matter, is the attempt to reactivate the transformative force of desire. Deleuze and Guattari try to do this by breaking the link between 'desire' and 'desire for'. Every 'desire for' is a closure: desire for revolution, desire for mastering nature, desire for recognition, desire for an identity, desire for not having an identity, desire for desire. This is the political move Deleuze and Guattari reinsert into the new materialism: to disrupt the view that the creativity of people, animals and matter can be viewed as a desire which can always be folded back into capitalist domination and valorisation. Every 'desire for' is already captured and appropriated. This is the spell capitalism casts upon life.

The key political ingredient of monist materialism is that desire needs to be disarticulated from its essential function as something which has a target and object. The diagnosis: 'desire for' is the way capitalism revolutionises itself. The radical political key to monist materialism is that it allows desire to be engendered in a way that can move beyond its recoding into the political closures of the counter-revolutions of the twentieth century. The prominent role of matter in Deleuze and Guattari is a small gesture of rebellion against the capture of earlier materialisms within a docile machine for constantly revolutionising capitalism. Deleuze and Guattari perform this small gesture of freedom by inserting indeterminacy into the way desire operates; and they do so by turning to the underlying indeterminacy of matter: matter is primarily unformed and in continuous variation, an oscillation between various intensities, closures and openings. Matter is a political exit. Matter is escape. The making of a life. Matter can break the capitalist spell.

The turn to matter becomes political when it is articulated in relation to this understanding of desire. That is why, despite the various attempts to read Deleuze and Guattari's materialism in a scientistic way – that is, as a cosmology attentive to science (see for example De Landa 1997) – what Deleuze and Guattari propose is a rather minor move, one which attempts to interrupt the appropriation of desire by grounding it in the indeterminate movements of matter. Deleuze and Guattari refer to this move also as a science but crucially a minor science (or a nomad, ambulant, itinerant science). In Proposition III of the War Machine chapter in *A Thousand Plateaus* they describe this as a practice which follows matter's immanent traits, confronts problems instead of applying theorems, pushes matter to the next threshold, connects practical effects and affects of practice. Against a science of matter or a technology to control it, Deleuze and Guattari emphasise practice as the key dimension of a minor science that knows how to surrender to matter. Minor science is a practice which is essentially experimental; rigorous but not systematic, it directly links activity with matter. It is here that the neo-materialism of the 1990s and after can once again become activist, with minor, nomad science on the one hand and the big, royal, imperial science of the state on the other: 'What we have ... are two formally different conceptions of science, and, ontologically, a single field of interaction in which royal science continually appropriates the contents of vague or nomad science while nomad science continually cuts the contents of royal science loose' (Deleuze and Guattari 1987: 367). If there is to be an activism of neo-materialism it will be developed in the decades to come from the practices of the nomad scientist, the artisan who operates within the constraints of matter, who follows singular material possibilities, and who thereby escapes state striation.

V. 2027

> Among the tortures and devastations of life is this then – our friends are not able to finish their stories. (Woolf 1992)

Minor science is embedded in a reality primarily defined by the centrality of scientific knowledge for the making of a polity in the societies of the Global North. Politics are increasingly performed through science itself (cf. Papadopoulos, forthcoming 2011). Physical, biological, chemical bodies can be thought as political in their own right (Protevi 2001). Minor science can respond to this tight articulation of politics and scientific knowledge. Simultaneously scientific knowledge is a constitutive element of a transformation traversing the societies of the Global North by becoming increasingly distributed in society (the so-called 'knowledge society'). The figure of the 'socialised worker' (Negri 2005) captures this move to a mode of production and circulation based on the valorisation of the totality of life and the intellectual creativity of the individual worker. In this context, scientific knowledge on the one hand becomes explicitly political and, on the other, permeates a wider range of social strata than ever before in the Global North.

Minor science is part of the social material conditions prevailing today; it operates below and outside state science and yet, as discussed in the previous section, it is continuously under pressure to be absorbed into the big science of the state.

> The fact is that the two kinds of science have different modes of formalization, and State science continually imposes its form of sovereignty on the inventions of nomad science. State science retains of nomad science only what it can appropriate; it turns the rest into a set of strictly limited formulas without any real scientific status, or else simply represses and bans it. (Deleuze and Guattari 1987: 362)

Even the very idea of minor science itself can be buried under the desire for the new grand theory which can be assimilated into state science. The minor science of matter can be deployed to support a new grand system of thought; a grand theory that uses all the fashionable and marketable concepts and ideas circulating today – complexity, event, affect, multiplicity, networks, assemblages, etc. – to create a new meta-framework with which to approach the world. Cosmopolitical assembling as a new cosmology. A new abstract theory. Producing a new grand theory is one possible trap for today's minor science. A Deleuzian century? This would be the end of every inspiring and transformative potential of today's neo-materialism. The unfinished story of contemporary minor science is that it can so easily become absorbed into the workings of state science, that is, become a 'desire for' a grand system, a philosophical materialism devoid of its activist element. This kind of philosophical materialism will then become nothing but a form of governance of things and events. Latour the governor, Badiou the priest, Žižek the buffoon: actors in the imperial court in which state science feeds on the practices of minor science to produce a new cosmology that shapes technoreality.

Minor science and state science are inextricably bound together. In fact, minor science exists in the very core of state science. Pamela Smith has shown how artisan production – probably the most vital aspect of minor science – was crucial for the emergence of the rationalist objectivist scientific world-view which came to dominate the western world increasingly after the sixteenth century. It was the artisans' work, an intellectual revolution from bottom up, that 'transformed the contemplative discipline of natural philosophy into an active one' (Smith 2006: 239). Artisan science was later codified and appropriated into a new disembodied epistemology of experimental science. But experimental science never abandoned artisanal production. In fact experimental science and imperial science always rely on artisanal production and the minor science of matter. It was thanks to the purported modesty of meticulous artisanal efforts that Boyle's bottom-up experimental laboratory science won out over Hobbes' top-down geometric science (Shapin and Schaffer 1985; Haraway 1997).

This is even more the case today. In experimental science, the 'discovery' of 'natural facts' and 'realities of matter' was a distinct procedure that preceded possible technological applications. With the rise of technoscience, such applications become the very drive behind basic research. Discovery *is* fabrication. Science is not about observation but about modification. This situation creates an even more intense pressure for maintaining minor science, making it part of the fast-moving world of technoscientific research. In other words, one of the main characteristics of minor science – its interventionist, direct, ambulant quality – is now a dominant feature of technoscience itself. Propelled by the post-Second World War rise of big science, the later proliferation of the assembly-line industrial scientist (see Shapin 2008), the spread of an entrepreneurial scientific culture, the neoliberalisation of research culture and the precarisation of intellectual and affective labour, science and its applications increasingly fold into each other. Minor science fuels the everyday workings of contemporary technoscience.

Scientific practices and objects are as much the result of artisanal work as they are of the precarised labour of industrial scientists and of the entrepreneurial investments of corporate and state science. The problem is not so much that minor science and state science meet and collide – an image which Deleuze and Guattari have pictured in their all too typical masculinist reading of science as an agonistic field in *A Thousand Plateaus*. Rather, minor science and state science co-constitute what Donna Haraway calls zones of implosion where the boundaries between human and non-human, nature and artificiality, are meaningless: 'the chip, gene, bomb, fetus, seed, brain, ecosystem, database'. Such imploded technoscientific objects make up the conditions of our actual material presence in the world, they are 'wormholes that dump contemporary travelers out into contemporary worlds' (Haraway 1997: 43).

The entanglement of minor and state science is the very reality in which our material existence unfolds. In these conditions the crucial challenge for minor science is to engage with radical activism again. Among the questions this activism is facing today are the following: How can minor science contribute to the immediate making of liveable words (Haraway 2007; Puig de la Bellacasa 2010; in press)? How can justice be inscribed in relation to our technological objects, our cells and organs, the water, the air, the soil? And how can material justice be instigated in a non-dualistic manner?

As minor science implodes into big state science and itself tends towards a grand system of thought, rather than theorise this implosion, it may be we need to fabulate. Thriving in communities which will only selectively make use of big state science the new activisms that will emerge in the decades to come will be truly operating on the level of matter. They will mobilise radical political interventions through intra-acting with and within matter. The remaking of matter engenders radical liberation projects. And thus perhaps our almost 200-year-old tale of emancipation will happily become a reality.

Note

I am grateful to Marcelo Svirsky for his insightful suggestions and encouragement. Special thanks go to Maria Puig de la Bellacasa, Hywel Bishop and Jan L. Harris for their critical engagement with the text.

References

Althusser, Louis (2001) 'Ideology and Ideological State Apparatuses: Notes Towards an Investigation', in *Lenin and Philosophy*, trans. B. Brewster, New York: Monthly Review Press, pp. 85–126.

Althusser, Louis (2006) *Philosophy of the Encounter: Later Writings, 1978–1987*, trans. G. M. Goshgarian, London: Verso.

Bennett, Jane (2010) *Vibrant Matter: A Political Ecology of Things*, Durham, NC: Duke University Press.

Blackman, Lisa, John Cromby, Derek Hook, Dimitris Papadopoulos and Valerie Walkerdine, (2008) 'Creating Subjectivities', *Subjectivity*, 22, pp. 1–27.

Bourdieu, Pierre (1987) *Sozialer Sinn: Kritik der Theoretischen Vernunft*, Frankfurt am Main: Suhrkamp.

Braidotti, Rosi (2002) *Metamorphoses: Towards a Materialist Theory of Becoming*, Cambridge and Malden, MA: Polity/Blackwell.

Butler, Judith (1997) 'Against Proper Objects', in E. Weed and N. Schor (eds.), *Feminism Meets Queer Theory*, Bloomington, IN: Indiana University Press, pp. 1–30.

Butler, Judith, Ernesto Laclau and Slavoj Žižek (2000) *Contingency, Hegemony, Universality: Contemporary Dialogues on the Left*, London: Verso.

Chekhov, Anton P. (1900) *Three Sisters*, Oxford: Oxford University Press.

Chesters, Graeme and Ian Welsh (2006) *Complexity and Social Movements: Multitudes at the Edge of Chaos*, London: Routledge.

Clifford, James (1986) 'Partial Truths', in J. Clifford and G. E. Marcus (eds.), *Writing Culture: The Poetics and Politics of Ethnography*, Berkeley: University of California Press, pp. 1–27.

Clifford, James and G. E. Marcus (eds.) (1986) *Writing Culture: The Poetics and Politics of Ethnography*, Berkeley: University of California Press.

Clifford, James (2000) 'Taking Identity Politics Seriously: 'The contradictory, stony ground...', in P. Gilroy, L. Grossberg and A. McRobbie (eds.), *Without Guarantees: In Honour of Stuart Hall*, London and New York: Verso, pp. 94–112.

Clifford, James (2001) 'Indigenous Articulations', *The Contemporary Pacific*, 13:2, pp. 468–90.

Connery, Christopher (2005) 'The World Sixties', in R. Wilson and C. Connery (eds.), *Worldings: World Literature, Field Imaginaries, Future Practices: Doing Cultural Studies Inside the U.S. Warmachine*, Santa Cruz: New Pacific Press, pp. 77–108.

Csordas, Thomas J. (1994) *Embodiment and Experience: The Existential Ground of Culture and Self*, New York: Cambridge University Press.

De Landa, Manuel (1997) *A Thousand Years of Nonlinear History*, New York: Zone Books.

Debord, Guy (1981) 'Perspectives for Conscious Alterations in Everyday Life', in K. Knabb (ed.), *Situationist International Anthology*, Berkeley: Bureau of Public Secrets, pp. 68–75.

Deleuze, Gilles (2001) 'Dualism, Monism and Multiplicities (Desire-Pleasure-Jouissance)', *Contretemps*, 2, pp. 92–108, http://www.usyd.edu.au/contretemps/contretemps2.html (accessed February 2007).

Deleuze, Gilles and Félix Guattari (1987) *A Thousand Plateaus: Capitalism and Schizophrenia*, trans. Brian Massumi, Minneapolis: University of Minnesota Press.

Dyer-Witheford, Nick (2006) 'Species-being and the New Commonism: Notes on an Interrupted Cycle of Struggles', *The Commoner*, 11, pp. 15–32.

Eco, Umberto (1989) *The Open Work*, trans. Anna Cancogni, Cambridge, MA: Harvard University Press.

Engels, Friedrich (1987 [1878]) 'Anti-Dühring. Herr Eugen Dühring's Revolution in Science', in K. Marx and F. Engels, *Collected Works*, vol. 25, London: Lawrence and Wishart.

Engels, Friedrich (1990 [1886]) 'Ludwig Feuerbach and the End of Classical German Philosophy', in K. Marx and F. Engels, *Collected Works*, vol. 26, London: Lawrence and Wishart.

Fausto-Sterling, Anne (2000) *Sexing the Body: Gender Politics and the Construction of Sexuality*, New York: Basic Books.

Gadamer, Hans-Georg (1989) *Truth and Method*, trans. Joel Weinsheimer and Donald G. Marshall (2nd revised edition), New York: Crossroad.

Gilbert, Jeremy (2008) *Anticapitalism and Culture: Radical Theory and Popular Politics*, Oxford: Berg.

Hall, Stuart (1986a) 'Gramsci's Relevance for the Study of Race and Ethnicity', *Journal of Communication Inquiry*, 10:2, pp. 5–27.

Hall, Stuart (1986b) 'On Postmodernism and Articulation: An Interview with Stuart Hall', *Journal of Communication Inquiry*, 10:2, pp. 45–60.

Hall, Stuart (1990) 'Cultural Identity and Diaspora', in J. Rutherford (ed.), *Identity: Community, Culture, Difference*, London: Lawrence and Wishart, pp. 222–37.

Hall, Stuart and Tony Jefferson (1976) *Resistance Through Rituals: Youth Subcultures in Post-war Britain*, London: Hutchinson.

Haraway, Donna J. (1997) *Modest_Witness@Second_Millennium: FemaleMan©_Meets_OncoMouse™: Feminism and Technoscience*, New York: Routledge.

Haraway, Donna J. (2007) *When Species Meet*, Minneapolis: University of Minnesota Press.

Harré, Rom (1996) 'The Necessity of Personhood as Embodied Being', *Theory and Psychology*, 5, pp. 369–73.

Harvey, David (1990) *The Condition of Postmodernity: An Enquiry into the Origins of Cultural Change*, Oxford: Blackwell.

Holland, Eugene W. (2005) 'Desire', in C. J. Stivale (ed.), *Gilles Deleuze. Key concepts*, Chesham: Acumen, pp. 53–62.

Jameson, Fredric (1981) *The Political Unconscious: Narrative as a Socially Symbolic Act*, London: Methuen.

Jordan, Zbigniew A. (1967) *The Evolution of Dialectical Materialism: A Philosophical and Sociological Analysis*, London: Macmillan.

Laclau, Ernesto and Chantal Mouffe (1985) *Hegemony and Socialist Strategy: Towards a Radical Democratic Politics*, London: Verso.

Lefebvre, Henri (1991) *Critique of Everyday Life, Vol. 1: Introduction*, trans. John Moore, London: Verso.

Lenin, Vladimir I. (1961 [1902]) 'What Is To Be Done? Burning Questions of Our Movement', in V. I. Lenin, *Collected Works*, vol. 5, Moscow: Foreign Languages Publishing House, pp. 347–530.

Lenin, Vladimir I. (1970 [1908]) *Materialism and Empirio-criticism: Critical Comments on a Reactionary Philosophy*, Moscow: Progress Publishers.

Marx, Karl (1975 [1844]) 'Economic and Philosophical Manuscripts of 1844', in K. Marx and F. Engels, *Collected Works*, vol. 3, London: Lawrence and Wishart.

Marx, Karl and Friedrich Engels (1976 [1846]) 'The German Ideology', in K. Marx and F. Engels, *Collected Works*, vol. 5, London: Lawrence and Wishart.

Mouffe, Chantal (2000) *The Democratic Paradox*, London: Verso.

Müller, Heiner (2000) 'Kinder, denkt an die Zwangsläufigkeit, Freiheit, Korruption, Konterrevolution: Ein Gespräch zwischen Sascha Anderson, Heiner Müller und A. R. Penck vor zehn Jahren', *Frankfurter Allgemeine Zeitung*, BS 3, Januar 20.

Negri, Antonio (2005) *The Politics of Subversion: A Manifesto for the Twenty-first Century*, trans. James Newell, Cambridge: Polity.

Overton, Willis F. (1998) 'The Arrow of Time and Cycles of Time: Concepts of Change, Cognition and Embodiment', *Psychological Inquiry*, 5, pp. 215–37.

Papadopoulos, Dimitris (2006) 'World 2: On the Significance and Impossibility of Articulation', *Culture, Theory and Critique*, 47:2, pp. 165–79.

Papadopoulos, Dimitris (2010) 'Insurgent posthumanism', *Ephemera: Theory and Politics in Organization*.

Papadopoulos, Dimitris (forthcoming 2011) 'Alter-ontologies: Towards Constituent Politics in Technoscience', *Social Studies of Science*.

Papadopoulos, Dimitris, N. Stephenson and V. Tsianos (2008) *Escape Routes: Control and Subversion in the Twenty-first Century*, London: Pluto Press.

Protevi, John (2001) *Political Physics: Deleuze, Derrida, and the Body Politic*, London: Athlone.

Puig de la Bellacasa, Maria (2010) 'Ethical Doings in Naturecultures', *Ethics, Place and Environment*, 13:3.

Puig de la Bellacasa, Maria (in press) 'Matters of Care in Technoscience: Assembling Neglected Things', *Social Studies of Science*.

Rorty, Richard (ed.) (1967) *The Linguistic Turn: Essays in Philosophical Method*, Chicago: University of Chicago Press.

Sahlins, Marshall D. (2002) *Waiting for Foucault, Still*, Chicago: Prickly Paradigm Press.

Sedgwick, Eve K. (1990) *Epistemology of the Closet*, Berkeley: University of California Press.

Shapin, Steven (2008) *The Scientific Life: A Moral History of a Late Modern Vocation*, Chicago and London: University of Chicago Press.

Shapin, Steven and Simon Schaffer (1985) *Leviathan and the Air-pump: Hobbes, Boyle, and the Experimental Life*, Princeton: Princeton University Press.

Slack, Jennifer D. (1996) 'The Theory and Method of Articulation in Cultural Studies', in D. Morley and K.-H. Chen (eds.), *Stuart Hall: Critical Dialogues in Cultural Studies*, London: Routledge, pp. 112–27.

Smith, Pamela H. (2006) *The Body of the Artisan: Art and Experience in the Scientific Revolution*, Chicago: University of Chicago Press.

Spivak, Gayatri C. (1999) *A Critique of Postcolonial Reason: Toward a History of the Vanishing Present*, Cambridge, MA: Harvard University Press.

Stephenson, Niamh and Dimitris Papadopoulos (2006) *Analysing Everyday Experience: Social Research and Political Change*, London: Palgrave Macmillan.

Warner, Michael (1999) *The Trouble With Normal: Sex, Politics, and the Ethics of Queer Life*, New York: Free Press.

Williams, Raymond (1980) *Problems in Materialism and Culture: Selected Essays*, London: Verso.

Woolf, Virginia (1992) *The Waves*, London: Penguin Books.

Activism, Philosophy and Actuality in Deleuze and Foucault

Paul Patton   University of New South Wales

Abstract

Deleuze and Foucault shared a period of political activism and both drew connections between their activism and their respective approaches to philosophy. However, despite their shared political commitments and praise of each other's work, there remained important philosophical differences between them which became more and more apparent over time. This article identifies some of the political issues over which they disagreed and shows how they relate to some of their underlying philosophical differences. It focuses on their respective approaches to the state, to 'actuality' and to the analysis of the present.

Keywords: Deleuze, Foucault, activism, state, actuality, history

> But the thought is one thing, the deed is another, and another
> yet is the image of the deed. The wheel of grounds does
> not roll between them.
> (Nietzsche 2005: First Part: 'The Pale Criminal')

Much of Deleuze's career as a political activist involved common causes with Foucault during the early to mid 1970s. These included his participation in the *Prisoner's Information Group* established by Foucault, Daniel Defert and others at the beginning of 1971, along with his role in the campaign later that year in support of immigrant workers and against racism that was sparked by the shooting of a young Algerian in the Paris neighbourhood known as the *Goutte d'Or* (Dosse 2010: 309–13).[1] Defert and Donzelot describe the interaction with the prison environment in and around the experience of the *Prisoner's Information Group* as a pivotal moment in the history of the forms of political

Deleuze Studies Volume 4: 2010 supplement: 84–103
DOI: 10.3366/E1750224110001145
© Edinburgh University Press
www.eupjournals.com/dls

activism that emerged in the aftermath of May '68, suggesting that it represented 'a transformation of political intelligence' (Defert and Donzelot 1976: 33). Elements of this transformation found expression in the efforts by Deleuze and Parnet to characterise a new politics and a new relationship between political and intellectual activism. The final chapter of *Dialogues*, published in 1977, develops the idea of radical politics as experimentation defined in terms of Deleuze and Guattari's theory of the different kinds of line or segments that make up a social field, but also in terms of the state as agent of realisation of the 'abstract machines' that overcode a given society. They invoke a 'becoming-revolutionary of people, at every level, in every place, instead of the Marxian concept of a revolution that changes everything by the capture of state power and the establishment of new social relations of production' (Deleuze and Parnet 2002: 147).

Foucault's work followed a different political trajectory. His 1975–6 lectures at the Collège de France, under the title 'Society Must Be Defended' (Foucault 2003), undertook a critical genealogy of the discourse of war and domination that had provided the language of much of his thinking about power. After a sabbatical in the United States in 1976–7, he embarked on a genealogy of the forms of exercise of sovereign power that led him to explore elements of liberal and neoliberal governmentality (Foucault 2007, 2008). From 1980, his focus shifted away from the exercise of power over others and towards forms of self-government as theorised by the ancient Greeks.

Both Deleuze and Foucault repeatedly drew connections between their own social and political activism and their respective approaches to philosophy. However, despite their shared political commitments and praise of each other's work, there remained important philosophical differences between them which became more and more apparent over time. Their political collaboration came to an end around the time of the campaign against the extradition of the Baader-Meinhof lawyer Klaus Croissant in 1977. In Foucault's case, as I will show, the political differences that emerged in 1977 carried over into his 1978 lectures on neoliberal governmentality. In Deleuze's case, the precise nature of their philosophical and political differences is partly obscured by the highly idiosyncratic account he gives of Foucault's approach to philosophy in interviews and in his *Foucault*, published in 1986 two years after Foucault's death.[2] The lesson to be drawn is that we should be wary of taking their views of the relationship between their respective approaches to philosophy and politics at face value. As Nietzsche's Zarathustra reminds us in the passage quoted above, the thinking that motivates human actions is one thing, the actions another, and neither of these are identical with the rationalisations or retrospective accounts given by the actors themselves.

The high point of their common political and theoretical engagement was undoubtedly the 'Intellectuals and Power' interview, conducted in March 1972 and published in the issue of *L'Arc* devoted to Deleuze later that year.[3] Together they outline a new conception of the relationship between 'theory' and 'practice' according to which practice is not the application of theory, any more than it is the source or inspiration of theory to come. They reject the idea that there is a single 'totalising' relation between theory and practice in favour of a more local and fragmentary conception. Theory is neither the expression nor the translation of a practice, but is itself a local and regional practice that operates as a series of relays from one practice to another, while practices are relays from one theoretical point to the next. It is in the course of this discussion that Deleuze advances the much quoted formula that epitomises the pragmatism of their approach: theory should be considered a tool-box, or a pair of spectacles that may or may not provide a useful view of the world. If a theory does not help in a given situation, the theorist-practitioner should make another (Deleuze 2004: 208).

This conception of the theory-practice relation as a series of relays within a multiplicity of elements at once theoretical and practical implies a novel conception of the nature and political task of the intellectual as a multiplicity that connects with other social forces rather than a subject who represents a class or a group. He or she is, to use Guattari's term, a 'groupuscule'. Deleuze attributes to Foucault the important lesson of the 'indignity' of speaking for others, as exemplified in the practice of the *Prisoner's Information Group* which sought to bring to the public at large the voice of those imprisoned. In turn, Foucault suggests that it was one of the lessons of the upsurge of direct political action at the end of the 1960s in France that the masses have no need of enlightened consciousnesses in order to have knowledge of their situation. The problem is rather that their own forms of knowledge are blocked or invalidated. The role of the intellectual therefore does not consist of bringing knowledge to or from the people but of working within and against the order of discourse within which the forms of knowledge appear or fail to appear. More generally, it consists of struggling against the forms of power of which he or she is both the object and the instrument.

Deleuze endorses the rejection of the distinction between reform and revolution that we find elsewhere in Foucault,[4] along with the idea that power itself forms a system that is inherently fragile and liable to unravel at any point. The continuity in the forms of exercise of power, its cynicism as well as its puerility, is manifest in the similarities between the treatment of prisoners, schoolchildren and factory workers that Foucault has demonstrated through his historical account of disciplinary power. Moreover, the then present (1972) political situation shows how the different kinds of repression directed at immigrants, workers, students and young people generally are readily totalised from the point of view of power. The political conclusion he draws is that it is not for those struggling against this process and this future to totalise or to work through existing representative institutions such as unions or political parties: the task is rather to establish 'lateral connections, a system of networks and popular bases' as well as different mechanisms for the circulation of information (Deleuze 2004: 210).

Foucault makes the connection between the problem of finding adequate forms of struggle and the present ignorance of the nature of power. It took until the nineteenth century to arrive at knowledge of exploitation, but we remain largely ignorant of the nature of power: certainly the existing theories of the state and state apparatuses are inadequate to understand the nature of power and the forms of its exercise, as is the theory of class power associated with Marxism. Foucault credits Deleuze's *Nietzsche and Philosophy*, as well as his work with Guattari, for advancing the manner in which this problem is posed (*Anti-Oedipus* was published in March 1972). He implicitly refers to his earlier comments about working within the order of discourse and knowledge in suggesting that identifying and speaking publicly about the centres of power within society is already a first step in turning power back on itself: 'If discourses such as those of prisoners or prison doctors are struggles it is because they confiscate at least for a moment the power to speak of the prison that is currently held by prison administrators and reformers alone' (Deleuze 2004: 211). Perhaps alluding to a lesson learned from their experience with prisons, he adds that it is not the unconscious that is challenged by such discourses of struggle but the secrecy that is all too often the condition of the exercise of power: 'The discourse of struggle is not opposed to the unconscious but to the secret ... The secret is perhaps more difficult to bring to light than the unconscious' (211–12).

Deleuze's response obliquely illustrates their differing attitudes towards psychoanalysis. He takes up Foucault's point about relative ignorance of the workings of power by outlining a summary version of the thesis developed in *Anti-Oedipus* concerning the difference between individual or group interests and desiring-investments: it is the nature of the desiring-investments in a social body that explains why people can act against their interests. Foucault agrees that there is a complex interplay between relations of power, desire and interest and that people can desire the exercise of power by those who act against their interests and even their lives, as occurred in the case of fascism (Deleuze 2004: 212).

Finally, Deleuze returns to the question: how to conceive of the necessary networks and transversal connections between the different sites of struggle against power, whether from one country to another (Vietnam-France) or within a given country? Foucault responds by describing the current revolutionary struggle as one against power rather than against exploitation and, as such, one in which the proletariat may be involved but not necessarily in a leading or pre-eminent role: the struggles of women, prisoners, conscripts, homosexuals and others also form part of the revolutionary movement. Their commonality derives not from a theoretical totalisation but from the system of power itself, which in countries like France is exercised in a way that maintains capitalist relations of exploitation. For this reason, Deleuze comments, 'Every partial revolutionary attack or defense in this way connects up with the struggle of the working class' (Deleuze 2004: 213).

Many of the points made in this landmark interview continued to reverberate through the work of Deleuze and Foucault in the years that followed, albeit in different guises. Much of Foucault's work during the latter part of the 1970s sought to develop new conceptual tools for understanding power and its relation to knowledge or theory. His 1982 text 'The Subject and Power' offers much the same analysis of the totalisation of micro-powers by a dominant or ruling power that he gave a decade earlier (Foucault 2000: 326–48). The first lecture of his 1976 course at the Collège de France takes up the question implicitly posed by his 1972 remarks about the relative lack of understanding of the nature of power and sets out a series of heuristic principles designed to reorient the study of power away from the juridical, political and ideological apparatuses of the state and towards the material operations of domination and subjectification throughout society, along with the formations of knowledge that accompany them. At the outset of this lecture, he returns to the inhibiting effects of global theories in relation to 'subjugated knowledges', defining his genealogical approach as one that targets 'a combination of erudite knowledge and what people know' – the technical knowledge of the practitioners of particular forms of power and the disqualified knowledge of those subject to them – and suggesting that this would not have been possible were it not for 'the removal of the tyranny of overall discourses, with their hierarchies and all the privileges enjoyed by theoretical vanguards' (Foucault 2003: 8).

The ideas canvassed in the 1972 discussion between Deleuze and Foucault continue to influence many of those concerned to develop mutually productive relations between political activism and academic theorising.[5] But this text also shows points of mutual incomprehension between them. At one point, for example, Deleuze endorses and attributes to Foucault the idea that theory is 'by nature opposed to power', even though Foucault has just suggested that theory always takes place within an order of discourse and knowledge that is governed by forms of power (Deleuze 2004: 208). Deleuze appears to understand 'theory' to mean something like the conception of philosophy as the creation of concepts that he later described as 'in itself' calling for 'a new earth and a people that do not yet exist' (Deleuze and Guattari 1994: 108). However, this conception of theory continues to rely on the repressive conception of power that Foucault soon came to challenge. Deleuze refers here to the radical fragility of the system of power and its 'global force of repression' (Deleuze 2002: 291; 2004: 208; translation modified).

Philosophically, there were always differences between them. Some of these differences become apparent after the publication of Foucault's *History of Sexuality Volume 1* in 1976. A letter that Deleuze wrote to him in 1977, subsequently published as 'Desire and Pleasure', sets out a number of disagreements over the nature of power and its relation to desire, the relative primacy of desire in relation to power, along with Deleuze's reservations about Foucault's attachment to concepts of truth and pleasure (Deleuze 2007: 122–34). Some of these differences were restated several years later in a footnote in *A Thousand Plateaus* that reaffirmed the priority of desire over power and the primacy of lines of flight or deterritorialisation in any given assemblage (Deleuze and Guattari 1987: 530–1).

In retrospect, it is not surprising that these differences should have emerged around 1977. That year was a turning point in the history of the French left, when the adherence to Marxism on the part of many who had participated in the forms of activism that flourished after 1968 began to crumble. The reasons for this were complex, but they coalesced around the issue of Soviet dissidence and the Gulag, along with the contemporaneous and brief popularity of the so-called 'New Philosophers'. For the most part, these were former students of the *École Normale Supérieur* who had been taught by Althusser and who had been engaged in the post-'68 Maoist left: Bernard-Henri Lévy, Jean-Marie Benoist, Michel Géurin, Christian Jambert and Guy Lardreau. Others such as André Glucksmann were also associated with this movement. His book *La Cuisinière et le mangeur d'hommes* (Glucksmann 1975) was one of the first to combine Foucauldian theses about the 'Great confinement' with evidence derived from Solzhenitsyn and others about the Soviet camps. Levy's *La Barbarie à visage humaine* (Levy 1977) also drew parallels between Foucault's account of confinement in *Histoire de la folie* and what happened in the USSR. He invoked Foucault by describing his own book as 'an archaeology of the present' and by drawing on the theory of disciplinary power outlined in *Surveiller et punir* to frame his account of modern totalitarianism. In this manner, David Macey comments, Foucault became 'part of the new philosophy's vulgate' (Macey 1994: 386).

Foucault's own engagement with the New Philosophers was more circumspect. Macey describes a three-page review of Glucksmann's *Les Maîtres penseurs*, published in *Le Nouvel Observateur* in May 1977, as his 'most significant gesture of support for the new philosophers' (Macey 1994: 387).[6] Foucault praised the book for tracing the horrors of the Soviet Gulag to the manner in which nineteenth-century German philosophy – Hegel in particular – linked the state and the revolution such that revolution promised a true and benign state while the state in turn promised the serene accomplishment of revolution. By contrast, one month later, Deleuze published a denunciation of the New Philosophers in which he expressed his disgust at their martyrology of the victims of the Gulag and of history more generally. He also accused them of trafficking in big empty concepts such as The Law, The Power, The Master and so on.[7] Macey suggests that the reference to power contained an implicit rebuke of Foucault and that their differing attitudes towards the New Philosophers contributed to their 'increasing estrangement' (388). Whether or not this was intended, it is true that Foucault and Deleuze tended to drift apart from the mid '70s, sometimes taking different positions on issues of the day. In what follows I focus on two moments at which important conceptual and political differences emerged between them. The first turns around the Klaus Croissant affair at the end of 1977 and their respective conceptions of the state. The second relates to the respective conceptions held by Deleuze and Foucault of 'the present' (*actualité*).

I. Genealogy and the State

The extradition of Klaus Croissant in November 1977 was a key episode that is often cited as a turning point in their relationship, especially by some of Foucault's biographers. François Dosse – following a written response by Deleuze to James Miller some years later, in which he insists that there was no single cause of their estrangement but a number of contributing factors – lists the Croissant affair as one among a series of political disagreements, alongside their different attitudes towards the New Philosophers and their deep divergence over Israel-Palestine (Dosse 2010: 314). Croissant had been one of the defence lawyers in the trial of members of the Red Army Faction (RAF) in 1975. After having been charged with supporting a criminal organisation and jailed on more than one occasion, he fled to France in the summer of 1977 and applied for political asylum. In response to his arrest by French authorities in September 1977, Foucault, Deleuze and Guattari were among those who joined a Committee established to oppose his extradition and agitate for his release from prison. Their activities were to no avail as Croissant was finally extradited on 16 November, shortly after the suicide of three leading members of the RAF, Andreas Baader, Gudrun Ensslin and Jan-Carl Raspe, in Stannheim and then the killing of abducted businessman Hanns-Martin Schleyer on 19 October. Foucault and Deleuze were among the small crowd of protesters outside *La Santé* prison when Croissant was removed. However, they took different positions in the public campaign in his favour. Foucault published several pieces against the extradition of Croissant, but he refused to sign a petition circulated by Guattari and signed by Deleuze among others. He considered it too lenient towards the RAF and preferred to restrict his support to the lawyer and to the right of accused parties to legal representation.[8] Macey claims that what Foucault found unacceptable in the petition was a characterisation of the West German state as 'fascist': 'In other words, Foucault was prepared to fight for Croissant's right to asylum, but he would not lend his name to any statement which lent support to a thesis associated with the Red Army Faction itself' (Macey 1994: 394). Eribon offers a slightly milder version of the unacceptable petition, describing it as presenting West Germany as drifting towards 'police dictatorship' (Eribon 1991: 260).

Foucault's reticence towards any support for the opinions much less the actions of the RAF has since been taken to imply that Deleuze and Guattari themselves supported terrorism. The editor of Foucault's lectures, Michel Senellart, describes Deleuze and Guattari's opinion piece in *Le Monde* on 2 November 1977 ('*Le pire moyen de faire l'Europe*'[9]) as one that 'gave backing to terrorist action' (Foucault 2007: 393 n. 26). It is difficult to reconcile this claim with the text of the article. The passage cited by Senellart follows comments on the characterisation of Baader and other members of the RAF by the press in Germany and France that sought to portray them as Nazis or the children of Nazis. Deleuze and Guattari write: 'Leaving aside the search for filiations, it is simpler to recall that the question of violence, and even of terrorism, as a response to imperialist violence, has constantly troubled the revolutionary and worker's movement since the last century in very diverse forms' (Deleuze 2007: 150). There is no evidence to suggest that Deleuze or Guattari ever condoned the violent actions of the RAF. There is evidence to suggest that Guattari in particular did not.[10] Both were well aware that the temptation to resort to violence was real among members of the post-'68 left across Europe and the passage from their article cited above simply acknowledges this fact. Deleuze and Guattari's text presents the issue of Croissant's extradition as raising questions about the role of Germany in the emerging European Union. They suggest that it has acquired a position of strength in relation to other European governments such that it is able to export its judicial, police and 'informational' model and to become the central organiser of repression in other countries such as France: a decision by the French court to allow extradition would in effect favour 'the importation of the German state and judicial model' (149).

Foucault's increasing distance from the views of his former friends is apparent in his own comments on 'the German model' in lectures delivered in the first half of the following year (Foucault 2008). These lectures were the only ones that Foucault devoted to issues arising directly from contemporary politics.[11] They make it clear that the role of 'the German model' in the immediate political context is part of the reason for undertaking these historical analyses of neoliberal governmentality, even as they develop an account of this model very different from that put forward by Deleuze and Guattari: 'The German model which is being diffused, debated and forms part of our actuality, structuring it and carving out its real shape, is the model of a possible neo-liberal governmentality' (Foucault 2008: 192). An immediate concern in these lectures is to show that policy shifts underway in France during this period, such as the abandonment of a social security system based on the wartime principle of national solidarity in favour of a system that would provide assistance to those unable to participate in the economic game without imposing additional constraints on the market, represent the radicalisation of themes found in German neoliberal social policy elaborated from the 1930s and adopted after 1945. Foucault's broader aim is to show that 'political actuality' is more complex than is recognised by many of the proponents of state theory. He points out that the work presented in these lectures was undertaken partly for what he calls 'a reason of critical morality' that amounts to a direct challenge to the 'state phobia' that was widespread in twentieth-century political thought and particularly amongst the French extra-parliamentary left during the 1970s. By 'state phobia' he means, firstly, the idea that the state possesses its own intrinsic tendency to expand, 'an endogenous imperialism constantly pushing it to spread its surface and increase in extent, depth and subtlety to the point that it will come to take over entirely that which is at the same time its other, its outside, its target and its object, namely: civil society' (187). Secondly, state phobia involves the idea that sovereign power is a phenomenon with its own essential characteristics. At the heart of this attitude is an essentialist conception of the state such that administrative, welfare, bureaucratic, fascist and totalitarian forms of state may all be regarded as expressions of the same underlying form: 'there is a kinship, a sort of genetic continuity or evolutionary implication between different forms of state' (187).

Elements of this approach can be found among a variety of Marxist theories of the state as instrument of class domination, or among anarcho-Nietzschean theories of the state as 'the coldest of all cold monsters' (Nietzsche 2005: 43).[12] The concept of the state outlined in Deleuze and Guattari's *A Thousand Plateaus* (1980) also retains elements of state phobia. They propose an abstract definition of the state-form as an apparatus of capture that exists whenever two fundamental conditions are met: the constitution of a milieu of interiority and the establishment of a standard or centre of comparison on the basis of which a surplus can be extracted (Deleuze and Guattari 1987: 444). As such, they suggest, there is a 'unity of composition' among different kinds of state that is not found in the diverse forms of nomadic war machine (Deleuze and Guattari 1980: 427). Deleuze and Guattari's conception of the state is by no means ahistorical: there is an evolution of forms of state and, even in the present, there are significant differences between totalitarian, fascist, social democratic and neoliberal states. Yet these different 'axiomatisations' also involve an isomorphism to the extent that all nation states are particular 'domains of realisation' of the underlying capitalist axiomatic (464).

Foucault objects to the essentialism of the state phobic conception that it licenses the 'interchangeability of analyses and a loss of specificity' (Foucault 2008: 188). His aim, by contrast, it to maximise specificity, for example by showing that the welfare state has neither the same form nor the same origin as 'the Nazi, fascist or Stalinist state' (190).[13] Second, the inbuilt dynamism of the state ensures that, whatever the context and whatever political process is under discussion, it can always be criticised by reference to the worse that will inevitably follow: 'something like a kinship or danger, something like the great fantasy of the paranoiac and devouring state can always be found' (188). As such, the state phobic conception allows its protagonists to deduce political analyses from first principles and avoid altogether the need for empirical and historical knowledge of contemporary reality. In this sense, Foucault argues that it sustains a critical discourse the value of which is artificially inflated since it enables its supporters to 'avoid paying the price of reality and *actuality*' (188; emphasis added). Foucault's analysis of governmentality seeks to disqualify this essentialist conception of the state from the outset. His approach does not seek to extract the essential nature of the modern state but to question it from the outside by 'undertaking an investigation of the problem of the state on the basis of practices of governmentality' (78). From this perspective, the institutions and policies of the state are nothing more than the residue or the effects of the ways in which more or less centralised power has sought to govern territories, populations, economic and social life: they are 'the mobile effect of a regime of multiple governmentalities' (77).

Foucault's final objection to state phobia points to its ignorance of the widespread suspicion of the state from within twentieth-century liberalism. His analysis of the origins and emergence of German neoliberalism shows how this kind of critique of the state and its 'intrinsic and irrepressible dynamism' was already formulated during the period from 1930 to 1945 in the context of efforts to criticise the whole range of interventionist policies from Keynesianism to National Socialism and Soviet state planning (Foucault 2008: 189). The influence of anti-state liberalism in the post-war period meant that all those on the left who participate in this state phobia are 'following the direction of the wind and that in fact, for years and years, an effective reduction of the state has been on the way' (191). A constant refrain of Foucault's criticism of state phobia is a plea for realism about the state and its origins. By implication, it is the lack of realism on the part of his former political companions that contributes to the emerging gulf between them. His genealogical sketch of neoliberal governmentality is one element of a broader methodological argument in these lectures against the kind of political criticism that interprets the present by reference to already given concepts of state and society. His aim is quite different: to investigate the particular ways in which sovereign power was conceived and exercised, in order to show the historical specificity of government. In this manner, he proposes 'to let knowledge of the past work on the experience of the present' (130). Deleuze and Guattari's treatment of the different forms of state past and present shows that the issue is not simply whether or not the political theorist takes history into account, but the precise means by which this is to be achieved.

II. Philosophy, Politics and 'Actuality'

The distance that separates the conceptions of 'theory' held by Foucault and Deleuze becomes apparent when we compare the latter's characterisation of the former and his attempt to pursue what he presents as a Foucauldian form of criticism of the present. For the most part, Deleuze does not undertake the same kind of genealogical interpretation of the present that we find in Foucault, even though he regularly compares Nietzsche's untimely and Foucault's *actuel* with the realm of becoming and pure eventness that is the object of his own philosophy. One exception to this is the diagnosis outlined in his 'Postscript on Control Societies', and in his 'Control and Becoming' interview with Negri, where he describes the present as the initial stages of a newly emerging 'control society'.[14] This diagnosis stands in stark contrast to the account of the present given in his 1972 discussion with Foucault, where Deleuze saw the political present as a period of repression after the social upheavals of '68 and its immediate aftermath: not only as a response to what occurred in '68 but as the concerted preparation and organisation of the immediate future by reinforcing the social structures of confinement. His diagnosis at this point effectively anticipated the New Philosophers in describing the present period by reference to Foucault's discussion of 'confinement'. In 1990, he offers a diagnosis that draws upon Foucault's discussion of political technology in *Discipline and Punish*, suggesting that this moment is witness to the birth of a society characterised by the predominance of a new type of political technology.

Just as the modern society described by Foucault in *Discipline and Punish* is characterised by a diagram of disciplinary power, so Deleuze describes the new society emerging at the end of the twentieth century as one characterised by a diagram of control. Control society comes next in the series identified by Foucault, in which each kind of society is defined by a particular diagram of power. Thus, sovereign societies were succeeded by disciplinary societies and now 'Control societies are taking over from disciplinary societies' (Deleuze 1995: 178). This raises the question: what is meant by 'control' in the context of this specific diagram of power? How does it differ from disciplinary power? In the first place, in so far as it is the name of a particular technique for the exercise of political power, we can say in the light of Foucault's later clarification of his concept of power that it involves a certain kind of action upon the action, or the field of possible actions, of others (Foucault 2000: 326–48). Control power is different from disciplinary power at the level of its primary material, its means, modalities and ends. At the level of primary materials, control does not operate on the individual but on 'dividuals', not on the mass of people but on samples or data-banks. Unlike disciplinary societies, control societies do not form individuals to fit certain moulds in order to produce docile bodies, obedient subjects and so on. Rather, they extract dividuals where these are not whole persons but a certain number of functional aspects, each one defined in relation to particular ends. The dividual is a bundle of aptitudes or capacities such as the financial means that ensure a capacity to repay a bank loan or the scholarly aptitudes that guarantee entry onto a given program of study. A multiplicity of dividuals do not constitute a mass of people but rather a sample or a data-bank that can be analysed and exploited for commercial, governmental or other ends.

At the level of the means of its exercise, control makes use of pass-words rather than order-words. Individuals are associated with an increasingly long and potentially endless chain of pass-words, including passwords for their computers, email servers, assorted bank and credit card logins, online shopping, travel agencies, journal subscriptions, professional associations and so on. In contrast to disciplinary societies, control societies do not establish institutional spaces of confinement but series of thresholds through which one can only pass with the right password. They establish different kinds of penalties as alternatives to imprisonment, such as fines, community service, compulsory rehabilitation and so on. They establish home medical care instead of hospitalisation, lifelong education and training instead of schools and colleges, and enterprises of various kinds instead of factories. Control operates in the open air rather than in confined spaces, by means of various digital and electronic technologies. To take an example that has emerged since Deleuze wrote his 'Postscript', consider the manner in which GPS location has become utilised in a whole series of devices, from personal direction-finders to electronic bracelets and other tracking devices. In the words of one commentator:

GPS represents the final stage of this evolution. Even the electronic bracelet remains essentially disciplinary, transforming the home into a prison and trapping the condemned as though in his apartment burrow. By contrast, mobile technologies of surveillance in real time liberate the individual. They liberate his energy and his desire so that he can work at his own always ephemeral and perfectible integration. (Razac 2008: 61)

At the level of the modality of action, control mechanisms do not impose particular moulds according to the nature of the institution in which they are employed, producing a certain kind of subject, body or relationships. Rather, they involve the continuous modulation of behaviours or performances in and by means of their relations to one another. In turn, this implies a series of replacements in different domains of social life. For example, the replacement of apparent acquittal by unlimited deferral of judgement in the judicial sphere; the replacement of manufacture by the sale of services or immaterial products in the economic sphere; the replacement of examinations by continuous assessment in the educational sphere. In each case, it is a question of abandoning disciplinary modalities in favour of other means of acting upon the action of people. Razac is not the only one to suggest that Foucault's analyses of 'security apparatuses' in the course of his 1977–8 lectures, 'Security, Territory, Population', played a more or less implicit role in Deleuze's characterisation of control society. The basis for this suggestion lies above all in the mode of regulation of a given material that is common to Foucault's security apparatuses and Deleuze's control societies: 'continuous modulation and the treatment of the object of power adapt in real time to what actually occurs' (Razac 2008: 40). At the same time, however, Razac points to the historical difficulty raised by this suggestion: Foucault situates the emergence of techniques of security at the end of the eighteenth century, whereas Deleuze situates the transition to control societies in the latter half of the twentieth century after the Second World War.

In other respects, too, the reference to Foucault, which is fundamental for Deleuze's definition of control society, is more troublesome than it first appears. Deleuze presents his diagnosis as though it corresponded fully with Foucault's method of undertaking an analysis or an archaeology of the present. In fact, it corresponds more with the manner in which Deleuze presents Foucault's method than it does with Foucault's own work. Following Nietzsche's way of writing a genealogy of the present, Foucault reinterprets past practices, institutions and forms of knowledge from the perspective of a hitherto unnoticed distance. His genealogies describe the discursive and non-discursive formations (*dispositifs*) from which we are separated by hitherto imperceptible fractures in the hermeneutical frameworks within which we live and experience the historical present. In this manner, he shows up the madness of incarcerating the insane, the arbitrariness and injustice of imprisoning convicts, the irrationality of making our identity as subjects depend upon our sexual behaviour. In the terms of his own retrospective account of his genealogical method in 'What is Enlightenment?' these are all examples of practices that were previously considered unproblematic or unavoidable but that we can now perceive as contingent and open to change (Foucault 1997: 315). Foucault describes the aim of his genealogies as pursuing this break with the past in a manner that might serve as a condition for further change.

Deleuze offers a different account in *What is Philosophy?* when he explains how Foucault's analysis of the present does not aim to capture the form of society in which we live at any given moment but rather the form of society that is emerging. He argues that, whereas he and Guattari identify becoming as the source of change, Foucault writes from the perspective of the actual (*actuel*). He does not mean *actuel* in the ordinary French sense of this word, which refers to that which is current or present, but rather something much closer to Nietzsche's 'untimely'. It is in this sense, according to Deleuze, that we must understand Foucault's use of the term 'actuality'. It is not a question of what already exists or is present in a given historical moment, but of what is coming about, of what is in the process of becoming.

Deleuze defends this reading of Foucault's use of *actuel* with reference to a passage in *The Archaeology of Knowledge* in which Foucault draws a distinction between the present (*notre actualité*) and 'the border of time that surrounds our present, overhangs it and indicates it in its otherness' in order to suggest that Foucault writes from this border between present and future (Foucault 1969: 172; 1972: 130). Even though Foucault's text does not describe it in this way, Deleuze suggests that this border between the present and the future is what he means by the actual. He offers a more extended commentary on this passage from *The Archaeology of Knowledge* in 'What is a Dispositif?':

The novelty of a *dispositif* in relation to those that precede it is what we call its actuality, our actuality. The new is the *actuel*. The *actuel* is not what we are but rather what we are becoming, what we are in the process of becoming, that is to say the Other, our becoming-other. In every *dispositif* we must distinguish what we are (what we are already no longer) and what we are becoming: the part of history and the part of the actual. (Deleuze 2007: 350)[15]

Deleuze employs the same form of words in *What is Philosophy?* in spelling out the proximity of his own 'becoming', Nietzsche's untimely (*l'inactuel* or *l'intempestif*), and Foucault's supposed *actuel* in suggesting that all three terms refer to 'that which is in the process of coming about': not what we presently are or recently were, but rather 'what we are in the process of becoming – that is to say, the Other, our becoming-other' (Deleuze and Guattari 1994: 112). The problem is that Foucault does not use the term in the manner that Deleuze suggests. His text actually contrasts this border region with 'our actuality' (Foucault 1969: 172; 1972: 130).

A second difficulty raised by Deleuze's reference to Foucault in elaborating his concept of control society emerges when, in his 'Postscript', he reminds us that Foucault himself was one of the first to point out that we no longer live in an age of discipline: 'we were no longer in disciplinary societies, we were leaving them behind' (Deleuze 1995: 178). According to this diagnosis of the present, disciplinary society is already disappearing. The techniques of disciplinary power are in crisis, and institutions such as the school, factory, hospital, army and prison have more or less reached their use-by date: 'It is simply a matter of nursing them through their death throes and keeping people busy until the new forces knocking at the door take over. Control societies are taking over from disciplinary societies' (Deleuze 1995: 178).

In other words, Foucault recognised the end of the relatively brief historical reign of the disciplinary model of power that followed the sovereign model and that had been progressively replaced by the control model since the end of the Second World War. In the course of a 1977 interview, 'The Eye of Power', he noted that 'disciplinary power was in fact already in Bentham's day being transcended by other and much more subtle mechanisms for the regulation of phenomena of population, controlling their fluctuations and compensating their irregularities' (Foucault 1980: 160).[16] Moreover, the fact that he had devoted *Discipline and Punish* to the detailed analysis of the disciplinary model is difficult to reconcile with Deleuze's thesis regarding the meaning of 'actuality' for Foucault. In the terms of Deleuze's hypothesis, *Discipline and Punish* should have analysed what we are in the process of becoming rather than confining itself to the disciplinary society that we were. It is true that in his lectures in the years that followed the publication of this book Foucault did focus on technologies of power that succeeded the disciplinary model, such as mechanisms of security. But this led him in an altogether different direction to that suggested by Deleuze's account of control society, namely towards the analysis of different forms of governmentality and a genealogy of liberal and neoliberal government. This project led him in the direction of a more and more refined study of the different means by which states sought to act on the actions of people. In the terms of Foucault's study of different forms of governmentality, the idea that a society might be defined by a single diagram of power in the manner that he had suggested in *Discipline and Punish* no longer played a role. Deleuze's Foucault is based upon an earlier moment of Foucault's thought but also upon a philosophical conception of history that does not have the same commitment to realism, or rather the same means of expressing historical reality. For Deleuze, it is the philosophical concept rather than historical knowledge of the past that is supposed to act upon our experience of the present.[17] In the end, they held very different views of the relation between activism and philosophy.[18]

Notes

1. The *Groupe d'information sur les prisons* (GIP) grew out of efforts to support Maoist militants imprisoned during the repression of leftist activity in 1970. Its aim was to gather and publish information about conditions in French prisons and it was organised as a decentralised series of groups around particular prisons. For further information see Deleuze's 'Foucault and Prison' (Deleuze 2007: 277–86) and Defert and Donzelot 1976.
2. As well as this book, a thorough treatment of their relationship would need to take into account the interviews in Deleuze 1995 as well as the interviews and other texts about Foucault in Deleuze 2007. The present article is well short of a comprehensive discussion of the topic but one that I hope will stimulate further investigation.
3. See Deleuze and Foucault 1972. This interview is reprinted in Foucault's *Dits et écrits*, tome III (Foucault 1994: 306–15). English translations appear in Foucault 1997: 205–17 and Deleuze 2004: 206–13. Page references are to the latter version, although the translations are modified.
4. See 'Powers and Strategies', a 1977 interview with the editorial collective of *Les révoltes logiques*, in Foucault 1980: 134–45.
5. See for example Chaloupka 2003 and Rowe and Dempsey 2004.
6. Foucault's review '*La grande colère des faits*' appeared in *Le Nouvel Observateur*, 625, 9–15 May 1977, pp. 84–6. It is reprinted in Foucault 1994: 277–81.
7. Deleuze's text, '*A propos les nouveaux philosophes et d'un problème plus général*', dated 5 June 1977, was first published as an interview in *Le Monde*, 19–20 June 1977. It was also printed as a supplement to the journal *Minuit* (no. 24, May 1977), and distributed free of charge in bookshops. It is included in *Two Regimes of Madness* as 'On the New Philosophers (Plus a More General Problem)' (Deleuze 2007: 139–47).
8. Eleanor Kaufman writes a propos their different attitudes towards the Croissant issue: 'Foucault's support was on legal grounds, and he did not sign the petition that expressed a more vehement condemnation of West Germany's totalitarianising tendencies. The clash between Foucault's position and Deleuze's

more extreme one seems to have been the principal ground for their falling-out' (Kaufmann 1998: 248). She cites Eribon 1991: 258–62, and Macey 1994: 392–7. See also Dosse 2010: 314.

9. Translated in *Two Regimes of Madness* as 'Europe the Wrong Way' (Deleuze 2007: 148–50). I have been unable to determine whether this article is identical to the text of the petition circulated by Guattari. It contains no characterisation of the West German State as fascist nor any suggestion that it was becoming a police dictatorship. However, since Senellart refers explicitly to this text it is appropriate to ask whether it might be read as implying support for terrorist action.

10. Dosse comments that Guattari's refusal to publicly condemn the actions of the RAF or the Italian Red Brigades in 1977–8 may perhaps be explained by his own underground efforts to dissuade many of those tempted by terrorism (Dosse 2010: 295). See also Guattari's review of the film *Germany in Autumn*, in which he comments that the only result of the RAF's actions 'will have been to echo the collective melancholia that has present-day Germany in its grip' (Guattari 1982: 108).

11. Michel Senellart comments in his essay contextualising the 1977–8 and 1978–9 lectures that the study of German neoliberalism and American anarcho-liberalism 'is Foucault's sole incursion into the field of contemporary history throughout his teaching at the Collège de France' (Foucault 2007: 385). Francesco Guala describes the lectures in 1979 as his one and only 'diversion into contemporary political philosophy' (Guala 2006: 429).

12. In the section of Part One of *Thus Spoke Zarathustra* entitled 'On the New Idol', Nietzsche writes: 'State is the name for the coldest of all cold monsters. Coldly it tells lies; and this lie crawls out of its mouth: "I, the state, am the people"' (Nietzsche 2005: 43).

13. Deleuze and Guattari develop their own detailed and complex analyses of fascism. A thorough comparison of their approach with Foucault's governmentality analysis would need to take this into account. See, for example, Holland 2008 and Protevi 2000.

14. The interview with Negri first appeared in *Futur antérieur*, no. 1, Spring 1990. The 'Postscript' first appeared in *L'autre journal*, May 1990. Both are reprinted in *Negotiations* (Deleuze 1995: 169–76; 177–82). See also the comments in 'What is an Act of Creation?' (Deleuze 2008: 317–29).

15. The original text reads: 'La nouveauté d'un dispositif par rapport aux précédents, nous l'appelons son actualité, notre actualité. Le nouveau, c'est l'actuel. L'actuel n'est pas ce que nous sommes, mais plutôt ce que nous devenons, ce que nous sommes en train de devenir, c'est-à-dire l'Autre, notre devenir-autre. Dans tout dispositif, il faut distinguer ce que nous sommes (ce que nous ne sommes déjà plus), et ce que nous sommes en train de devenir: la part de l'histoire, et la part de l'actuel' (Deleuze 2003: 322).

16. Earlier in the same interview, he commented that 'the procedures of power that are at work in modern societies are much more numerous, diverse and rich' (Foucault 1980: 148). See also *Dits et écrits*, tome III, 'La société disciplinaire en crise' (Foucault 1994: 532).

17. Deleuze acknowledges the difference between his own and Foucault's commitment to history in commenting in an interview that he did not approach things 'through structure, or linguistics or psychoanalysis, through science or even through history, because I think philosophy has its own raw material that allows it to enter into more fundamental external relations with these other disciplines' (Deleuze 1995: 89).

18. I am grateful to Marcelo Svirsky and an anonymous reader for helpful comments on an earlier draft of this paper.

References

Chaloupka, William (2003) 'There Must Be Some Way Out of Here: Strategy, Ethics and Environmental Politics', in W. Magnussen and K. Shaw (eds.), *A Political Space: Reading the Global Through Clayoquot Sound*, Minneapolis: University of Minnesota Press, pp. 67–90.

Defert, Daniel and Jacques Donzelot (1976) 'La charnière des prisons', *Le magazine littéraire*, 112/113, pp. 33–5.

Deleuze, Gilles (1986) *Foucault*, Paris: Éditions de Minuit.

Deleuze, Gilles (1990) *Pourparlers, Paris*: Éditions de Minuit.

Deleuze, Gilles (1995) *Negotiations 1972–1990*, trans. Martin Joughin, New York: Columbia University Press.

Deleuze, Gilles (2002) *L'Île Désert et Autres Textes: Textes et Entretiens 1953–1974*, ed. David Lapoujade, Paris: Éditions de Minuit.

Deleuze, Gilles (2003) *Deux Régimes de Fous: Textes et Entretiens 1975–1995*, ed. David Lapoujade, Paris: Éditions de Minuit.

Deleuze, Gilles (2004) *Desert Islands and Other Texts 1953–1974*, trans. Michael Taormina, ed. David Lapoujade, New York: Semiotext(e).

Deleuze, Gilles (2007) *Two Regimes of Madness: Texts and Interviews 1975–1995*, trans. Ames Hodges and Mike Taormina, ed. David Lapoujade, New York: Semiotext(e) (Revised Edition).

Deleuze, Gilles and Félix Guattari (1972) *L'Anti-Oedipe*, Paris: Éditions de Minuit.

Deleuze, Gilles and Félix Guattari (1980) *Mille plateaux*, Paris: Éditions de Minuit.

Deleuze, Gilles and Félix Guattari (1987) *A Thousand Plateaus: Capitalism and Schizophrenia*, trans. Brian Massumi, Minneapolis: University of Minnesota Press.

Deleuze, Gilles and Félix Guattari (1994) *What Is Philosophy?*, trans. Hugh Tomlinson and Graham Burchell, New York: Columbia University Press.

Deleuze, Gilles and Félix Guattari (2004) *Anti-Oedipus*, trans. R. Hurley, M. Seem and H. R. Lane, London: Continuum.

Deleuze, Gilles and Michel Foucault (1972) 'Les intellectuels et le pouvoir', *L'Arc 49: Deleuze*, pp. 3–10.

Deleuze, Gilles and Claire Parnet (2002) *Dialogues II*, trans. Hugh Tomlinson and Barbara Habberjam; 'The Actual and the Virtual', trans. Eliot Ross Albert, London: Continuum.

Dosse, François (2010) *Gilles Deleuze and Félix Guattari: Intersecting Lives*, trans. Deborah Glassman, New York: Columbia University Press.

Eribon, Didier (1991) *Michel Foucault*, trans. Betsy Wing, Cambridge, MA: Harvard University Press.

Foucault, Michel (1969) *L'Archéologie du savoir*, Paris: Éditions Gallimard.

Foucault, Michel (1972) *The Archaeology of Knowledge*, trans. A. M. Sheridan Smith, London: Tavistock.

Foucault, Michel (1977) *Language, Counter-Memory, Practice: selected Essays and Interviews*, trans. Donald F. Bouchard and Sherry Simon, ed. Donald F. Bouchard, Ithaca: Cornell University Press.

Foucault, Michel (1980) *Power/Knowledge: Selected Interviews and Other Writings 1972–1977*, trans. C. Gordon, L. Marshall, J. Mepham, K. Soper, ed. Colin Gordon, Brighton: Harvester Press.

Foucault, Michel (1994) *Dits et écrits*, tome III, Paris: Gallimard.

Foucault, Michel (1997) *Essential Works of Foucault 1954–1984, Volume 1, Ethics*, trans. R. Hurley et al., New York: New Press.

Foucault, Michel (2000) *Essential Works of Foucault 1954–1984, Volume 3: Power*, trans. R. Hurley et al., ed. James D. Faubion, New York: New Press.

Foucault, Michel (2003) *Society Must Be Defended: Lectures at the Collège de France 1975–1976*, trans. David Macey, ed. Mauro Bertani and Alessandro Fontana, New York: Picador.

Foucault, Michel (2007) *Security, Territory, Population: Lectures at the Collège de France 1977–1978*, trans. Graham Burchell, ed. Michel Senellart, Houndmills, Basingstoke and New York: Palgrave Macmillan.

Foucault, Michel (2008) *The Birth of Biopolitics: Lectures at the Collège de France 1978–1979*, ed. Michel Senellart, trans. Graham Burchell. Houndmills, Basingstoke and New York: Palgrave Macmillan.

Guala, Francesco (2006) 'Critical Notice: *Naissance de la biopolitique. Cours au Collège de France, 1978–1979*, Michel Foucault. Edited by Michel Senellart. Seuil/Gallimard, 2004', *Economics and Philosophy*, 22, pp. 429–39.

Guattari, Félix (1982) 'Like the Echo of Collective Melancholia', *Semiotext(e), The German Issue*, 4:2, pp. 102–10.

Glucksmann, André (1975) *La Cuisinière et le Mangeur d'Hommes: Réflexions sur l'État, le marxisme et les camps de concentration*, Paris: Seuil.

Glucksmann, André (1977) *Les Maîtres penseurs*, Paris: Grasset.

Holland, Eugene (2008) 'Schizoanalysis, Nomadology, Fascism', in Ian Buchanan and Nicholas Thoburn (eds.), *Deleuze and Politics*, Edinburgh: Edinburgh University Press, pp. 74–97.

Kaufman, Eleanor (1998) 'Madness and Repetition: The Absence of Work in Deleuze, Foucault, and Jacques Martin', in E. Kaufman and K.J. Heller (eds.), *Deleuze and Guattari: New Mappings in Politics, Philosophy, and Culture*, Minneapolis: University of Minnesota Press, pp. 230–50.

Lévy, Bernard-Henri (1977) *La Barbarie à visage humain*, Paris: Grasset.

Macey, David (1994) *The Lives of Michel Foucault*, London: Vintage.

Nietzsche, Friedrich (2005) *Thus Spoke Zarathustra*, trans. Graham Parkes, Oxford: Oxford University Press.

Protevi, John (2000) 'A Problem of Pure Matter: Fascist Nihilism in *A Thousand Plateaus*', in K. Ansell-Pearson and D. Morgan (eds.), *Nihilism Now! Monsters of Energy*, London: Macmillan, pp. 167–88.

Razac, Olivier (2008) *Avec Foucault, Après Foucault: Disséquer la société de contrôle*, Paris: L'Harmattan.

Ross, Kristin (2002) *May '68 and its Afterlives*, Chicago: University of Chicago Press.

Rowe, James K. and Jessica Dempsey (2004) 'Why Poststructuralism is a Live Wire for the Left', in Duncan Fuller and Rob Kitchin (eds.), *Radical Theory/Critical Praxis: Making a Difference Beyond the Academy?*, Kelowna: Praxis (e)Press.

Politics in the Middle: For a Political Interpretation of the Dualisms in Deleuze and Guattari

Rodrigo Nunes   Pontifícia Universidade Católica do Rio Grande do Sul

Abstract

The paper identifies three recent lines of interpretation of the politics that can be derived from Deleuze and Guattari, all of which share a way of reading the dualisms in their work that can be traced back to how they understand the actual/virtual partition, and to an alleged pre-eminence of the virtual over the actual. It is argued that this reading is not only inaccurate, but obscures the political dimension of Deleuze and Guattari's work. Clarifying the latter requires a reinterpretation of the dualisms involved (as dyads rather than binaries), of the relation between virtual and actual (as a formal distinction where one acts back upon the other), and the drawing of a clear distinction between what Deleuze calls a 'transcendent exercise' of thought and sensibility and the properly metaphysical exercise that sets up the distinction between virtual and actual. What then appears is an image of Deleuze's and Guattari's thought that is far more concerned with practical questions and with a situated political practice of intervention.

Keywords: dyad, immanence, univocity, virtual, actual, intervention

That dualisms play a major structural role in Deleuze's and Guattari's work, both solo and collaborative, is a fact that will have escaped no reader. One could, in effect, speak of three ways in which dualism appears in it as a problem. At first, dualism itself is identified as the problem, a target and mark of what to avoid in philosophy: 'the only

Deleuze Studies Volume 4: 2010 supplement: 104–126
DOI: 10.3366/E1750224110001157
© Edinburgh University Press
www.eupjournals.com/dls

enemy is two' (Deleuze 1973), ultimately the One/Multiple opposition behind both monism and dualism. It is exactly the false choice between these two pairs that the concept of 'multiplicities' is supposed to disarm. But the alternative that follows is set up as an irreconcilable opposition – in the end, 'one can only think in either monist or pluralist terms' (Deleuze 1973). Inevitably, this will raise the recursive suspicion that such a dichotomy is itself still mired in dualistic thinking. Finally, this will in turn cast suspicions over all the other dualisms that run through Deleuze and Guattari's work. They acknowledge as much in the introduction to a book whose dualistic nature is most obvious:

> We make use of a dualism of models only so as to arrive at a process that would refuse every model. . . . To arrive at the magical formula that we all search for: PLURALISM = MONISM, going through all the dualisms that are the enemy, but the absolutely necessary enemy, the furniture we are constantly moving around. (Deleuze and Guattari 2004a: 31)

It is obvious why they would find it necessary to exorcise such suspicions: the threat they represent is nothing less than the ultimate failure of some of the highest avowed goals of their philosophy. If the point is to affirm the univocity of Being, then allowing any form of dualism to creep in risks reintroducing a categorial distinction within Being that returns it to its Aristotelian equivocity. If the point is to affirm an absolute immanence 'immanent to nothing but itself' (Deleuze and Guattari 2003: 49), then the danger is the re-institution of a metaphysical supplement outside the plane of immanence, thereby reintroducing the dative relation that is the sign of transcendence.

Alain Badiou is the most prominent commentator to have stressed how these dualisms can be traced back to the crucial distinction between actual and virtual: according to him, 'the nominal pair virtual/actual exhausts the deployment of univocal Being' (Badiou 1997: 65). While it is not, as I hope to show, a matter of simply reducing all other oppositions to this one, or even of mapping them onto either side of the line, Deleuze's own final statement on his philosophical project would seem to warrant such a conclusion. In his last published essay, the flag of his early 'transcendental empiricism' is unfurled into the presentation of a pure plane of immanence or transcendental field by which the given is given to empirical representation, a field containing nothing but 'virtuals [which] become actualised in a state of affairs and a lived state' (Deleuze 2003c: 363). If it plays such a central part in Deleuze and Guattari's thought, it is inevitable that the virtual/actual distinction should also have a determinant role in interpretations of their work – and thus also in the assessments that have been made of its political consequences, which is our specific concern here. Looking at recent examples of the latter, I suggest there are three general lines along which they appear, all of which can be traced back to a shared manner of reading the virtual/actual dualism – which, in turn, affects their approach to other dualisms more generally, and to politics specifically. My contention is that the errors common to all three approaches obscure the ways in which Deleuze and Guattari can be useful for thinking political practice. Proposing an alternative reading – in which their dualisms appear as *dyads* instead of *binaries* – coupled with an analysis of these errors, may thus shed some new light on what an activist practice inspired by Deleuze and Guattari *can be*, as well as aiding the negative task of pointing out what (*contra* these three lines of interpretation) it *is not*.

I. Three Times Two Equals One

Let us start by identifying these three different ways of thinking the relationship between Deleuze and Guattari's thought and politics, the first of which expresses a positive evaluation, the other two a negative one. The first approach generally corresponds to a dominant strain in the 'revival' enjoyed by the two thinkers since the 1990s (itself largely due to their English-language reception), in various academic disciplines as well as in some political and artistic circles. Here, Deleuze and Guattari appear as proponents of a politics of 'movement'. Not only a politics of flux over stasis, but also one that pitches social movements (in the broad sense) against institutions (state, parties, unions, etc.), and values openness over identity, nomadic displacement over attachment, the temporary, the mobile, the small-scale and the micropolitical over larger, more permanent and cohesive forms whose horizon would be macropolitical.

It is obvious that this approach finds much support not only in explicit statements made by Deleuze and Guattari themselves, but in many of their overt political commitments and practices.[1] While this interpretation runs diffusely through several texts and political or aesthetic practices, it was arguably the publication of Hardt and Negri's *Empire* (2000) that provided it with a focal point, and the reasons for its prevalence are to some extent tied in not only with that book's success, but with the conditions that enabled it: a worldwide tide of political mobilisation, the protagonists of which by and large fell outside more traditional organisational forms, and which, having first tasted the subversive potential of new communication technologies, articulated a politics that pointed beyond the limits of the nation state towards a transnational space created by the consolidation of the global capitalist market. It seemed natural that some of those taking part in this moment would find resonances in Deleuze and Guattari's politics. For its positive take on their work, and for the importance this acquired in certain political milieus, one could call this the *activist* line of interpretation.

The centrality suddenly achieved by two such eccentric (in every sense of the word) thinkers has elicited a critical reaction in which we can identify the two other main lines of interpretation. Here, Deleuze and Guattari appear as either *anti-political/depoliticising* or else as *political despite themselves*. In the first case, they are charged with retreating from the site of politics itself into either a quasi-mystical contemplation of the boundless power of creation, of which actuality is only a limitation, or into the purity of a utopianism lacking any footing in the concrete constraints of practice. From this perspective, Deleuze and Guattari are ultimately indifferent 'to any notion of change, time or history that is mediated by actuality' and to the relations and 'politics of this world' (Hallward 2006: 162), caught up in the aristocratic *askesis* of a thought that reaches beyond the actual towards a reunification with an all-productive One-All (Badiou 1997: 22–3); or else are incapable of understanding the most fundamental insight of Marxism-Leninism, for which the question of strategy lies precisely at the point where necessity and liberty cease to be opposed in absolute terms and become related in the situatedness of political action (Badiou 1977: 37–8). In the second case, the equation of resistance with an affirmative desire as power to differ turns Deleuze and Guattari into the unwitting apologists of a capitalism that works precisely through the modulation of desire and the production of difference: here, in short, they become the 'ideologist[s] of late capitalism' (Žižek 2004: 184). If '"enjoy in your little corner"' is 'the maxim of rhizomatic multiplicities' (Peyrol[2] 1977: 50), this can either be read as a call away from political work proper into self-indulgent, inconsequential distraction, or, worse, as the promise of an unfettered expression of desire that may have appeared radical in the 1970s, but which has since then been recuperated into the mechanisms of capitalist accumulation and political legitimation. When resistance has become effectively indistinguishable from capitalism, it can offer no answer to the question: 'how, then, to revolutionise an order whose very principle is constant revolutionising?' (Žižek 2004: 213).

From the point of view of the virtual/actual partition and the other dualisms, it is immediately striking that the image of Deleuze and Guattari's thought that can be extracted from each alternative is ultimately quite similar. In fact, the first stands in an inverted relation to the other two, so that what appears as positive on one side is negative on the other, and vice versa. This inversion overdetermines the evaluation of all the dualisms whose political sense is more immediately obvious: major/minor, molar/molecular, *dispositif*/line of flight, state/nomad, macro/micropolitics, re/deterritorialisation... In all three versions, the series of first terms is placed on the side of the actual, while the series of second terms falls on the side of the virtual. Not only do they take the distinction as a starting point, they are also clearly premised on a prevalence of the virtual side over the other: 'we need two names for the One *in order to experience that it is from only one of them that springs the ontological univocity designated by the nominal pair*' (Badiou 1997: 65; original emphasis). As a consequence, the image of Deleuze and Guattari's thought that emerges is one that ascribes philosophical and political eminence to the second series to the detriment of the first: a philosophy and a politics of the virtual, the minor, the molecular, the micropolitical, nomadism, lines of flight, and (absolute) deterritorialisation.

It is important to notice that, although both critics and advocates share this *doxa*, each arrives at it in a different way. While the two tomes of *Capitalisme et schizophrénie* tend to be enthusiasts' main point of reference, Badiou's critique is mostly predicated on Deleuze's solo work, where political concerns are much less explicit, and gives little attention to Guattari. Žižek, on the other hand, insists on a sharp break and change of direction taken by the 'original', 'good' Deleuze – from the sterile Sense-Event as the effect of bodily causes towards a notion of becoming as the virtual production of the actual – under the '"bad" influence' (Žižek 2004: 20) of the activist Guattari. Hallward is the only one to grant the same weight to the collaborative works, which would stand in continuity to the others in so far as they also subscribe to a logic where the stress placed on the virtual empties the relations among actual elements/bodies in favour of the direct relation of each actual thing to its virtual 'ground'.

This inverted relation explains the tone common to the three critiques of Badiou, Žižek and Hallward: that of 'revealing' the true face of a thought misread by its 'disciples'. 'Which Deleuze?', Badiou starts by asking; and the answer is quickly forthcoming: we must uncover, behind the usual image of the affirmation of difference and multiplicitous heterogeneity, a 'metaphysics of the One' (Badiou 1997: 20) in which the impulse of thought, though singular each time, is always reconnected to its source in the One-All. Against the same misconception, Hallward offers a portrait of a philosophy in which what matters is 'the redemptive re-orientation of any particular creature towards its own dissolution', a 'spiritual, redemptive' Deleuze who is unconcerned with matter, nature or the world, an '*extra*-worldly' thinker of '*dis*-embodiment and *de*-materialisation' (Hallward 2006: 3; original emphasis). Žižek's position is slightly different, as for him one must rescue the true Deleuze and his politics from 'the deadlock and impotence of the "popular" Deleuzian politics' and 'the popular image . . . based on the reading of the books he co-authored with Félix Guattari' (Žižek 2004: xi–xii). While not spelled out in Badiou, this political dimension also figures in Hallward, who closes his book with the suggestion that 'those of us who still seek to change the world and to empower its inhabitants will need to look for our inspiration elsewhere' (Hallward 2006: 164).

At any rate, and whatever one makes of these critiques, it is clear how they aim at the heart of Deleuze's project, solo or with Guattari. In Badiou's and Hallward's *anti-political* account, the weightiest charges are at least three. First, that the professed immanentism is in fact a philosophy of emanation; as such, Deleuze and Guattari fail to make the 'conversion' by which 'univocal Being is said of difference and, as such, revolves around beings' (Deleuze 2003a: 91) and instead make the actual/creatural entirely dependent on the creative, self-differentiating power of an extra-worldly One. Second, and consequently, that a categorial distinction ultimately subsists between virtual and actual, entailing a failure to sustain the univocity of Being and a slippage between immanent and eminent or emanating cause.[3] Third, that the resulting thought of individuation is ultimately grounded in what Deleuze calls the pre-critical 'negative of limitation' – and one should recall here Deleuze's entreaty that 'every reduction of individuation to a limit [i.e., as the finite that is said by limitation of the infinite] or complication of differenciation compromises the whole of the philosophy of difference' (Deleuze 2003a: 318). The *political despite themselves* version of the critique, on the other hand, returns to Hegel's critique of the tautology of Spinoza's Substance and gives it a Marxian twist: anything that affirms the world is inevitably too compromised by it; genuine critique can only come from negating it; and so Deleuze and Guattari can only capture their time in a mystified form, by (re)producing its ideology.

Now, if all three interpretative lines – one positive, two negative – only invert the values of a common basic understanding, a defence of the political significance of Deleuze and Guattari's thought will have to share with the critiques a certain task of 'demystification'. In other words, we may have to rescue Deleuze and Guattari from (some) friends as much as from their foes. If that is the case, the best way to proceed is by working back towards what the three alternatives share – an emphasis on the virtual/actual distinction, and on the pre-eminence of the former over the latter.

II. The Flux *and* the Party?

We could, in fact, start precisely with a situation in which Guattari publicly disagrees with someone attempting to reclaim his thought. In the early 1980s, Guattari travelled to Brazil on the invitation of fellow psychoanalyst and cultural critic Suely Rolnik, where he took part in various encounters and more or less formal debates with several groups from the political milieu that, at that time, was consolidating itself into the Workers' Party (PT). Alongside other texts – including a dialogue between Guattari and a then thirty-something Lula, fresh out of leading the metalworkers' strikes of the late 1970s and running for office for the first time – these debates were collected by Rolnik in *Molecular Revolution in Brazil*, a quietly influential book in Brazil that has only recently appeared in English.

As we have seen with Žižek, Guattari can sometimes be presented – especially by philosophers – as the 'activist' who drew Deleuze away from his rigorous philosophical path. For pretty much the same reason, he finds a warmer reception in the *activist* line of interpretation. This makes it all the more remarkable to discover him involved in the following exchange, in which his interlocutor begins by praising 'what I understand of what Guattari thinks' – that there is a need for 'various molecular revolutions . . . a multiplicity of feminist, lesbian-feminist, black, and other groups, questioning patriarchal or phallic structures' that should invest in constructing 'new forms of performance, assemblages that seek to question those power structures' that, like the party, reproduce 'the patriarchal structure' (Guattari and Rolnik 2008: 123–4). Guattari replies:

> If the movement works like that, OK. But there might also be situations in which it falls apart. I'll give a historical example: all the different components of the *Autonomia* movement in Italy broke down, and often because of this kind of discourse. . . . They organized themselves in structures – very interesting ones, actually, such as publishing houses and cooperatives – which within a few months became completely depoliticized. . . . No doubt this process would have appeared at some point in history, one way or another. Nevertheless, a different script could have been written: the autonomization

of the feminist members operating as a factor to reinforce the effectiveness of movements [instead of their] collapse into a black hole. Just imagine if all the women in the PT . . . suddenly decided to say: 'That's it, we've had enough of Lula and all that, we're off.'

Comment: And then they'd organize themselves into women's groups. I think that would be great!

Guattari: Maybe. But to think it great that a movement like the PT should disappear is debatable, to say the least. (Guattari and Rolnik 2008: 124–5)

This exchange is located at the intersection of two series: that of a country (Brazil) reaching the end of a military dictatorship that had prevented various micropolitical transformations brewing throughout the 1970s, and whose main point of convergence in the 1980s would become the PT, from entering into compositions that lent them consistency and urgency; and that of a European (Guattari) processing the sometimes tragic defeats of the previous decades, the double edge of Mitterrand's electoral victory, and the onset of the *années d'hiver* of Integrated World Capitalism. The caution and nuance shown in Brazil perhaps have something to do with this descendent curve. It is certainly easy to follow a difference in tone in his collaborations with Deleuze, from the post-1968 heat of *L'Anti-Oedipe* to the exhortations to restore our faith in this world in *Qu'est-ce que la philosophie?* Had they lost faith in movement, in micropolitics, in the molecular – in all those things we recognise the *activist* Deleuze and Guattari for – and settled instead for the reform that you could get, the *change you could believe in*? Or was there never an a priori choice between micro- and macropolitics, molecular and molar, minor and major in the first place?

We must take note that even *L'Anti-Oedipe*, an exalted book if there ever was one, does not speak of a *choice* as such. In fact, the opposition between molecular and molar is presented as a 'theory of the two *poles*' (cf. Deleuze and Guattari 2008: 406ff.). This is because

there is molar *and* molecular everywhere: their disjunction is a relation of inclusive disjunction, which varies only according to the two senses of subordination, depending on whether the molecular phenomena are subordinated to the large ensembles, or subordinate them instead. (Deleuze and Guattari 2008: 407; original emphasis)

How are we to conceive of a dualism that is not a choice? In speaking of two 'poles', what may well have been in Deleuze's and Guattari's minds is the Simondonian *dyad*. This Platonic notion, which interestingly does not figure in Deleuze's review of Simondon's *L'Individu et sa genèse physico-biologique* (Deleuze 2004b: 120–4), plays arguably as structural a role in Simondon's thought of individuation as does the virtual/actual pair for Deleuze; it is certainly through it that, 'in Simondon's dialectics, the problematic replaces the negative' (122). For a dyad is a relation of inclusive disjunction between two indefinite terms in a dynamic relation of tension that constitutes a field in which the terms themselves become singularised. It is the mistake of the hylemorphic schema to assume the extremes as already individuated givens; the primacy of the pre-individual entails that there is only a polarised directionality between two indefinite extremes, so that 'every realised quality appears as a measure in an indefinite dyad of absolute and opposed qualities' (Simondon 2005: 163).

It seems perfectly clear that the overarching opposition of *L'Anti-Oedipe* and *Mille plateaux* – capitalism and schizophrenia – is meant not as a binary, but as a dyad. Between the two, neither is desirable: 'we have only spoken of a schizoid pole in the libidinal investment of the social field, to avoid as much as possible the confusion of a schizophrenic process with the production of a schizophrenic' (Deleuze and Guattari 2008: 455). 'One does not attain the BwO, or its plane of consistency, by de-stratifying wildly' (Deleuze and Guattari 2004a: 199). But this logic should be extended to the other dualisms: if we understand the opposition between molar and molecular (major and minor, macro and micropolitical etc.) as dyadic, there is no contradiction between Guattari's apparent support of the (seemingly) macro against micropolitical forms in the quotation above. What he saw in that moment of Brazilian history was the PT as the focus for a process of convergence that intensified the heterogeneous desires and groups that went into its constitution, while managing to stop their differences from just being annulled; and Lula, the charismatic figure relayed by the mass media, not as ' "the Father of Oppressed" or "the Father of the Poor"', but 'the vehicle of an extremely important vector of dynamics in the current situation', for 'nowadays one can't consider the struggles at all the levels without considering this factor of the production of subjectivity by the media' (Guattari and Rolnik 2008: 240). This is Lula not (or hopefully not) as the mirror that would become the fixed other of transference, but as a 'transitional object' that could be reappropriated by those projecting themselves onto him.

We must indeed conclude that Deleuze and Guattari establish *no* absolute opposition between, to borrow the title of Badiou's (1977) polemic, 'the flux' and 'the party'. There is no *a priori* choice concerning the forms in which the virtual may become actualised, since that would be to assume these forms as self-identical givens, rather than to think them as singular solutions within a problematic field defined by two extremes. What matters is that 'there be' virtuality, deterritorialisation, or potential each time – and that it be, as it were, 'cultivated'. To be sure, one can point out the greater arborescent tendency inherent in the party-form, or the risks inherent in the growing identification of a movement with a charismatic, mediatic leader (who then ceases to be a transitional object and becomes the mirror of transference). But to dismiss either outright on the grounds that they possess a 'transcendent' form is precisely to think in a transcendent way: separating the actual from its virtual conditions, reducing it to an a priori form 'filled' each time with content, rather than a singular being each time.

III. To Have Done With Dualisms

Yet does this not take us back to that point common to all three approaches to Deleuze and Guattari's politics: the preponderance of the virtual over the actual? If the 'real' movement, even in the political sense, is that of the virtual, does one not end up with precisely what a philosophy of immanence was supposed to counter: a negation of this world, its vicissitudes and the challenges it imposes on us, and a search for comfort beyond it? Are the critics not correct in pointing out a tendency towards pointless idealism, or the risk of celebrating all one opposes by always discounting actual processes and effects in favour of their potentials? Given practical application, does all this not effectively tend towards an exclusive emphasis on the 'small' or the 'local', and ultimately a refusal of any form of concerted action, scalability, negotiation, institutionalisation, mediation...? A stubborn refusal to see the larger picture in which one may, after all, be complicit – or a condemnation to self-satisfied subcultural irrelevance?

The crucial element here is the verb *to tend*. It is undeniable that the various critiques play on tendencies found in Deleuze and Guattari; the question is what we can gain from resisting their downplaying of other tendencies, and what image of their thought emerges when it is taken as a whole, rather than in half. To that end, we must return to the philosophical questions concerning the virtual/actual distinction. 'In order to suppress the opposition between the One and the Multiple' – precisely the one in which Deleuze and Guattari would be entangled – one must make 'one and multiple cease to function as adjectives in order to give place to a noun: there are only multiplicities' (Deleuze 1973). The point is, precisely, that 'there are two kinds of multiplicities' (Deleuze 2004a: 33), as per Bergson's modification of Riemann. The one is characterised by 'exteriority, simultaneity, juxtaposition, order, quantitative differenciation, *difference in degree*, a numerical multiplicity, discontinuous and actual'; the other is 'internal, of succession, fusion, organisation, heterogeneity, qualitative discrimination or *difference in nature*, a *virtual and continuous* multiplicity that is irreducible to number' (Deleuze 2004a: 30–1; original emphasis). In the first case, there is only actuality, actual relations. In the other, a 'line that goes from the virtual to its actualisation', an indivisible line whose each division amounts to a change in nature, that is, to an actualisation that happens 'through differenciation, along divergent lines'; the virtual 'to the extent that it becomes actualised [*en tant qu'il s'actualise*], in the process of becoming actualised [*en train de s'actualiser*], inseparable from the movement of its actualisation' (Deleuze 2004a: 36).

In this one finds the elements with which to dispel once and for all the myth of a political 'cult of the small' in Deleuze and Guattari: if the virtual is continuous, and thus foreign to number – if the operation of counting belongs to the actual, and is therefore a way of bringing the virtual into actualisation – then micro or molecular politics is not defined by its opposition to large numbers or scalability. Through its focus on the virtual, it is in fact entirely indifferent to scale, size, or measurement itself, in the same way that the opposition between singularity and totality (the latter being the category that would define dialectical, and as such Marxist, thinking) does not entail the automatic conclusion that 'small is beautiful'. If 'small' can only be said of discontinuous, actual multiplicities, 'micro' and 'molecular' refer to the virtual, continuous multiplicities that are implicated in *any* discrete multiplicity, *big or small*. This is why there is no a priori choice that excludes any actual existing party or leader, or the party-form and the leader-form as such. It is clear, then, that the 'cult of the small', whether celebrated by 'activists' or countered by critics, is premised on a very elementary confusion between the two kinds of multiplicity, when the whole point is exactly not to oppose the Multiple to the One, '*but on the contrary to distinguish two kinds of multiplicity*' (Deleuze 2004a: 31; original emphasis). The extensively 'small' is only 'beautiful' to the extent that it envelops more intensive potential; it can otherwise be quite ugly, turning in upon itself in a passive flight, a suicidal 'black hole', or a reactionary reterritorialisation. It is, in fact, the same distinction at work in the opposition between majoritarian ('not a relatively greater quantity, but the determination of a state or standard according to which greater as well as smaller quantities will be said to be minoritarian') and minoritarian ('one must not confuse "minoritarian" as a becoming or process and "minority" as an ensemble or state') (Deleuze and Guattari 2004a: 356).

It is important to notice that, unlike all the oppositions it founds, the one between actual and virtual multiplicities is in itself not dyadic. The crucial thing, however, is that the difference between them *not* be taken as categorial, as that would mean that Being itself is irremediably split, and is thus not said in *one*, but *two* senses. It is clear that, for Deleuze, they are to be understood in the same way as he interprets the attributes of extension and thought in Spinoza: as two *formally* (qualitatively, quidditatively), not *ontologically*, distinct sides of the real (cf. Deleuze 2002a: 30–1). Ontologically the same, they can be distinguished in *thought*. This is why the heart of *Différence et répétition* is a chapter on the 'image of thought', which almost 20 years later Deleuze will describe as 'the most concrete and necessary, and leading onto the following books, up until the researches with Guattari, when we invoke... a rhizomatic instead of an arborescent thought' (Deleuze 2003b: 283): for the task of 'transcendental empiricism' is none other than to institute a new image of thought.

Throughout Deleuze's oeuvre, including the books with Guattari, it is possible to discern two meanings of 'thought'; two different levels that one could roughly map onto Spinoza's first two modes of knowledge. First, there is thought as representation, which can be understood, with Kant, as the subsumption of a (differential) manifold under conceptual identity. It is never a case of ascribing a secondary reality to the actual, disputing the rights of representation, or arguing that it does not give us something true about the world – that it is a simulacrum or illusion that hides from us the true, virtual realm of Being. On the contrary, Deleuze (and Guattari) are, like Bergson, perfectly happy to acknowledge its practical utility, or that of science: being able to recognise identities is an evolutionary advantage to the extent that it imposes some degree of predictability on the world. The illusion lies not in representation itself, but in the hypostasis of the empirical/actual as the totality of Being. This is why we need a second level of thought that allows us to see the actual as the singular expression of virtual conditions. Given the same phenomenon, this second level allows us to perceive what appears as an identity for the first as being itself constituted by differences *that differ in time*; the empirical is cracked open by what undermines its self-identity and delivers it to new becomings. We can thus say at once that what appears to us is always new, and that it is only from the perspective of a higher, 'transcendent exercise' (Deleuze

2003a: 258) that it can appear as new. Every thought in the first sense appears as new, every repetition as productive of difference – every arborescence traversed by the rhizomatic, every assemblage by lines of flight, every majority by minoritarian becomings, every molarity by the molecular, etc. – when the actual is conceived in relation to its virtual potentials. The evolutionary advantage brought by representation must thus be qualified: the transcendent exercise that uncovers the differential conditions of existence of the empirical is above all a *practical* matter of liberating the potentials given in the present, of seeing the given actual as not necessary, but as open to transformation.

Clearly, however, if the transcendent exercise of thought *relies* on an actual/virtual partition, it cannot *found* it in itself. It requires a 'third mode' of knowledge, a properly *metaphysical* exercise of thought, to provide it. This is why Deleuze – celebrated by Badiou in this regard – remained entirely indifferent to the theme of the 'end of metaphysics' (cf. Badiou 1997: 69). If the point is to advance a new image of thought capable of connecting to what falls *outside* the reduction of the real to *the empirical*, only a *meta*-physics will do. Yet this metaphysics cannot be founded on the immanent movement of history, nor in any apodictic way – since the new image defines thought precisely as the *problematic* expression of virtual ideas. The key here is the Kantian distinction between knowledge and thought. While we need a metaphysics to *think* what this realm of virtuality may be, it is itself premised on the possibility of a transcendent exercise: it is *because* there is a transcendent exercise of sensibility that *senses* (but does not *perceive*) virtual intensities, and a transcendent exercise of thought that *expresses* (but does not *experience*) virtual ideas, that a metaphysical *thought* (and not *knowledge*) is possible.

Once the possibility of a new image of thought has been established – once the 'transcendental' moment has been dealt with – it is no longer a matter of providing a philosophical account of how problems are determined, but of determining them: of experimenting (with) immanence, with what it means to live 'in' (or maybe 'live out') immanence. 'In my earlier books, I tried to describe a certain exercise of thought; but describing it is not yet exercising thought in that way', says Deleuze; 'proclaiming "Long live the multiple" is not yet doing it, one must do the multiple' (Deleuze 2006: 13).

This allows us to understand the importance acquired by concrete ethico-political questions, in particular the dialogue with Marx and the confrontation with the capitalistic plane of immanence, in the two volumes of *Capitalisme et shchizophrénie*. But the goal of instituting a new practical reason had been clear from the start: 'none of this would matter if it were not for the practical implications and the moral presuppositions of [the representative] distortion' – the 'conservatism' that turns us away 'from the highest task – that of determining problems, of applying to them our decisive and creative power' (Deleuze 2003a: 344). That metaphysics is necessary for an ethics, but must be measured by the latter's effects: this, and not a direct rational (or mystical) intuition of the One-All, is Deleuze at his most Spinozist.[4]

IV. 'Do the Multiple'...

Once the partition of virtual and actual has been attained, it can be applied to the practical task of orienting oneself in the world. We have seen that, for Simondon, orientation always presupposes a position along an indefinite dyad (indefinitely cold/hot, high/low, etc.). A dyad, in fact, is nothing other than a continuous multiplicity that changes in nature (that is, differenciates into a discontinuous multiplicity) when divided; thus, for example, it is along a continuum of indefinitely more painful/pleasurable that sensations can be individualised into perceptions of 'pain' or 'pleasure'. Now, if what we could call Deleuze's and Guattari's *dualisms of orientation* are such continua, it is necessary to conclude that the oppositions they establish define two indefinite *virtual* directions along which actualisations take place. This implies, firstly, a relation of 'more or less' in any actualisation: an actuality can be(come) *more or less* rhizomatic, molecular, minoritarian, smooth, *more or less* arborescent, molar, majoritarian, striated... Secondly, it affords two different registers by which to analyse one and the same assemblage: according to the (virtual) 'lines of segmentarity that stratify, territorialise, organise, signify, attribute it', or the (virtual) 'lines of deterritorialisation through which it flees incessantly' (Deleuze and Guattari 2004a: 16). Evidently, (re)territorialising potential will tend to the stabilisation of some actual forms, which in turn act back upon the virtual conditions of the assemblage as whole. This means that the first register of analysis always necessarily includes actual forms (state apparatus, institutions, binary molarities), though not simply as opposed to and cut off from virtuality; thus, for instance, the concept of totalitarian state 'is only valid on a macropolitical scale', but 'fascism is inseparable from molecular foyers that pullulate and go from one point to another *before* they resonate all together in the national-socialist state' (Deleuze and Guattari 2004a: 261).[5]

In all such dualisms there is, strictly speaking, *only* the middle: if they constitute virtual continua, it would be absurd to ascribe an actual existence to either pole. Moreover, the formal distinction of actual and virtual effectively forbids anything being actualised as, say, 'purely' molar or 'purely' molecular: a purely molar assemblage would be one without any virtual potential (which, as we have seen, is only the way in which actualities *appear* in representation), while pure virtual potential is by definition not actual. To put it schematically, one could say that the 'less virtual' pole has as its limit an actuality with a minimal degree of virtuality *above zero*; while the limit for the 'less actual' pole is the knowable and livable: the point beyond which there is only a chaos where no actuality takes hold.

This designation of 'less virtual' and 'less actual' is evidently inappropriate, since we are talking about two *virtual* directions along which elements are *actualised* as more or less open to variation, as possessing more or less virtual potential. But putting it in such terms can help us understand why it cannot be a matter of *choosing* one extreme over the other: the choice is simply impossible, as beyond each limit there is only impossibility – an actuality without virtuality or chaos.

But what does it mean to speak of 'limit' here? There is a common thread to the *apolitical* and other-worldly Deleuze and Guattari, the *political despite themselves* apologists of a boundless power of deterritorialisation that is ultimately capital's own, but also to a certain aestheticised *activist* celebration of tiny exceptions and infinitesimal local subversions, and to Hardt and Negri's substantialisation/anthropomorphisation of absolute deterritorialising power in the form of the multitude: all of them collapse *metaphysical* and *transcendent* exercises of thought into one another, and thus erase the crucial distinction between *knowledge* and *thought*. For if metaphysics can pose a plane of immanence as absolute deterritorialisation in *thought*, it does not deliver any *empirical knowledge* of the plane *as such*. 'Empirical knowledge of absolute deterritorialisation' is by definition a nonsensical formulation, since absolute deterritorialisation, as pure chaotic virtuality, entails the inexistence of any (actual) subject for whom it could appear as an (actual) empirical object.

The 'transcendent [exercise of a faculty] does *not at all* mean that it addresses itself to objects *outside of the world*, but, on the contrary, that it grasps *in the world* that which concerns it exclusively, and which gives birth to it in the world' (Deleuze 2003a: 186, emphasis added). This is why the 'highest task' of 'determining problems, of applying to them our decisive and creative power' is a concrete, *practical* question through and through: the transcendent exercise that Deleuze invites us to engage in consists in thinking the actual in relation to its virtual conditions so as to liberate the potential for the new in the present – but precisely *not* as a leap into unbounded potentiality. It is a matter of activating the virtual of *this* actual, '*to the extent* that it becomes actualised [*en tant qu'il s'actualise*], *in the process of* becoming actualised [*en train de s'actualiser*], *inseparable from the movement* of its actualisation' (Deleuze 2004: 36; emphasis added). We never experience virtual totality *in itself*, but only virtuality *in so far as it is mediated by an actual encounter*. If truth is 'in every respect a matter of production, not adequation' (Deleuze 2003a: 200) – problematic and not apodictic – it is because the transcendent exercise does not *know* the virtual, but *expresses* it each time in a new, singular way.

Evidently, the idea of an actual 'mediation' must be said not only of the actualisation of thought, but of actualisation in general. In fact, it is *only* if we conceive of the actual as acting upon the virtual as much as the other way round that the partition of the two can be shown to be formal, not categorial or hierarchical (where one would be the other's ground, in a unidirectional relation).[6] If Deleuze speaks of a 'static genesis' that goes from virtual to actual, it is in order to provide an account of the asymmetrical, novelty-producing character that necessarily falls away if one remains at the mechanistic level of dynamic, actual causes – not to eliminate them. 'The event is of a different nature from the actions and passions of the body. But it *results* from them: [it] is the effect of corporal causes and their mixtures' (Deleuze 2002b: 115; original emphasis). But if there is a difference in nature between the two serial causes, the relation between them cannot itself be causal. The event of an actual encounter between two bodies, being determined by mechanical causality, cannot create the new itself; but it determines new relations among virtual conditions, effecting a virtual Event that produces a new actualisation. A *metaphysical* exercise can think the virtual as a continuous Whole of relations; but the intersection between the two series that effects the Event (the object of a *transcendent* exercise) is necessarily mediated by an actual event.

It is no surprise that all interpretations that posit a pre-eminence of the virtual over the actual will tend to miss the proper place of event, individuation and agency in Deleuze's (and Guattari's) thought: the intersection (and also re-commenced scission) between actual and virtual series. This is evident in Hallward (2006), who faults Deleuze for eliminating individuation and individuality in favour of a boundless creating power. But also in Badiou (1997), whose exposition of the virtual as ground is by and large premised on the second synthesis of time, thus erasing the 'ungrounding' that supervenes on it with the third synthesis/Event. Žižek, on the other hand, does at one point consider the possibility that the two different ontologies he identifies – virtual as sterile event-effect of actual causes; virtual as productive of the actual – could be the two sides of the same one; but then, not uncharacteristically, decides that the model for such a two-sided ontology can only be symbolic castration (Žižek 2004: 84–5).

V. . . . Then Do It Again

If Deleuze speaks of a '*decisive* and *creative* power', it is because to view the present as contingent and to liberate its potentials for becoming-other necessarily involves an element of decision. Not the autonomous act of an unfettered subjectivity or noumenal agent, since we are dealing with conditions that we neither control nor can make exhaustively clear; but a wager that extracts a new dice-throw not guaranteed by any knowledge. Such is the case with politics, 'not an apodictic science. It proceeds by experimentation' (Deleuze and Guattari 2004a: 575).

What the dualisms of orientation offer us is a series of bipolar axes and double registers with which to consider the potentials of the actual: both to view it as a singular, contingent solution of different problematics, and to guide our choices when acting on it. These choices concern identifying the givens of present problems and producing new solutions to them – *not* choosing one pole over the other, as if they could be treated as actualities. To put it in a formula: no choice between the *two poles*, because one can only ever choose *in between* them. Politics is where life is, and '[t]hings do not begin to live except in the middle' (Deleuze 2006: 41).

In his virtuosic treatment of *Capitalisme et schizophrénie*'s dualisms, Jameson refers to them as a key part of the 'fictive mapping' that organises its materials 'into force fields', but does not linger on the implications of the metaphor: a force field is a dyad, an intensive continuum defined by two or more attractors. He is absolutely right in pointing out that the insistence of dualisms in those two books 'always tempts us to reinsert the good/evil axis . . . and to call for judgment where none is appropriate', so that 'the reader feels perpetually solicited to take sides with the Schizo against the Paranoid . . . and with the Nomads against the State' (Jameson 1997: 412) – but this is exactly what is prevented if we read them dyadically. Famously, it was as an ethics that Foucault suggested *L'Anti-Oedipe* should be read, listing some 'essential principles' of its 'art of living contrary to all forms of fascism': a series of general guidelines rather than a system of moral judgements attributing good and evil (Foucault 2001: 134–5). The first of these – liberating action from 'every unitary and totalising paranoia' – should then be understood as having the same relation to the others as the self-referential item ('included in this classification') in Borges' Chinese encyclopaedia cited at the start of *Les mots and les choses*. It is the in-built unsettling of the ensemble that pre-emptively exposes as paranoid in itself any attempt to transform those ethical principles into a morality.

If it is true that Deleuze and Guattari place a higher value on deterritorialisation, this value is subordinated to the practical problem of resisting the conservatism that reduces the real to the given and turns the latter into necessity. That this error should be opposed *in act* entails that it is never a matter of saying that *everything is possible*, which is practically vacuous, but of saying that, in every *here* and *now*, there are *potentials* that can be *acted upon*. If the political practice to be derived from this attitude can be given a name, it is *intervention*.

> For an authentic analysis (a schizoanalysis, a molecular analysis, what we call it isn't important) the first concern won't be interpretation, but *intervention*. What can we do to clear up a situation? ... What's the point of trying to determine the role of the father, the mother, the national education system, Knowledge, Power, the Economy, if we don't offer to intervene in any way and to work through these different components? (Guattari 2009: 52; original emphasis)

An intervention singularises a situation as the contingent production of certain conditions, decomposes it into different levels and registers (macro- and micropolitical, molar and molecular, etc.), identifies the potentials and the points that one can get a grip on, and tests its present limits by liberating what may be latent in it. It is premised on *experimenting* with the virtualities 'of this actual', and never (*pace* Hallward) on an *experience* of the virtual Whole as such, in dissolution of every actual tie. While the plane of immanence as absolute deterritorialisation *sub specie aeternitatis* can be the object of a metaphysical *thought*, a direct, unmediated experience of immanence is tantamount to death, or psychosis. A philosophy of intervention is not at all a 'philosophy of death' (Badiou 1997: 24), but a practical work of removing the blockages that stop life.

> To unmake the organism was never to kill oneself, but to... install oneself on a stratum, to experiment with the chances it offers us, to search for a favourable place in it, eventual movements of deterritorialisation, possible lines of flight, to experiment with them [*les éprouver*], to ensure conjunctions of flows here and there... (Deleuze and Guattari 2004a: 198–9)

That death is one of the poles of the 'master' dualism, deterritorialisation–reterritorialisation, shows us that in our *experience* there are only ever relative deterritorialisations – and that this applies even to the most molar, majoritarian, arborescent formations. To deny that would amount to falling prey to representative thought. Here Deleuze and Guattari's methods must be applied back to them in order to show that the sustained critique of revolutionary groups in a book like *L'Anti-Oedipe* was a singular and local response to a certain *style* of militancy that they saw around them at the time; it is neither a critique of any form of organisation whatsoever, nor a principled hostility to militancy as such. We can call the political practice they propose an 'involuntarism' (cf. Zourabichvili 1998; Thoburn 2010: 136), provided we take every care to distinguish this from 'inaction', and see it as strictly opposed to 'voluntarism'. That is, while every action involves a wager that can only be verified in practice, it will be more or less capable of adequately expressing the problematic coordinates of the situation (and thus of successfully intervening therein) to the extent that it is more or less immanent to it, more or less connected to these coordinates. The egoic investment of a group that isolates itself as the subject that acts (the 'activist') is an obstacle to this 'dissolution' into the situation, in so far as it locks the intervention into a duality that detaches an 'active force' from a 'passive matter' by obscuring the several levels in which the two communicate. Deleuze and Guattari's Blanchotian paradox consists in saying: the more passivity is contracted, the more powerful the action; the more one opens up to exteriority, the more one can fold into an intimacy (Deleuze and Guattari 2003: 59); the more one affirms powerlessness, the greater the power that can be extracted from it (Deleuze 2003a: 257–8).

This 'dissolution', however, does not in itself imply a *negation* of organisation. On the contrary: in a situation such as community organising, one can perfectly well imagine that it would take a good degree of internal consistency for a group to be able to sustain an intervention that 'dissolves' itself in the life of its constituency so as to connect to all the flows that traverse it on various levels (the constitution of space, memory, economic or interpersonal relations, etc.).

But how far do these dyads take us from a trivial aestheticisation of infinitesimal change? If we are willing to go as far as accepting that in every nomad there is a state and in every state there hides a nomad (however little), what effect can this really have against an order that survives by 'revolutionising itself'? Deleuze and Guattari will be the first to admit that there is no guarantee: 'smooth spaces are not in and of themselves liberating', but only the place where 'the struggle changes, becomes displaced': 'Never believe that a smooth space will suffice to save us' (Deleuze and Guattari 2004a: 625). No guarantee; only intervention. Lines of flight can turn out bad, either because they find paranoid reterritorialisations, or because they become isolated and turn in upon themselves, or because we are never far from finding out that what we struggled for objectively led to the opposite of what it was we desired. (The French free radio movement, in which Guattari was very active, managed to open the airwaves to non-state actors, only to see them colonised by commercial ones.)

Yet we have already seen how there is nothing in Deleuze and Guattari that is *contrary* as such to the scalability, mass mobilisations or forms of organisation that more radical transformations may demand; the front is always both micro- and macropolitical. And if there is some fairness in identifying in *L'Anti-Oedipe* an 'apocalyptic accelerationism' (Noys 2010), this was never simply premised on the idea that deterritorialisation in and of itself would suffice to save us.[7] To affirm deterritorialising power does not mean saying yes to all deterritorialisations, but knowing how to *select*[8]: hence relative deterritorialisations are never separated from the problem of constructing a *plane of consistency* that allows for mutually reinforcing transversal connections–to the point, at times, of open antagonism. '[W]e cannot allow ourselves a dualism or dichotomy, even under the rudimentary form of the good and the evil.... Good and evil can only be the product of an *active* and *temporary* selection to be recommended' (Deleuze and Guattari 2004a: 16; emphasis added). It is never just a matter of fleeing, but of constructing an *active* flight:

Flights are everywhere, they are born again each time from the displaced limits of capitalism. And undoubtedly revolutionary flight (the *active* flight . . .) is not the same thing as other kinds of flight, the schizo flight, or the druggie [*toxico*] flight. But this is precisely the problem of marginalities: to make all lines of flight connect on a revolutionary plane. (Deleuze and Guattari 2004b: 376; emphasis added)

To faithfully repeat Deleuze and Guattari today consists not in the dogmatic assertion of an *ortho-doxa*, but in a renewed attempt to identify the problems that determined their solutions so as to ascertain to what extent they may still be our own, and in the permanently recommenced search for ways of determining our problems by individualising new solutions in the present. Solutions which, once determined, cannot bypass the problem of producing consistency, nor be satisfied with a vacuous celebration of the virtual, but must negotiate paths between molecular and molar, micro- and macropolitics, de- and reterritorialisation, the clinical and the critical. 'Practice does not come after terms and their relations have been established, but actively participates in the tracing of lines, confronts the same dangers and variations as them'; for 'before Being, there is politics' (Deleuze and Guattari 2004a: 249).

Notes

1. It also downplays others: the non-ideological flexibility in dealing with parties and governments (which characterised Guattari's work at La Borde, with the *Centre d'études, des recherches et des formations institutionelles*, in the free radio movement, and his approximation to Communist, Socialist and Green parties at different points); but also their stances, neither condemning nor condoning, towards armed struggle in Europe and the Palestine Liberation Organisation.
2. Pseudonym of Alain Badiou.
3. For Badiou, it is either this, or the two collapse into each other, in which case the virtual is no more than '*ignorantie asylum*' (Badiou 1997: 81).
4. 'Spinoza does not call his book an Ontology . . . he calls it *Ethics*. Which is a way of saying that, whatever the importance of my speculative propositions, you can only judge them at the level of the ethics that they envelop or implicate' (Deleuze 1981).
5. It must be noted that, despite the recurrent provisos that they are not opposed by 'size, scale or dimension, but by the nature of the system of reference' (Deleuze and Guattari 2004a: 264), the sometimes equivocal use of those pairs that suggest dimensions (molar/molecular, macro/micropolitics) can be a source of confusion. Furthermore, there is one case where the poles are not virtual: in 'double articulation', molar and molecular are both actual and opposed in scale, even if only relatively (the cell is molecular in relation to the organism, the individual in relation to the species, etc.). In this case, the virtual 'matter' is identified with 'unstable flow-particles' (cf. 55).
6. Among commentators, John Mullarkey (2006) has gone the farthest in contesting the primacy of the virtual in Bergson/Deleuze, finding support in a reading of the former to counteract the latter's tendency of overstressing the virtual to the point of placing the processual character of his metaphysics at risk. To do so, Mullarkey argues that the virtual should be understood as the infinite series of successive, actual *Chronos* indefinitely embedded in each other, eliminating the need for an eternal *Aion* of pure, virtual events. He concurs, nevertheless, that it is a matter of playing some tendencies in Deleuze's thought

off against others – and provides an excellent discussion of why and how Deleuze requires all of them, and their tension, to be simultaneously maintained.

7. I believe Noys' coinage does capture a real tendency in Deleuze's and Guattari's work, as well as in other strains of twentieth century and contemporary thought, and that it raises important questions as to how we might strategically conceptualise the relation between capitalism and resistance, especially in the present conjuncture. It is certainly a relatively accurate description of some authors who have appropriated Deleuze and Guattari's thought, such as Hardt and Negri, and (particularly) Nick Land. Where I would depart from Noys' analysis is in what seems to be the almost 'programmatic' status that he attributes to 'accelerationism' *in Deleuze and Guattari*, seemingly implying that they espouse a linear teleology in which an intensification of deterritorialising 'production' (in the very broad, ontological sense) would, necessarily and in and of itself, beat a path out of capitalism through its very acceleration. There certainly are passages, in *L'Anti-Oedipe* above all, that could suggest this reading. I would, however, argue that not only is it countered by many other statements that can be found throughout their work, not least their stringent remarks on neoliberalism from the 1980s on, but also by some fundamental traits of their philosophy. An accelerationist 'programme' sits uncomfortably with a radical ontological commitment to contingency and an opposition to any teleologism. Furthermore, (absolute) deterritorialisation, as a veritable ontological principle, is independent from and irreducible to its historical embodiment in capitalism; it neither relies on the latter exclusively in order to take place, nor would it fail to apply even in a putative 'post-capitalist' world. Rather than a generalised goal or an invariable strategic bet, the stress on deterritorialisation points to situated, tactical engagements against structures and blockages that are given. In other words, to *relative* deterritorialisations that are never entirely separated from the formation of new assemblages: 'the collective recapturing of those dynamics that can destratify the moribund structures and reorganize life and society in accordance with other forms of equilibrium, other worlds' (Guattari 2002: 260).

8. As far back as *Nietzsche et la philosophie*, Deleuze already made it clear: 'The real as such is an ass' idea.... Affirmation understood as ... affirmation of what is, as truthfulness of the true or positivity of the real, is a false affirmation. It is the ass' "yes".... The Dyonisiac "yes", on the other hand, is that which knows how to say "no".... To affirm is to create, not to carry, to bear, to take on' (Deleuze 2001: 208–13).

References

Badiou, Alain (1977) 'Le flux et le Parti', *Cahiers d'Yénan*, 4, pp. 26–41.
Badiou, Alain (1997) *Deleuze: La clameur de l'être*, Paris: Hachette.
Deleuze, Gilles (1973) 'Cours Vincennes: Monisme, Dualisme, Multiplicités. 26/03/1973'; http://www.webdeleuze.com/php/texte.php?cle=166&groupe=Anti%20Oedipe%20et%20Mille%20Plateaux&langue=1
Deleuze, Gilles (1981) 'Cours Vincennes, 25/11/1981'; http://www.webdeleuze.com/php/texte.php?cle=15&groupe=Spinoza&langue=1
Deleuze, Gilles (2001) *Nietzsche et la philosophie*, Paris: PUF.
Deleuze, Gilles (2002a) *Spinoza et le problème de l'expression*, Paris: Minuit.
Deleuze, Gilles (2002b) *Logique du sens*, Paris: Minuit.
Deleuze, Gilles (2003a) *Différence et répétition*, Paris: PUF.

Deleuze, Gilles (2003b) 'Préface à l'Edition Américaine de *Différence et répétition*', in *Deux régimes de fous*, Paris: Minuit, pp. 280–3.

Deleuze, Gilles (2003c) 'L'immanence: une Vie', in *Deux régimes de fous*, Paris: Minuit, pp. 359–63.

Deleuze, Gilles (2004a) *Le bergsonisme*, Paris: PUF.

Deleuze, Gilles (2004b) 'Gilbert Simondon, *L'Individu et sa genèse physico-biologique*', in *L'Ile desérte*, Paris: Minuit.

Deleuze, Gilles (2005) *Le Pli: Leibniz et le Baroque*, Paris: Minuit.

Deleuze, Gilles and Claire Parnet (2006) *Dialogues II*, trans. Hugh Tomlinson and Barbara Habberjam, London: Continuum.

Deleuze, Gilles and Félix Guattari (2003) *Qu'est-ce que la philosophie?*, Paris: Minuit.

Deleuze, Gilles and Félix Guattari (2004a) *Mille plateaux*, Paris: Minuit.

Deleuze, Gilles and Félix Guattari (2004b) 'Sur le capitalisme et le désir', in *L'Ile déserte*, Paris: Minuit, pp. 365–80.

Deleuze, Gilles and Félix Guattari (2008) *L'Anti-Oedipe*, Paris: Minuit.

Foucault, Michel (2001) 'Préface', in *Dits et écrits*, vol. II, Paris: Gallimard, pp. 133–6.

Guattari, Félix (2002) 'The Left as Processual Passion', in Gary Genosko (ed.), *The Guattari Reader*, London: Blackwell, pp. 259–61.

Guattari, Félix (2009) 'Institutional Intervention', in *Soft Subversions*, trans. Ernest Wittman, ed. Sylvère Lotringer, Cambridge, MA: Semiotext(e), pp. 33–63.

Guattari, Félix and Suely Rolnik (2008) *Molecular Revolution in Brazil*, trans. Karel Clapshow, Brian Holmes and Rodrigo Nunes, Cambridge, MA: Semiotext(e).

Hallward, Peter (2006) *Out of This World: Deleuze and the Philosophy of Creation*, London and New York: Verso.

Hardt, Michael and Antonio Negri (2000) *Empire*, Cambridge, MA: Harvard University Press.

Jameson, Frederic (1997) 'Marxism and Dualism in Deleuze', *The South Atlantic Quarterly*, 96:3, pp. 393–416.

Mullarkey, John (2006) *Post-Continental Philosophy: An Outline*, London: Continuum.

Noys, Benjamin (2010) 'Apocalypse, Tendency, Crisis', *Mute magazine*; http://www.metamute.org/node/13114

Peyrol, Georges [Alain Badiou] (1977) 'Le fascisme de la pomme de terre', *Cahiers d'Yénan*, 4, pp. 42–52.

Simondon, Gilbert (2005) *L'individuation à la lumière des notions de forme et d'information*, Grenoble: Jerôme Millon.

Thoburn, Nick (2010) 'Weatherman, the Militant Diagram, and the Problem of Political Passion', *New Formations*, 68, pp. 123–40.

Žižek, Slavoj (2004) *Organs Without Bodies: Deleuze and Consequences*, New York: Routledge.

Zourabichvili, François (1998) 'Deleuze et l'impossible (de l'involontarisme en politique)', in Eric Alliez (ed.), *Gilles Deleuze: une vie philosophique*, Paris: Synthélabo, pp. 142–58.

The Greek Gloom and the December 2008 Uprising

Ioulia Mermigka   National and Kapodistrian University of Athens

Abstract

This paper employs the notion of apparatus of capture in the context of the historical formation and transformations of the Greek nation state. The aim is to demystify the overcoding poles of political sovereignty as they are expressed in different chronological periods and to sketch an analysis of the appropriations of social living forms, social movements and war machines into regimes of signs. The term war machine is deployed as a key term for grasping the variables of content and the variables of expression that are encountered in the different historical circumstances. The order word modernisation illustrates not only the machinic enslavement but also new social subjections within a society of the spectacle and global capital. The account given here of the December 2008 uprising in Greece offers an insight into the political event and attempts a pragmatic analysis of the December war machine.

Keywords: apparatus of capture, war machine, history, modernisation, uprising, Greece

The following essay offers a student perspective on activism that attempts to make sense of the chapter '7000 B.C.: Apparatus of Capture' from Deleuze and Guattari's *A Thousand Plateaus* and records a fragmented trajectory of modern Greek history. The record outlined here is chronological, moving from the early stages of the formation of the Greek nation state to the series of modernisations that took place in the closing decades of the twentieth century. The final section provides an account of the December 2008 uprising and describes the political activism that accompanied the events. The term war machine is used

Deleuze Studies Volume 4: 2010 supplement: 127–141
DOI: 10.3366/E1750224110001169
© Edinburgh University Press
www.eupjournals.com/dls

abstractly throughout for different expressions of war, violence and resistance. The aim is to synchronise an outline of major Greek history with Deleuze and Guattari's theories of the state and minor politics.

The Greek historical climate is analysed in terms of vertical and horizontal political significations, national suppressions and regimes of resistance. Analysis of the Greek economy and the state is combined with an account of semiotic transformations arising within the society of the spectacle. The spectre of anarchy is tracked through the symbolic and political transitions of recent decades and an account given of the social violence erupting on the street and in the university.

Finally, I attempt to touch upon aspects of modernisation in terms of Greekness, the proletariat, the middle class, the Left, the so-called anarchist 'space', and resistance against authority and police repression. Here the account is mainly concerned with outbreaks of street violence and the principles of autonomous resistance.

I. 1821–96: The Double-Headed Eagle

The year 1821 marks the beginning of the Greek war of independence against the Ottoman Empire. The struggle of the bandits becomes an armed mobilisation essentially directed against the Ottoman state (Vournas 1974: 31–4). The war machine is soon captured. A double-headed eagle, a symbol of the revolution, looks in opposite directions, one head to the east, the other to the west. In one of its variations the eagle is crowned and holds a globe with a cross in its left foot, and a lance in its right (Herzfeld 1989). The double-headed eagle suggests a double articulation of political sovereignty.

The east-facing head implies both an overcoding pole, encapsulating the Christian-orthodox and despotic signifiers, and a pole signifying the supersession of those signifiers in the parliamentary function and the processes of national subjection. Conspiracies are hatched and town revolts erupt when the state's overcoding itself provokes decoded flows: whether the economic and social privileges of chieftains of the revolution in regional towns or the constitutional or cultural demands of the centralised political forces. The first governor of Greece, Kapodistrias, is assassinated in 1831 and the Bavarian king Otto has to deal with regional revolts during his reign until 1862 (Omada Enantia stin Lithi 1996: 359–400; Deleuze and Guattari 2004: 477–80). Moreover, despite the church's alignment with the state, the crown and the sultan, there are flows of Christian irredentism that bring about crises over the Eastern Question (Skopetea 1988: 251–71; Stathopoulou 1991: 166–204).

The west-facing head resonates with the glorifications of classicism and rationalism in western thought. Archaeology has discovered among the ancient Aegean civilisations highly evolved empires that had solved the western problem of how to 'take advantage of the oriental agricultural stock without having to constitute one for themselves' (Deleuze and Guattari 2004: 497). Classicism and the Enlightenment entail not just philosophy or aesthetics but an art of war, based on flows rather than codes.

The Greek state born out of the revolutionary machine enters into a series of financial pacts and military alliances with the quasi-imperialistic European states. This western alignment effectuates the public parliamentary function (with pro-French, pro-British and pro-Russian parties) and determines the financial and diplomatic arrangements of the Greek state while overcoding it with notions of Hellenistic and ancient Aegean glory. In the vacillating poles of political sovereignty the capitalist axiomatic of flows is introduced into a glorified archaeological democracy. In 1896 Athens mounts the revived Olympic Games.

The disjunction between the nationalists and the modernists after 1875 illustrates the knots at the western pole (Vournas 1974: 498–535): The oriental solution of the nationalists and the resonances of Hellenist-Christian irredentism on the one hand; the western solution of the modernists aligned with the capitalist axiomatic for the territories that would be annexed on the other. 'It is as if two solutions were found for the same problem, the oriental solution and then the western one, which grafts itself upon the first, and brings it out of the impasse while continuing to presuppose it' (Deleuze and Guattari 2004: 498).

II. 1914–22: The National Schism

In 1912, in the first Balkan War, the newly formed Christian states of Greece, Bulgaria, Serbia and Montenegro go to war against the Ottomans. The Balkans claim autonomy for the Christian populations in the Ottoman territories but the Ottomans ignore their ultimatum. The outcome of the war falls in favour of the Balkan League. The Great Powers consent to the annexation of some territories but raise objections with regard to others, leading in 1913 to the second Balkan War. The outbreak of the First World War the following year places the Greeks in an ambivalent position. The liberal Prime Minister Venizelos joins forces with the Allies, while the German-friendly king Constantinos holds to a supposedly neutral position. In 1916 the Greek state is split between two capitals: the pro-Venizelists in Thessaloniki and the royalists in

Athens. When the French occupy Athens, battling with the royalists and blocking all commercial flows, angry royalist supporters blame the liberals as traitors. Venizelos is excommunicated by the Orthodox Church, and in December 1916 thousands of people gather in Athens to throw signed stones of anathema in protest at the 'Satan-traitor' (Delta 1988: 277–80).

In 1917, with support from the British and the French, Venizelos returns to Athens and Greece enters the Great War. The outcomes are positive for Greece and in 1919 Greek troops land in Asia Minor to protect the Christian population. Venizelos wages a war of diplomacy, and of gradual territorial annexation, so as to pursue the 'Great Idea' of a 'Greece of five seas and two continents'. The romantic-nationalist pole, however, wins the elections of 1920 and the Greek army marches deeper into Turkey. The result is the 'Asia Minor Catastrophe' of 1922 and the first compulsory population exchange, involving approximately 2 million refugees.

The formation of the new Turkish state under Kemal Atatürk coincides with the waning of the 'Great Idea', along with the definitive collapse of the Ottoman Empire. Kemal's war machine against the sultan and the Greeks, and his pacts with the Allies, seeds the birth of the Turkish state in the pattern of the *Zeitgeist*. The Great Powers have to negotiate with another isomorphic albeit heterogeneous player. The Greek–Turkish friendship from then on becomes a recurrent issue.

III. The Greek Language Question and the People's Refrain

The Greek language question reveals not only the suppressive mechanisms involved in the birth and coming of age of the nation state but also how it was transformed by 'nationalitarian' phenomena (see Deleuze and Guattari 2004: 504). From 1830 to 1890 the major language of bureaucracy and the political elites is a purifying version that settles the tension between archaic and modernist-colloquial varieties in favour of archaic constants (especially ancient Athenian Greek). However, the demotic or vernacular language gradually comes to affect the major language. From 1888 a linguistic radicalism in favour of the demotic language begins to tip the balance towards modernist constants with socialist, romantic, nationalistic, or even racist variations (see Fragkoudaki 2001).

Over the following years more literature is written in the demotic language, but despite attempts at educational reforms the archaic varieties continue to dominate. The indirect discourse they are based upon entails a diachrony with ancient Greek and a synchrony with the archaic religious language of Orthodoxy, and in general with the dogmas of Hellenist-Christianity. After the collapse of the 'Great Idea' and the relocating of the enemy from the external (the Turks) to the internal (the communists), the demotic language also comes to be linked more closely with the workers' movement and the Left.

In an implementation of realpolitik, the liberal Venizelos passes a series of educational reforms in favour of the demotic language, but also in 1929 issues a legal order word, the *idionymon*, that penalises insurrectional ideas and aims in particular to prosecute communists and anarchists and to enforce repression against unionist mobilisations. With the coming of the Great Depression, Venizelos is forced to default on Greece's national debt, built up from loans for industrial modernisation and the housing of refugees from Asia Minor.

The refugees bring with them a sound of the east, a people's refrain. The *bouzouki* and other oriental instruments become orchestrated with the Greek voice. The refugee songs, known as 'Rebetika', relate tales of love couplings, dominations and subjections, either to authority or to addictions. The Rebetika are censored by government, while the Left passes moral judgement on their delinquent content. Nevertheless, they are the seed that would transform a recurring Greek sound. Musical matters of expression and the Greek voice merge at this particular period into a Greek chromatic sound that will become popular from the 1950s onwards.

IV. 1950–74: The Repressive Modernisation

During and after the Second World War the Greek milieu becomes polarised between the eastern Soviet pole and the western Anglo-American pole, both with their limits and thresholds. The Greek civil war lasts from 1944 to 1949. The communist resistance attempts to prevent a capitalistic state but it also anticipates it: radical socialist elements of people's power and gender equality coexist alongside property rights and the operation of the state as coordinator of private relations (Hart 1996: 273). By the 1950s the Greek milieu will definitely belong to the western neighbourhood of the capitalist megamachine (Deleuze and Guattari 2004: 480).

The right-wing Greek state overcodes its national sovereignty by means of a structural violence. The Communist Party is declared illegal and the military and police issue an order word obliging citizens to sign a certificate of national (anti-communist) beliefs. Many Leftists are imprisoned or sent into exile on rocky islets. As Athens becomes rapidly populated by new proletarian flows from the countryside, urban planning by army technocrats striate the city, ensuring that highway constructions and administrative centres provide easy military access and facilitate police control. This is a new technical machine. On the basis of this urban rationale military groups seize Athens and usurp power in 1967 (Anonymous 2002: 55–80).

The modern social subjection also derives from the organisation of housing policies, which aim at promoting private property in newly built blocks of flats. In this way, people living in refugee slums and working-class neighbourhoods lose their social networks and tend to be assimilated into a new urbanised middle class. The state's recognition 'that workers work better when they have a decent house' resonates with the greed of the new class of building contractors (Anonymous 2002: 80–72; Deleuze and Guattari 2004: 1989: 499–505); the resulting urbanisation of the period is described in Greek as a 'construction orgasm'.

The repressive modernisation of the period is also related to the rise of a public sphere with a mixed semiotics. In 1952, women gain the right to vote and be elected, but they still represent servants for the reproduction of the nation and guardians of the family (Komninou 2003: 69). Through the spectacle and the culture industry, capitalism advances its own limits of a libidinal economy. In the commercial Greek cinema of the period there is an overloaded investment in a modern version of a deviant femininity that decodes traditional gender relations, but the recurrent narrative ending is either a happy orthodox marriage or a life condemned in sin and shame (Athanasatou 2001: 342–6). The new task of the state apparatus consists in 'organizing conjunctions of decoded flows as such' (Deleuze and Guattari 2004: 498); in the Greek case this entails not only the participation of women in the labour market, in the public sphere and in the spectacle, but also their social subjection to a folded patriarchy. A modern house, a modern family and a night out at the *bouzoukia* clubs smashing plates: these are some of the prerequisites for the new social subjection.

There is also an international aspect to the national subjection. The dominant patriotic regime resonates with the desire for the union of mother Greece with Cyprus, but negotiates this revived irredentism with NATO and the USA. On the other hand, there is also a patriotic counter-signifying regime which turns away from the West to enunciate a polemical anti-Americanism (Stefanidis 2008: 285–306). The escalating left-wing mobilisations of the early 1960s share this patriotic passion, but direct it towards the East and the Third World struggles of the times.

The strategy of the repressed Left is to wear the face of Greekness, but provide another post-traumatic consciousness for it. In poetry and music this is expressed in the glorification or relative deterritorialisation of both the Greek *topos* and the victimised heroism of the people (Gavriilidis 2007). This radical patriotism integrates the war machine of the 1960s into a mixed semiotic (Deleuze and Guattari 2004: 131). In December 1960 it is the construction builders who first clash with the police and initiate a cycle of violent protest. Unionist mobilisation then escalates, making specific professional demands on the state, but also fighting against the structural violence of the police (Lampropoulou 2008: 220–41). Over the next years, the workers' and students' demand for democratisation of the state crystallises around the Left. From 1963 the Left aspires to gain power and gradually bring about a socialist transformation. Until 1963 it encouraged the counter-violence of the movements but from then on strives to pursue the struggle at the level of axioms. The situation comes to a head with the political assassination of the pacifist MP G. Lamprakis in 1963 and the killing of a student by police in the summer of 1965, when for over 40 days thousands of people take collective action on the street and clash with police (Katsaros 1999: 49–70).

This war machine should not be identified with the Left. It is rather what escapes from both the conjugation of capitalist flows of the repressive state and from the hierarchical organisations of the Left. If it is identified with the Left, it must be considered to have been defeated, since in 1967 the colonels' tanks march into the same streets and take over the power. From 1974, after the fall of the junta, the Left becomes assimilated into political games within social democracy. The war machine is rather the unnameable revolutionised mass of the period. It creates sheets of past that relate to the coexistence of a proletarian consciousness and a flight from the plane of capital (Deleuze and Guattari 2004: 521), and its peaks of present always involve its zone of indiscernibility between the poles of political sovereignty.

Such a high point of the war machine is the Polytechneio uprising in 1973. It begins as a students' revolt against the junta liberal reforms. The revolutionised youth creates a snowball effect and thousands take on to the streets. The spontaneity of the uprising and the heterogeneity of the crowds inhibits any organisation from the Left in terms either of armed revolt or public negotiations. The reformists accuse the revolutionary Left of being inciting agents. Everybody anticipates the intervention of the army that eventually suppresses the uprising. The consequences are another coup in Greece and in Cyprus, which results in the Turkish invasion and the division of the island.

In 1974, Karamanlis, the engineer of the repressive state of the 1950s, returns to secure national unity and consolidate democracy. He makes the date of the Polytechneio uprising a national anniversary, legalises the Communist Party and resolves the language question by establishing the demotic as the official language. Moreover, the monarchy is abolished by plebiscite. The right-wing government, despite the lure of neoliberalism, added social welfare axioms in order to meet the requirements of the European Community.

V. 1981–2004: The Populist Modernisation and the Spectre of Anarchy

In 1979–80, without the consent of the organisations of the Left, students occupy some of the universities and demonstrate against the educational reforms planned by the right-wing government. The students are labelled as anarchists. On the anniversary of the Polytechneio Uprising in 1980 a 21-year-old worker and 26-year-old student are killed by the police. Riots break out, because the government bans the rally from accessing the American embassy.

The ultra-populist Papandreou, leader of the Panhellenic Socialist Movement (PASOK), wins the election of 1981 under the slogan 'change'. He had promised withdrawal from NATO and the then EC and the closing down of the US military bases, but none of these are actualised. In 1981 Greece is officially a member of the EC. Papandreou adds more axioms signalling a shift in the style of government, but not in substance. His reforms bring Greece out of the national closet: civil marriage is introduced against stiff opposition from the church, adultery is removed from the catalogue of criminal offences and the dowry system is, legally at least, abolished. Papandreou also amends the family law and adds axioms at practically all levels of social policy (Clogg 1994: 183–4). He becomes so popular that Greeks refer to him by his first name, Andreas.

PASOK's decentralised socialism involves the nationalisation of problematic companies already indebted to the largely state-controlled banks. This, far from bringing with it any noticeable improvement in productivity, merely provides an opportunity to continue the former right-wing patronage by way of expanding the pay-roll. Via the leader's populism, the new policies regulate anti-production with social welfare policies and bounteous financial opportunism (Clogg 1994: 188). The slogan 'change' orders that capital will continue to produce surplus value thanks to the government's rescue of capitalists, and on the other hand that the state will regulate public debt. The public sector and bureaucracy grows gigantic; consent is secured by appointments in the public sector based on clientist relations; alliance with the party and favouritism for its members serves the interests of individuals and families and masquerades as realising the socialist liberal desire for the promised civil society. Andreas, despite his socialist polemic, ensures social subjection within the wider capitalist axiomatic.

Andreas functions as a libidinal image that symbolically occupies a limit but at the same time signals the displacement of capitalist desire. It is striking how he obscurely fascinates the crowds when, in an outspoken way, he dumps his feminist wife, a figure of some political standing, for a much younger air hostess, and even more striking how, when he is accused of being bribed by a capitalist, he still remains adored as a political icon. An oedipal detail of the 'dirty 89', the year a series of scandals breaks, is that the money is hidden in nappy boxes. The same year, radio and TV broadcasting are deregulated and the Adam Smith complex replaces the Oedipus complex. The resulting so-called deregulation is related to the wider re-structuring of communication systems and the new forms of machinic enslavement and media ecology.

In between, anarchists and autonomists with no clear outlines along with intellectuals and artists and other members of what is generally referred to as the underdog political culture, begin to settle in Exarchia, a neighbourhood close to the Polytechneio. In 1984 the police pursue a gentrification policy in the area, since the youth's abstract politicisation and radical culture can not be easily assimilated by the state apparatus. On the anniversary of the Polytechneio uprising in 1985 a 15-year-old student is shot by the police. The Polytechneio and the Chemistry department nearby are occupied and violent protests take place. The police invade the buildings, despite the university asylum which forbids the police and the army from entering university premises. The state demonstrates its capacity for 'socialist' structural violence. At the same time a war machine against the monopoly of state violence forms. It is rooted in an anarchist polemic which endangers it but also effectuates a space of unlimited and vital political expression.

In 1990–1 there is a high-school student mobilisation and another cycle of contention. The educational reforms introduced by the right-wing government include anachronistic measures like compulsory school uniforms, prayer and hoisting of the flag, and generally a tendency to limit student rights in favour of an arbitrary school. Moreover they increase competition for university entry and do not by any means resolve the issue of fee-paying crammer schools. Overall, education is to be based more on memorisation than critical thinking.

The wave of high-school occupations sweeps the country. In Athens the demonstrations are violently repressed by the police. It is during this time that I first encounter political theories and become involved in political activism. The period remains significant not so much for our eventual victory in resisting the government's measures but for the fact that the seeds of a proletarian consciousness were sown, at a critical distance from party and other groupuscules, in spite of the desire for belonging.

The situation culminates in the events of 1991 when a left-wing teacher is killed by far-right thugs and four civilians die when a building is set alight during a demonstration the next day. The blame is placed on the anarchists for their agitation against the social order, despite the fact that the fire most probably resulted from the extensive use of tear gas by the police. It is at the beginning of the '90s that an anarchist 'space' becomes more articulated, in contrast with the vertical organisations of the Left. From then on, arson becomes a virtuality haunting this 'space'.

Not long after, in 1993, the government pursues the privatisation of public transport and other conservative reforms. The bus drivers are polarised and strikers clash with the police. However, a shift is marked during this time, as the flow of Albanians and other immigrants from around the globe become the new constant capital. Greek capitalists exploit this development, while the state does little to secure the immigrants' civil integration and public-opinion gate-keepers cultivate a climate of xenophobia. This racial class rupture will mark the atrophy of the proletarian consciousness over the next few years.

The anarchist movement that gains momentum mainly among the youth detaches itself from struggles at the level of axioms, since its relation to labour is one of precariousness, of a proclaimed negation of wage labour and of inertia in regard to capitalist relations. The figure of the proletarian will be replaced in some anarchist factions with the figure of the revolutionary, the scarlet slogan 'revolt' taken to justify its avant-garde position. In 1995 at the anniversary of the Polytechneio uprising, anarchists occupy the university. University asylum is again violated when the building is burned and more than 500 are arrested and filed as extremists. Some anarchists from then on tend to appropriate the Polytechneio as their symbol of revolt. It is in this way that the 'space' is striated in police files and in the area around Exarchia.

The rupture in proletarian consciousness will be even more obvious in the next few years as the order word 'modernisation' takes on new

forms of circulation. The stock-market crash of 1999 involves lower-
and middle-class civilians, even in remote regions of Greece, who invest
their microcapital in so-called bubble stocks and lose their savings as a
result. Elsewhere, the events in Seattle and Genoa inspire a mobilisation
in Greece during the EU–Western Balkan Summit in Thessaloniki in
2003, where the Black Bloc attempt a more organised presence in terms
of social counter-violence within the anti-globalisation movement.

In 2004 Athens hosts the Olympic Games and national pride in the
cradle of democracy is revived. However, with foreign and public debt
escalating, the right-wing government proves to be iniquitous. A series of
public scandals break out, involving almost all levels of social authority:
judges, priests, bankers, MPs and ministers, civil servants, journalists...
The slogan now becomes 'shed light', but the gloom is thick. On the
one hand, the processes of subjectification have managed to cultivate
indifference, cynicism and atavistic consumerism; on the other hand,
the counter-signifying regime is either appropriated by the mainstream
Left or endangered by the sublimation of social war by the anarchists.

VI. The December 2008 Uprising

One further precursor of the December 2008 uprising is the student
movement of 2006–7. The state's programmes for education reform
generally try to link the public university with the axioms of private
education. In response, student organisations on the Left, following
a logic of hegemony, try to dominate the students' assemblies and
impose a parochial politics. In June 2006 and March 2007 proletariat
youth fight against police repression and the mobilisation turns into
an uprising. The situation is already complicated as the students – the
so-called 'generation of 700 euro' (the minimum wage), who somehow
have to invent a life within the new capitalist relations – merge on the
street with the anarchists and the lumpenproletariat.

This unnameable student proletariat affiliates more closely with the
conscientious labour objectors than it does with the myopic Left (cf.
Thoburn 2003). There is, however, a tendency to relate the student
mobilisations with labour issues and with new forms of activism, like
the blocking of public transport, occupations of radio stations, protests
in workers' neighbourhoods and reclaim-the-streets parties. What has
remained from these mobilisations are the networks of social relations
that ensued from the occupations, a spirit of solidarity that grows
out of autonomous forms of organisation, and a student community

that, even if it didn't manage to intensify qualitatively the mobilisation, nevertheless discovered new lines of flight.

In the summer of 2007, a series of forest fires break out across Greece leaving the land scorched. Many mourn and others covet the ready-to-be-built-upon land. The echoes of the financial crisis reach Greece. In December 2008 in the area of Exarchia – a sanctuary for political underdogs – a 15-year-old student is cold-bloodedly shot dead by the police. The murder releases a flow of resistance and affect. A war machine forms against state repression and the capitalist colonisation of everyday life. The line of flight it traces is a line of fire, and one that is not easily put out. Police repression meanwhile escalates; the city chokes with tear gas and the mainstream media churn out legalistic nonsense, promoting bad conscience and binary divisions between good and bad demonstrators.

Even though it is the anarchists who trigger the line of fire, in the demonstrations, behind the barricades, and in the assemblies the war machine is formed by a multiplicity of crowds. Anarchist politics germinates the seeds of the politics of the act, but the war machine exceeds their political signals (see Day 2008). The social composition of the uprising is not polarised between political or ideological milieus but involves bevies of high school and university students, unnameable proletarians, lumpenproletarians, refugees, immigrants and civilians who have no prior fixed political allegiance but choose to participate in the violent expression against the police, against chain stores as symbols of the society of the spectacle, against the banks as symbols of financial capital, and against public buildings as symbols of the state (Kalamaras 2009: 21).

Following the early days of 'burning and looting' a smoother urban space is created: Universities in Athens and Thessaloniki are occupied by political activists; high-schools and university departments by students; the HQ of the Workers Confederation by insurgent workers; the HQ of the News Editors Union by media activists, the National Opera House by artists. From occupied municipal buildings and other public spaces in many Greek cities there are calls for people's assemblies; public TV and radio stations are interrupted briefly by activists. The December uprising is a feast of activism, a feast in the most original sense. This is because the series of events are organised by the revolutionary assemblages themselves and the duration of the uprising depends on their political will and creativity and ability to overcome fatigue.

A pragmatics of the war machine deals with how it is appropriated. The dominant raison d'être of the two major political parties wants the Left to be undermining democracy by inciting social violence. The Greek-style culture of violence, according to this regime of signs, is a return of the repressed of the Left: the Left must suppress all revolutionary ideas and practices in order to aspire to parliamentary power. Left intellectuals in response implement a minimum abstraction in relation to the uprising's materialism, seeing it as a cultural event or an expression of apolitical rage on the part of the youth. They proclaim that the uprising lacked political articulation and that violence must be condemned wherever it comes from. In this way the Left exorcises its defeat in the civil war and the ghost of a Stalinist revolutionary totalitarianism. It interprets its revolutionary peaks like the Polytechneio uprising of 1973 as a legitimate resistance in a state of exception. Its bad conscience and its subjection to the apparatus enforces the state of exception of the legitimate state in violently repressing the uprising and the rhizomes that spread in its aftermath. In general it confirms its vertical hegemony in relation to social struggles by projecting its integration within democratic institutions (see Flesh Machine 2010: 69–97).

The anarchist 'space' is outlined by its resistance against the monopoly of state violence. From the 1990s on that principle of resistance has transformed the 'space' into a counter-signifying regime that makes critical statements on the functions of democracy and capitalism and has been attracting a growing number of people. In the December event, the right to social counter-violence as a matter of expression brings to the foreground the potentiality of a war against the *logos* and the law of the democratic state, and of a grounding of a people's *nomos*. Other features of the anarchist 'space' include an emphasis on the political values of autonomy in the post-Fordist era, self-organisation amongst craft unions, direct democracy in decision making, and horizontal networks of free-spirited relations outside consumerist frameworks. Some anarchist fractions, however, take war against the state as their sole mission.

These fractions are composed by the lumpenproletariat (see Thoburn 2003). The affiliation of the anarchist 'space' with the lumpenproletariat and with political activists outside or on the margins of the law is one of the revolutionary connections that transform this 'space' into a counter-signifying regime. Especially after December there is an urgent need to conjugate the variables of content and the variables of expression of the uprising so as to open up its assemblages to a patient and sober, but revolutionary, line of flight (Deleuze and Guattari 2004: 97). This line of flight will have to entail the involution of the genealogy of social violence in regard not only to the national context but also to the trans-national militarisation of the policing of protests. Through the spectacle of violence and police repression the new conception of security reconstitutes the war machine in conformity with the requirements of the capitalist axiomatic, which promotes a special kind of secured peace (Deleuze and Guattari 2004: 516).

As far as the circumstances of the current crisis in Greece are concerned, the transformational work being done in relation to autonomous craft-unionism, the unnameable proletariat and minorities, refugees, immigrants, social centres and queer politics within the anarchist 'space', is endangered by the post-subjectification of some anarchists as the revolutionary avant-garde of the movement. On 5 May 2010, during a massive demonstration against austerity measures imposed by the government, the IMF and the EU, three bank employees and a foetus are killed during an arson attack on a bank. While this event does not represent the anarchist 'space', it is a virtuality that haunts that 'space' and becomes actual when the line of fire turns into a line of abolition. More than ever there is a need for sober collective analysis of the anarchist subjectifications and for new revolutionary connections with the lumpenproletariat and with minorities.

The situation looks as though it has reached an impasse in regard to the conjunctions of the capitalist axiomatic within the current crisis. The gloom grows thicker. The hegemonic Left deepens the inertia of the proletariat by proclaiming occasional strikes; some anarchist fractions hold to their tight solidarity with anarchist prisoners, political criminals and armed struggle terrorists; the decentred anarchist 'space' rallies and tries to effectuate anew its abstract machine outside the strata, on the strata and between the strata. It is from within the unnameable proletariat, the unemployed and the minorities that new lines of flight will be drawn and vital connections made against the automation of the capitalist axiomatic and its bureaucratic programming (Deleuze and Guattari 2004: 522).

Allow me to conclude with a slogan from the December uprising: 'Freedom does not exist, all we have is choice.'

References

Anonymous (2002) 'Πολεοδομία και δημόσια τάξη' ['Urban Planning and Public Order'], *Text*, Athens: Ekdosi tis lesxis kataskopon tou 21ou eona.
Athanasatou, Ioanna (2001) *Ελληνικός Κινηματογράφος 1950–1967. Λαϊκή Μνήμη και ιδεολογία* [*Greek Cinema 1950–1967. Popular Memory and Ideology*], Athens: Finatec.
Clogg, Richard (1994) *Greece in the 1980s*, Hampshire: Macmillan.

Day, Richard (2008) *Gramsci is Dead: Anarchist Currents in the Newest Social Movements*, trans. Panagiotis Kalamaras, Athens: Eleutheriaki Koultoura.

Deleuze, Gilles and Félix Guattari (2004) *A Thousand Plateaus*, trans. Brian Massumi, London: Continuum.

Delta, Pinelopi (1988) *Ελευθέριος Βενιζέλος [Eleutherios Venizelos]*, Athens: Ermis.

Flesh Machine, Ego Te Provoco A (2010) *Violence*, Athens.

Fragkoudaki, Anna (2001) *Η Γλώσσα και το έθνος 1880–1980 [Language and the Nation 1880–1980]*, Athens: Alexandreia.

Gavriilidis, Akis (2007) *Η αθεράπευτη νεκροφιλία του ριζοσπαστικού πατριωτισμού [The Incurable Necrophilia of Radical Patriotism]*, Athens: Futura.

Hart, J. (1996) *New Voices in the Nation: Women and the Greek Resistance 1941–1964*, London: Cornell University Press.

Herzfeld, Michael (1989) *Anthropology Through the Looking-glass: Critical Ethnography in the Margins of Europe*, Cambridge: Cambridge University Press.

Kalamaras, Panagiotis (2009) 'Κύριοι αγαπάτε μας και αξύριστους, ξυρισμένους μας αγαπάνε όλοι' ['Gentlemen, love us also unshaved, when shaved everybody loves us'], Panoptikon, 12.

Katsaros, Stergios (1999) *Εγώ ο προβοκάτορας, εγώ ο τρομοκράτης [Me the Inciting Agent, Me the Terrorist]*, Athens: Mavri Lista.

Komninou, Maria (2003) *Από την αγορά στο θέαμα [From the Market to the Spectacle]*, Athens: Papazisis.

Lampropoulou, Dimitra (2008) 'Κοινωνικά δικαιώματα και πολιτικη σύγκρουση στην αυγή της 'σύντομης' δεκαετίας. Η απεργία των οικοδόμων τον Δεκέμβριο του 1960' ['Social Rights and Political Conflict at the Dawn of the 'Short' Decade: The Builders strike in December 1960], in A. Rigos, S. Seferiadis and E. Chatzivasileiou (eds.), *Η 'σύντομη' δεκαετία του '60 [The 'Short' Decade of the '60s]*, Athens: Kastaniotis.

Omada Enantia stin Lithi [Group Against Oblivion] (1996), *Κυριαρχία και κοινωνικοί αγώνες στον 'Ελλαδικό Χώρο' [Domination and Social Struggles in the 'Helladic Space']*, Athens: Anarchiki Archeiothiki.

Skopetea, Elli (1988) *Το 'Πρότυπο Βασίλειο' και η Μεγάλη Ιδέα. Όψεις του εθνικού προβλήματος στην Ελλάδα [The 'Model Kingdom' and the Great Idea: Aspects of the National Problem in Greece]*, Athens: Politipo.

Stathopoulou, Theoni (1991) *Το κίνημα του Παπουλάκου [The Movement of Papoulakos]*, unpublished PhD thesis.

Stefanidis, Ioannis (2008) 'Ο αλυτρωτισμός την δεκαετία του 1960 – Η περίπτωση της κινητοποίησης για το Κυπριακό ζήτημα' ['Irredentism in the 1960s: The Case of the Mobilisation on the Cyprus Question'], in A. Rigos, S. Seferiadis and E. Chatzivasileiou (eds.), *Η 'σύντομη' δεκαετία του '60 [The 'Short' Decade of the '60s]*, Athens: Kastaniotis.

Thoburn, Nicholas (2003) *Deleuze, Marx and Politics*; http://libcom.org/library/deleuze-marx-politics-nicholas-thoburn-3

Vournas, Tasos (1974) *Ιστορία της Νεώτερης Ελλάδας 1821–1909 [History of Modern Greece, 1821–1909]*, Athens: Tolidis Brothers Publications.

Life Resistance: Towards a Different Concept of the Political

Brad Evans   University of Leeds

Abstract

In an attempt to reaffirm Deleuze's Nietzschean affinities, this article argues that it is possible to detect in his thought an alternative concept of the political which gives ontological priority to difference. In order to map this out, a Deleuzian reading of the Zapatista experience will be provided, with particular attention given to the manner in which power is re-conceptualised, resistance strategised, subjectivities recast, and political solidarities formed anew. Once this has been established, the paper will argue that not only does Deleuze provide us with a meaningful basis for political action, he offers us possibilities for creating new forms of political solidarity that no longer take Hegelian inspired dialectical enmity or dangerous Kantian unfulfilment as their point of theoretical departure.

Keywords: total war, resistance, concept of the political, difference, the Other, politics of friendship

I. Deleuze's Resistance

Michael Hardt and Antonio Negri's trilogy remains the most ambitious attempt at making Deleuze relevant to today's political climate (see Hardt and Negri 2000, 2004, 2010). Foregrounding Deleuze as the affirmative theorist of micropolitical nomadism, Hardt and Negri's project places him in direct confrontation with the two great modernist thinkers who dominate contemporary political thought: Immanuel Kant and George Wilhelm Hegel. 'The leitmotif of Kantian philosophy',

Deleuze Studies Volume 4: 2010 supplement: 142–162
DOI: 10.3366/E1750224110001170
© Edinburgh University Press
www.eupjournals.com/dls

they suggest, is the 'necessity of the transcendental, the impossibility of every form of immediacy, the exorcism of every vital figure in the apprehension and action of being' (Hardt and Negri 2000: 81). While their anti-Hegelianism, contra Fanon, results in a scathing critique of the dialectical method for the manner in which it re-produces the colonial mind: 'Colonialism constructs figures of alterity and manages their flows in what unfolds as a complex dialectical structure... *Reality is not dialectical, colonialism is*' (124, 129). One could argue that these battles are altogether Deleuzian. Deleuze did not hesitate to call Kant 'the enemy' (Deleuze 1990: 6). Neither did he refrain from accusing Hegel of 'inspiring every language of betrayal' (Deleuze 2004: 144). While Kant was singled out for his deceitful 'politics of compromise', which allows us to question certain parameters of knowledge, truth and morality while refusing to bring thought to bear on these terms in themselves (Deleuze 2006: 83, 84), Hegel, caught in a double Kantian bind, stands accused of infecting all political struggle with a 'spirit of revenge' so that political triumphs always define the 'weak *as* weak', with the victory of the slaves written into the world as their 'victory *as* slaves' (109). What is being uncovered here is the process wherein a state of mind becomes a 'mind of state': where Kant's *Cogitatio Universalis* demands a higher unity in order to tame the multiplicity of forces which potentially troubles the unification of the faculties of reason (Deleuze and Guattari 2002: 367), Hegelian dialectics perpetuate this drama with greater inner purpose by conceiving '*power as the object of a recognition, the content of a representation, the stake in a competition, and therefore mak*[*ing*] *it depend, at the end of a fight, on a simple attribution of established values*' (Deleuze 2006: 9–10). Either way, the political as a function of difference is the problem to be solved.

Whatever problems one may have with Hardt and Negri's wider project they nevertheless pose a critical question about the relationship between imperial 'war machines' and canonical 'images of thought'. Kant is a somewhat easy target. His universal disposition directly relates the singular predilection for difference to the problem of war. This is no small matter. Whereas Hobbes taught us that there can be no politics without security, and no security without the State, Kant encourages us to believe that there can be no security without universality, and no universality without moral progress towards the unification of the species. Hegel's legacy is more complicated. If Kant inaugurated the modern age, it was with Hegel that modernity became problematic in so far as its inner workings became visible and self-consciously theorised (see Habermas 1987). Hegel is therefore for many the founder of the modern theory of *resistance*. While Hardt and Negri recognise this, they find this approach problematic on two distinct counts. Historically speaking, since the dialectical method has been implicit in recreating the master/slave dichotomy out of the ashes of liberation, inscribed into the fabric of its counter-hegemonic discourse has been a profound distaste for anything which differs from the orthodox Eurocentric schema. Now that all social relations are underwritten by networked thinking, ideas concerning linearity, teleology and limit conditions have been firmly displaced by notions of complexity, contingency and emergence. As a consequence, even if dialectics did once harbour the potential for political transformation, it now has little or no relevance to the operation of contemporary power which works at the level of pure strategy. From this perspective then, while the Kantian attempt to realise the unification of the species for the sake of its own protection arguably makes him the imperial philosopher whose time has come, Hegel and his descendents have no political relevance in the post-dialectical field of play.

Dialecticians have invariably fought back. John Holloway was among the first to take critical aim at Hardt and Negri's project. 'Politically', he explains, while 'the emphasis on the power of the working class has an obvious appeal... the understanding of labour and capital in terms of an external relationship leads to a... failure to explore the internal nature of the relation between labour and capital leading the autonomist analysts to underestimate the degree to which labour exists *within* capitalist forms' (Holloway 2002: 174). Dialectics then becomes the only method capable of providing 'the escape plan, the thinking-against-the-prison, thinking-against-the-wrong-world, a thinking that would no longer make sense if we were outside of the prison of the wrong world'. Holloway thus calls upon us to 'strengthen negativity', 'make the scream more strident' and in the process negate in whatever way we can the negativeness of our existence – the negation of the 'untruth of the world' (8). To his credit, Holloway is not blind to the failures of the past, but he believes that since it is possible to move away from the 'logic of synthesis' (which he takes to be the focus of concern for Hardt and Negri) and on to the 'movement of negation', it is possible to negate the present without colonising the future. Slavoj Žižek has been less forgiving. Lamenting that 'Deleuze more and more serves as the theoretical foundation of today's anti-global Left' (Žižek 2004: xi), Žižek insists that in-vogue tendencies to invoke Deleuzian notions such as becoming, multiplicity, nomadism, micropolitics, and the power of the affirmative, make him at best a compliant apologist: 'There are, effectively, features that justify calling Deleuze the ideologist of late capitalism' (185). Since Deleuze lacks the negative power of truth, Žižek effectively ascribes to him a truly nihilistic agenda which claims the resistance of everything and yet, being ill-equipped to pose the right questions, actually ends up creating nothing, offering only a life of endless becoming which in the end shows an allegiance to 'the infinitely divisible, substanceless, void within a void' (24).

Deleuzian scholars have responded to these critiques by suggesting that Deleuze's relationship with Kant and Hegel was actually more complex than the literal Nietzschean reading ordinarily suggests. Paul Patton's response, for instance, has no problem reconciling Deleuze with the constitutional tradition of political liberalism (see Patton 2008). While Ian Buchanan and Adrian Parr strike a now familiar note by explaining that

> Too many people are content to say Deleuze, like Nietzsche, was against Hegel without ever asking why... But this critique is only meaningful to the extent that it is read in terms of Deleuze's conception of philosophy's purpose, which is precisely Marxian to the extent that, like Marx, they hold that the point of philosophy is not to understand society, but to change it. (Buchanan and Parr 2006: 1)

While these efforts to nuance Deleuze's thought have their benefits, there is a danger here that in *re*-acting to such criticisms Deleuzian Studies either becomes the victim of a dialectical entrapment or attempts to become all things to all people in a frantic search for acceptance. The suggestion is not, of course, that Deleuze needs to be authenticated, still less that we should refrain from using his concepts wherever appropriate. But having said this, to argue in favour of a Deleuze who is open to all forms of interpretation (affirmative/negative, creative/compromised, micro/macro, singular/universal, nomadic/sedentary, non-Statist/Statist) not only risks confirming what Žižek contends – that Deleuze is an ultimately substanceless political philosopher whose arbitrary positioning at best inspires an allegiance to the purely contingent – it also invites those 'bad readings or displacements' derived from 'arbitrary selections' of his works (not least the well-documented appropriation of Deleuze's ideas by various advocates within military academies) that he was so keen to warn us against in the particular context of Nietzsche's fate (Deleuze 2004: 17).

For Deleuzian scholarship what is at stake here centres on his relationship with Nietzsche. Should this be read in purely philosophical terms? Or might it offer to us something more *politically* than do those attempts to reconcile Deleuze with the best of the Enlightenment tradition? While the style of Deleuze's *Nietzsche and Philosophy* does allow for some distancing in the sense that it is written from the perspective of the commentator exploring his target's thought processes, it is undoubtedly clear that this is done out of admiration rather than denunciation (unlike in the study of Kant). Keith Ansell-Pearson (2004) is therefore correct to insist that Deleuze's political 'battle cry' should not be divorced from its Nietzschean affinity. Such a severance would only undermine Deleuze's ontological commitment to the affirmation of difference, his belief in the creative dimension to resistance, his distaste for dialectics, his preference for the genealogical method, and his allegiance to Dionysian forces (nomadic, singular, micro and multiple) over Apollonian forces (sedentary, total, macro and universal). Moving away from the proposition that resistance is a creative process there is also a danger that Deleuze's contribution to our understanding of the political will simply be made to reaffirm well-established antagonistic terms of engagement.

Moving beyond this impasse, this paper will argue that it is possible to detect in Deleuze's thought an alternative concept of the political which gives ontological priority to difference. In order to gain a tangible purchase on this, a Deleuzian reading of the Zapatista experience will be presented, thereby countering the ludicrous assertion that Deleuze is merely some 'other-worldly' philosopher who provides us with no meaningful basis for normative political action.

II. Total War

When power takes life to be its object, resistance to power already puts itself on the side of life and turns life against power: 'life as a political object was in a sense taken at face value and turned back against the system bent on controlling it' (Deleuze 1999: 76). Life in other words not only 'becomes resistance to power when power takes life as its object, but invoking a special and particular "right to life", when power becomes bio-power, resistance becomes the power of life, a vital power that cannot be confined within species, environment or the paths of a particular diagram' (77). With life therefore said to be already richer in possibilities, the life which exceeds expectations *becomes a life of resistance*. Inevitably, since life resistance combats the forms of confinement (capture) and technical strategies (overcoding) so essential to forms of species manipulation, it equally refuses to accept the dangerously unfulfilled categorisation which power necessarily imposes in order to control and transform existence. This is crucial to our understanding of contemporary political struggles. Contemporary warfare is not simply about containing the problem. By-passing the classical concern with sovereign integrities, it is fought over the modalities of life itself (see Smith 2006). As Tony Blair reiterated on numerous occasions (e.g. Blair 2007), Westphalia aside, the battle today is for the global value space. It is about bodies that matter. Somewhat ironically then, sanctioned in the name of lasting human peace, this global will to war is also triumphed to be an advance in Liberal reason (see Ignatieff 2003). It is the surest of indicators that humanity can be brought together through the necessary battles which are waged against unnecessary species endangerment. War is no longer therefore simply fought in order to destroy those terroristic elements which occupy an epistemic place of exteriority to the normal order of things; rather, for the most part, it is now waged by 'other means' upon maladjusted insurgent populations which, although dangerous, are open to remedy and demand lasting engagement (see Bell and Evans 2010).

While counter-insurgency literatures present this as the latest strategic thinking (see Kilcullen 2009), indigenous populations have been mapping these biopolitical contours for some considerable time. Writing some four years after the first uprising against the 'New World Order', Subcomandante Marcos, a spokesperson for the indigenous Zapatistas of Mexico, published a highly original article in *Le Monde diplomatique* (Marcos 2002). Entitled 'The Fourth World War', this article offered a remarkably concise genealogy of modern warfare which begins by navigating through the three major wars which shaped the twentieth century: the First and Second being the familiar Great Wars, the Third synonymous with the Cold War. Marking a new departure, the Fourth War thus refers to a post-Cold War condition which, although revealing many commonalities, presents some distinct strategic turns:

Afterwards came the Fourth World War, which destroyed everything from before, because the world is no longer the same, and the same strategy cannot be applied. The concept of 'Total war' was developed further: it is not only a war on all fronts; it is a war which can be anywhere, a total war in which the entire world is at stake. 'Total war' means: at any moment, in any place, under any circumstances. The idea of fighting for one place in particular no longer exists. Now the fight can take place at any moment.

As Marcos sees it, 'the problem' begins to appear when one poses the question 'Who is the Enemy?':

We are saying that humanity is now the enemy. The Fourth World War is destroying humanity as globalization is universalizing the market, and everything human which opposes the logic of the market is an enemy and must be destroyed. In this sense, we are all the enemy to be vanquished: indigenous, non-indigenous, human rights observers, teachers, intellectuals, artists. Anyone who believes themselves to be free and is not.

Hence, for Marcos, since 'Total War' implies that the entire planetary biosphere is at stake: 'There are no longer civilians and neutrals. The entire world is part of the conflict... Everyone is a part, there are no neutrals, you are either an ally or you are an enemy.'

This abandonment of political neutrality is not incidental. It is fully indicative of the contemporary strategic landscape which has witnessed the blurring of all conventional demarcations (see Dillon 2007; Dillon and Reid 2009). One only has the think for instance of the notion of Humanitarian War to give credence to this fact. This undoubtedly raises some challenging political questions. Not least, what does it mean to be politically active when activism itself is openly recruited into a veritable state of war? The Zapatistas have undoubtedly been at the forefront of these recombinant dynamics. Their insurgency has been unique for a number of reasons: 1) The first movement to ever declare outright war on an internationally recognised agreement [NAFTA], they forced strategic analysts to begin conceptualising warfare beyond the confines of the State (see Arquilla and Ronfeldt 1997). 2) Moving beyond reified sovereign conceptions of power, i.e. US hegemony, what the Zapatistas emphasised was the need to reconcile political power with a more general economy of biopolitical production. 3) Since their resistance reveals how life consciously struggles against all aspects of biopolitical control, especially imposed forms of 'good governance', they have become testament to the fact that the life which resists finds its most potent (hence more problematic) expression through the political affirmation of *life's differences*. As Marcos writes: 'when confronted with the search for hegemony, "the first task" is to recognise that there are "differences between us all" and that in light of this we aspire to a politics of tolerance and inclusion. You cannot aspire to eliminate the other, that which is different, and neither can you ignore it' (cited in Duran and Higgins 1999: 270).

Difference is not explained here dialectically. Difference already registers in the affirmative:

We are 'other' and different... we are fighting in order to continue being 'other' and different... And what we are – far from wanting to impose its being on the 'other' or different – seeks its own space, and, at the same time, a space of meeting... that is why Power has its armies and police, to force those who are 'other' and different to be the same and identical. But the 'other' and different are not looking for everyone to be like they are ... The 'everyone doing his own thing' is both an *affirmation of difference*, and it is a respect for other difference. (Marcos 1999c)

While this commitment to 'the Other' has prevented the Zapatistas from oedipalising their cause, hence remarkably making non-violence a strategic option (see Evans 2009), there is a perhaps more important point to be made here: When life becomes the principle object for political struggles, one no longer ties political strategies or analysis to conventional limit conditions. Conditioning the possible, modes of active production instead define the biopolitical field of operations. This is not of course to suggest that wretched conditions cannot be defined as unjust or intolerable, but neither is it to play by the pre-set rules of political engagement. This exposes the fundamental difference between biopolitics and dialectics. Where a dialectical logic presupposes contradictory elements within a realm that it ultimately unifies, biopolitical logics presuppose connectable elements within a field in which everything is recombinant. With complex forms of self-organisation therefore replacing linearity, limit conditions are efficiently seconded by a general economy of political production. That is to say, once the strategic assumption that the universe is heterogeneous firmly displaces the dialectical assumption that the universe is homogenised, power struggles become a matter of pure strategy.

III. Fugitive Subjects

Compound life has become the 'permanently temporary' habitual reality for many of the worlds *sans-papiers* (see Bauman 2002). Even sovereignty itself, as Green Zones testify, has become nodal. Nevertheless, while encamped life is undoubtedly wretched and de-politicising, foregrounding the spatial figuration of the camp may lead us to underestimate how contemporary wars have become wars of movement (Virilio 2003). While Giorgio Agamben (1995, 2005) has provided us with some insightful commentary on the de-politicising nature of encamped life, his *Camp as Nomos* hypothesis remains tied to the static sovereign view of the world. If however we accept that biopolitical rule is in the ascendancy then the general ordering of the earth becomes a *Nomos of Circulation* (Evans and Hardt 2010). It is no coincidence then that some strategic analysts have been arguing that success in contemporary theatres of war is dependent upon mastering the network form (see Arquilla and Ronfeldt 2001). Not only do they allow one to operate more effectively in today's dynamic and radically interconnected world, network forms also benefit those who are *pro-active* in their strategic pursuits. It has thus all become a planetary game of 'GO'. Invariably, since the principal message here is that nothing is strategically marginal – that is to say, emergency is written into the fabric of all emergence – what potential there is for terror is placed into the heart of all possible *event*ualities (see Evans 2010). Knowing that we don't know thus registers at one and the same time as a wonderful condition of possibility and as the source of all our anxieties. With this in mind, given that the principal task for security practitioners is to pre-empt radical emergence, any ontological form of nomadism (animate/inanimate, actual/virtual) become *ipso facto* potentially dangerous (think illegal migration, shadow economies, unknown viruses, so forth). To put it another way, since the autonomous/emergent political subject cannot be left to chance, there is a simple choice to be made: either conform to the liberal attempts at making life live compliantly or become *politically fugitive*.

Here the Zapatistas are particularly instructive. While their *de facto* autonomous process has rightly received considerable attention (see in particular Burguete Cal y Mayor 2003; Mattiace 2003; Ross 2005, 2006; Sierra-Sierra 1995); the role *movement* plays in their struggle is often overlooked. Indeed, not only are they forcing us to re-conceptualise physical space, but, more profoundly, it is evident that their revolution offers a distinct nomadic disposition which has radicalised the intellectual political terrain. Since their uprising on New Year's Day 1994, the Zapatistas' ability to traverse space has been politically significant. This event in particular epitomised what Nietzsche termed the 'untimely'. A momentary appearance which truly unsettled the natural political order of things, its success was testament to the power of a revolutionary-becoming which, at the point of its emergence, proves to be completely imperceptible within conventional political registers. This tendency to move collectively en masse, while subsequently evacuating those off-limit territories without a trace, has repeatedly enabled the Zapatistas to display their autonomous power by entering politically sensitive areas to which they would not *Other*-wise belong. Such excursions have in numerous instances been political dynamite. On 12 September 1997, for instance, the Zapatistas kept their promise as a delegation of 1111 unarmed members travelled from Chiapas to the Federal District of Mexico City. In 1999, 5000 Zapatistas descended upon the republic for a referendum on the indigenous people's right to define their own meaning of rights. In the spring of 2001 they would join forces with the National Indigenous Congress (Congreso Nacional Indigena) to march through 17 Mexican cities as the Zapatista motorcade embarked on a two-week journey that would end with some 200,000 sympathisers filling the *Zocalo* in Mexico City infamously chanting 'Todos Somos Marcos' (We are All Marcos).

Marcos has more recently toured the entire nation as part of the 'Otra Campana' (Other Campaign). While this tour witnessed some remarkable acts of political theatre – e.g. Marcos actually gaining entry into a maximum security prison – la Otra perhaps best illustrates how movement has been placed at the heart of revolutionary thought and practice. La Otra was first announced by the Zapatistas in their *Sixth Declaration from the Lacandon Selva* on 6 June 2005. This declaration was for many a significant moment, not least because many political commentators had felt that the Zapatistas' time had passed.[1] Facing such suggestions John Ross has noted that 'La Sexta [the Sixth Declaration] shows once again the Zapatistas at their most politically savvy, whenever you expect them to be outspoken they respond with a barrage of silence, and when they are assumed to be a thing of the past they show, with a barrage of communiqués – they keep compounding us by being one step ahead'.[2] In a remarkable moment of self-criticism, the Zapatistas felt that there was something missing from their project: namely, oppressed constituencies which were not necessarily indigenous:

> The first thing we saw was that our heart was not the same as before, when we began our struggle. It was larger, because now we had touched the hearts of many more good people. And we also saw that our heart was more hurt; it was more wounded. It was not wounded by the deceit of the bad governments, but because, when we touched the hearts of others, we also touched their sorrows. It was as if we were seeing ourselves in a mirror.[3]

The Zapatistas therefore recognised that they had reached a new moment in their revolutionary process – 'a point in which we could possibly lose everything we have if we do not move forward'. This called for a 'new step forward in the indigenous struggle' to 'unite with other social sectors that suffer'.

The Other Campaign sought to instigate another type of politics, 'a different way of doing politics' which fully recognises that genuine autonomy cannot simply be achieved by remaining static. Reflecting the dynamism of the world around, the Other Campaign therefore sought to reconcile autonomy with a willingness to continuously create reciprocal adaptive networks, so that differences can be made to work together to produce new and alternative spaces. Hernandez Navarro believes this enables the Sixth Declaration to go well beyond the 'indigenous question' and 'announce a more far-reaching political initiative' which not only 'predicts the collapse of the political class' but seeks to depart from the rigidness of the 'traditional Left' (cited in Marcos 2006a: 15). The real strength of this new initiative is 'born of social energy generated in the heat of *mobilisation*'. This has been reflected by Marcos in what he termed *the Other Geometry* of the campaign. This calls for the creation of 'new realities which are already emerging, and which will go on appearing further ahead, need another theoretical reflection, another debate of ideas' (Marcos 2006b). Given that autonomy must therefore be receptive to political change in order for this project to work, openness must be built in to the revolutionary struggle: 'In our dreams we have seen another world... This world is not a dream from the past, it was not something that came to us from our ancestors. It came from ahead, from the next steps we are going to take' (Marcos 1994). *Nomadic tendencies* invariably come to the fore:

> In our theoretical reflection we talk about what we see as tendencies, not consummated or inevitable acts, they are theoretical reflections about the 'way we move', that is why we reject attempts at universality and eternity in what we say or do – 'what matters above all is the path, the direction, the tendency' – we are doing so not only in order to know what is happening and to understand it, but also, and above all, in order to try and transform it. (Marcos 2003b)

These tendencies provide us with a meaningful insight into what Deleuze and Guattari termed the 'Pure Idea of War': 'the distinction between absolute war as Idea and real wars seems to us to be of great importance... The pure Idea is not that of the abstract elimination of the adversary but that of a war machine *that does not have war as its object* and that only entertains a potential or supplementary synthetic relation with war' (Deleuze and Guattari 2002: 420). Not having war as its object, the war machine is a 'pure Idea' that is aphoristic and imperceptible to conventional political registers. It is not predicated on some original enmity; neither does it begin by negating the world. This pure idea of war as a nomadic becoming only therefore appears in the form of an antagonism directed against all forms of capture and overcoding once appropriation has occurred. When the imperceptible becomes perceptible! As such, what may appear to be an antagonistic refusal to follow the imperial production of peaceful subjects already registers in the affirmative. As Deleuze writes, 'the aim of war machines isn't war at all but a very special kind of space, *smooth space*, which they establish, occupy, and extend. Nomadism is precisely this combination of war machine and smooth space... War machines tend to be much more revolutionary, or artistic, rather than military' (Deleuze 1990: 33). Revolutionary-becoming, in other words, is markedly different from violent revolution. Nietzsche thus returns here with renewed force in relation to the recasting of political solidarities:

> the nomadic adventure begins when they seek to stay in the same place by escaping the codes. As we know, the revolutionary problem today is to find some unity in our various struggles without falling back on the despotic and bureaucratic organisation of the party or State apparatus: we want a war machine that would not recreate a State apparatus, a nomadic unity in relation with the Outside, that would not recreate the despotic unity. This is perhaps Nietzsche at his most profound, a measure of his break with philosophy, as it appears in aphorism: to have made thought a war machine, to have made thought a nomadic power. And even if the journey goes nowhere, even if it takes place in the same place, imperceptible, unlooked for, underground, we must ask: who are today's nomads, who are today's Nietzscheans? (Deleuze 2004: 260)

IV. The Solidarity of Rights

Political activism cannot be divorced from the creation of solidarities with those deemed to be at the raw end of power. The activist is more often than not defined by the actions they undertake on behalf of those disenfranchised populations existing on the global periphery. From this perspective, while political realists have generally been lauded for their self-serving agendas, liberal theorists and practitioners have positioned themselves as the exemplars of political activism. Setting aside concerns for sovereign integrities, their commitment to alleviating unnecessary suffering is presented as the basis for a cosmopolitan ethic that will bring a new world community together. However, despite the self-declared *human*itarianism this account offers, one question tends to escape considered critical attention: How are political rights actually realised? If one takes the well-established juridical approach to liberal power then one locates the rightful act in the commitment to uphold legal declarations. Exalting the best of the positive law tradition, what is right then becomes synonymous with the legal protections offered to distant others. This, however, is only part of the story. Economic conditions have continually disrupted and transformed any static semblance of legal rights. Indeed, while some liberals continue to tell an abstract juridical tale, at the level of policy it is now widely accepted that in order to achieve genuine social cohesion a commitment to political rights must be accompanied by a commitment to dealing with the problems of maladjusted economic subjects. A mere glance at the United Nations Declaration of Human Rights provides us with sufficient evidence for this fact. While it pays due attention to necessary protections from legal transgressions, it is the Declaration's Human Security guarantees (regarding access to resources essential for survival, education, healthcare, shelter, clean drinking water, and so on) which are seen as a triumph of the liberal conscience.[4] As Richard Falk suggests, thinking about security in human terms allows us to envisage a political 'community for the whole of humanity which overcomes the most problematic aspects of the present world scene... [and where] difference and uniformities across space and time are subsumed beneath an overall commitment to world order values in the provisional shape of peace, economic well-being, social and political justice, and environmental sustainability' (Falk 1995: 243).

While poststructuralist theorists are well aware of the limitations associated with juridical approaches to freedom, rights and justice (see Braidotti, Colebrook and Hanafin 2009), less attention is paid to the way in which a biopolitical approach might offer a critical perspective on the de-politicising nature of liberal humanitarianism in practice.[5] That is to say, while there is sufficient evidence of how the commitment to sovereign forms of right necessarily leads to the creation of abandoned lives reduced to 'bare life' through the sovereign encounter (see Agamben 1995, 2005), insufficient attention has been paid to the more positive power dynamics at play which, working in the name of human development and progress, actually serve to de-politicise alternative forms of political subjectivity *within* the remit of humanitarian discourses and practices. This offers an important corrective to Agamben. Whereas his concept of 'bare life' begins with the de-politicisation of others in order to construct political and moral registers, bare life in a biopolitical sense begins with the promotion of others in order to facilitate the elimination of that which is seen to be undesirable/regressive. Not then a form of bare life in the sense of legally suspended or abandoned; rather the 'bare activity' of a species life whose wretched conditions permit interventionist forces to act out of necessity. When life as such is reduced to the level of a victim incapable of providing even for the 'bare essentials', it is through the subsequent alleviation of suffering that all life is reduced to mere technology.

Deleuze and Guattari understood this all too well. Human rights, they argued, were merely 'axioms'. That is to say, what are presented as inviolable universal rights can quite easily 'exist on the market with many other axioms', or else can simply be suspended when the 'determinate inequalities of development dictate' (Deleuze and Guattari 1994: 106, 107). Human rights as such actually tell us 'nothing about the immanent modes of existence of people provided with rights'. The Zapatistas have learned this well. Their non-juridical approach to rights is well established (see Higgins 2004). Less attention, however, has been given to their conscious refusal of the human security prescriptions, which in the process of challenging imposed conditionality provides for critical reflection on the practice of saving strangers. Marcos understood early in the struggle that through the politicisation of aid warfare was taking place by other means (Marcos 1999a). This would have a profound impact upon the Zapatistas' entire relationship with all non-governmental organisations (see Marcos 2001, 2003a). While an inevitable side-effect of this has been self-deprivation,[6] it has nevertheless led to the creation of entirely new forms of solidarity which have redefined the benefactor/recipient relationship in a more reciprocal and locally sensitive manner (see Earle and Simonelli 2005; Olesen 2000, 2005). Development projects still happen; but not in order to meet statistical quotas set by technocrats in order to give a minimum valuation on the stock of life; rather, to enrich the indigenous communities' control over their own political affairs. Inevitably, since this conscious decision has effectively undermined the prevailing human security principle that underdevelopment is dangerous, the Zapatistas have in the process of exposing the de-politicising nature of biopolitical technologies forced the political back into conflict analysis (Evans 2008). One cannot propose scientifically deduced cause/effect remedies for a struggle which does not agree with the underlying economising logic. Neither can one deploy an army of technocratic ameliorators with a mandate for social transformation into a political crisis zone when those within the zone do not believe that they are the problem to be solved. A critical redefinition of the political itself is needed, in order to move from tolerance to genuine hospitality towards that which is different.

V. A Different Concept of the Political?

Jacques Derrida once said that the 'the rapport of self-identity is always a rapport of violence with the other; so that the notions of property, appropriation and self-presence, so central to metaphysics,

are essentially dependent on an oppositional relation with otherness'
(Derrida 1984: 117). The Zapatistas have seemingly taken note of this
modern truism. Centuries of indigenous persecution easily cultivates hate
and resentment. Once mobilised into a political force, these historical
animosities tend to re-cast old dialectical foes against one another in
a perpetual struggle for mastery. Had the Zapatistas follow this trend,
Marcos believes, they would have simply produced another brand of
'fundamentalism, converting the Zapatista movement into a movement
against another race' (El Kilombo 2007: 18). Importantly then, for
Marcos, since there are 'historical arguments which back up the idea
that from *there* comes the pain', in order for the Zapatistas to create
a 'new horizon' it is essential that from the outset one begins with a
'respect for the Other who is different'. Only then can they 'eliminate
from us the possibility of fundamentalism'. In light of this attempt to
proactively thwart fundamentalist tendencies, Deleuze's call in his study
of Bergson to 'think differences of nature, independent of all forms of
negation' (Deleuze 1988: 41) reads than more than an expression of
admiration for a bygone philosopher. Intensifying the normative basis
for affirmative politics, the concept of the political itself is recast to give
ontological priority to difference. This represents a radical departure
from conventional political referents. The orthodox approach begins
with the political as a problem in the context of establishing the order
and demarcations of battle, but for those advocating lasting peace, the
political only gains meaningful currency when as the source of this
enmity it is foregrounded as *the* problem to be solved.

   The idea that the political should be conceptualised through a
dialectical enmity is well established.[7] Realists deploy it in order to
maintain their allegiance to epiphenomenal tensions. This enables them
to present a world of neat sovereign demarcations through which
it is possible to clearly identify other/self, them/us, outside/inside,
enemy/friend and so on. Liberals on the other hand have openly recruited
this Schmittean approach in order deploy it against itself. The politics of
exceptionalism thus becomes the principal rallying cry for those who
advocate a globally inclusive imaginary in order to rid the world of
unnatural spatio-determined divisions. There is a tragic irony to all this.
In order to save humanity from itself, liberals take the worst aspects
of Schmitt's thought (i.e. ontologically prior enmity) in order to use it
against its resulting tensions. Furthermore, the idea of separate sovereign
orders is brought into question in order to re-establish a true planetary
basis for sovereign power. Schmitt's nightmare vision of the fall of
jus publicum Europaeum is therefore recast as the liberal condition of

possibility. Through selective appropriation of his ideas, Schmitt comes to represent the diagnostician in chief along with the chief adversary to be vanquished at all costs. If this renders Schmitt the bastard child of Hegelian disdain, no recourse to Kant will provide us with the political solution. The focus of concern here is not with the highly abstracted and reified account of sovereign power which tends to underwrite post-Kantian politics. Neither is it with the debilitating idealism of Kantian universality. What concerns us lies beneath the surface of this architecture. A shameful deceit, Kantian universality masks an altogether more sinister biopolitical imperative which, casting suspicion over all human life, means that all life is recruited into a perpetual state of internal war without distinction.

To explain this it is necessary to point out the irresolvable dilemmas upon which Kantian rule depends: Kant preaches universality but accepts that the universal is beyond the realms of lived experience. He preaches the international virtues of law but accepts that one's encounter with moral law has to be contingent. He demands that all life strive towards the unification of the species yet acknowledges that this is always going to be met with internal revolt and political strife. He insists upon autonomy even though he starts his analysis by offering an account of freedom in which man has fallen to the guilt of his own unmaking. He promotes human progress yet puts forward the thesis of infinite regress to highlight humankind's imperfections. And he claims that all life has an original predisposition to good while at the same time a natural propensity to evil. Taken together, while Kant therefore demands that life must be made to live for the sake of its own protection; he knows full well that to live in this Kantian way reveals how the capacity to be unnecessarily dangerous is inherent to all species of life. As such, not only does he condemn all life to a temporal purgatory, i.e. life is always guilty of the moral deficiencies of the past, yet incapable in its own right of exorcising them in the future. He also demands these imperfections in order for life to prove its moral and political worth. Hence, although Kantianism undeniably moves beyond the familiar geo-strategic epiphenomenal tensions (friend/enemy, outside/inside, bios/zoe), what takes their place is the biopolitical proposition that all life is always somehow dangerously unfulfilled.

Marcos cuts to the chase when he argues that 'the problem is respect towards the Other ... Whatever political relationship that is not based in respect is manipulation. Well-intentioned or bad-intentioned, it doesn't matter, because it is manipulation ... That's why we said, starting there, we can construct respect or we can construct a relationship of domination' (El Kilombo 2007: 29, 30). How then does this respect for the Other who is already different manifest itself politically? Gregg Lambert (2008) and Charles Stivale (2008) have pointed us in the right direction in their attempts to explore the meaning of the Deleuzian notion of 'friendship'. Lambert, for instance, detects in Deleuze's later work a desire to place the Other at the forefront of our philosophical enquiry. This he believes forces an entire re-evaluation of the meaning of friendship as a political and philosophical concept that appears ontologically prior to the friend/enemy distinction: 'that is prior to any presupposition of a social commonality or relationship to identity, before we can even begin to think of the possibilities of friendship again' (Lambert 2008: 50). For Stivale, friendship cannot be divorced from Deleuze's political philosophy since it is intimately bound both to the creation of philosophical concepts and to active engagement:

> Deleuze's understanding of friendship is not that of a common or ideal bond and can hardly be encapsulated in a neat definition... However, Deleuze's myriad practices of friendship stand in sharp contrast to any ultimate recognition of friendship as distress, for such a defeatist view would fail to acknowledge that this distress constitutes but a complementary fold in the active engagement of friendship. (Stivale 2008: xiii)

For Stivale then, the question is not 'Who is the friend?' but more pertinently 'What can friendship do?' If we can say that that a Deleuzian notion of friendship is intimately bound up with our becoming in this world, forcing us indeed to find reasons to believe in this world, perhaps we can therefore say that friendship is precisely what he had in mind when he found in Nietzsche a philosophical ally who 'break[s] with philosophy, as it appears in the aphorism: to have made a war machine of thought, to have made thought a nomadic power' (Deleuze 2004: 260). It was Nietzsche after all who enabled Deleuze to move away from the morally reductive concern with 'how should we live?' towards considering the ethical possibilities of 'how might we live?' (May 2005: 7).

This certainly takes us into some fertile conceptual territory. While Derrida may provide us with obvious points of further connection, Agamben also appears to have something in common. As he recently stated: 'I maintain, rather, that "friend" belongs to the class of terms that linguists define as non-predicative; these are terms from which it is not possible to establish a class that includes all the things to which the predicative in question is attributed' (Agamben 2009: 29). Friendship in other words is not a referent to be captured. It does not possess some objective denomination through which one might expose some transcendental essence. Friendship is a 'pure experience' of the world (30). Politically speaking, it is irrevocably bound to the 'pure fact of being': 'Friends do not share something (birth, law, place, taste): they are shared by the experience of friendship. Friendship is the con-division that precedes every division, since what has to be shared is the very fact of existence, life itself. And it is this sharing without an object, this original consenting, that constitutes the political' (26). Importantly, for Agamben, since the concept of friendship is equipped with an *intensity* that registers as political potential, he equally gestures towards a concept of the political which no longer needs to be based on enmity or some profound suspicion that political difference is *the* problem to be solved. Providing a more thorough and meaningful basis for this is perhaps the most difficult and yet most urgent task we face today.

Notes

1. For instance, in January 2005, Vincente Fox called the Zapatistas 'practically a thing of the past' with the 'people of Chiapas looking forward . . . with a new face'. See W. Weissert, 'Mexico's Fox Calls Guerrilla Movement a Thing of the Past', Associated Press, 12 January 2005.
2. Interview conducted in Mexico City, 17 December 2005.
3. See the EZLN 'Sixth Declaration from the Lacandon Jungle'.
4. Amongst an abundance of literature dedicated to this, see in particular Booth 1991, 2005; Buzan 1991; Buzan et al. 1998; and Wyn-Jones 1999.
5. A notable exception to this is the work of Mark Duffield (see in particular Duffield 2007).
6. As June Nash observes 'The resistance of the Zapatista communities is also expressed in their rejection of government handouts in every form, be it textbooks, medical supplies and interventions, immunization programs, and other programs that might well benefit communities' (cited in Earle and Simonelli 2005: xi).
7. In his *Politische Theologie* (1922), Carl Schmitt first made his now well-established claim that sovereign power refers to 'he who decides upon the state of exception' (Schmitt 2006: 21). This would be developed more fully into a 'Concept of the Political' in the volume bearing that name (Schmitt 1996).

References

Agamben, Giorgio (1995) *Homo Sacer: Sovereign Power and Bare Life*, trans. D. Heller-Roazen, Stanford: Stanford University Press.
Agamben, Giorgio (2005) *State of Exception*, trans. K. Attell, Chicago: University of Chicago Press.
Agamben, Giorgio (2009) *What is an Apparatus?*, trans. D. Kishnik and S. Pedatella, Stanford: Stanford University Press.

Arquilla, John and David Ronfeldt (eds.) (1997) *In Athena's Camp: Preparing for Conflict in the Information Age*, Santa Monica, CA: RAND.
Arquilla, John and David Ronfeldt (eds.) (2001) *Networks and Netwars: The Future of Terror, Crime and Militancy*, Santa Monica, CA: RAND.
Bauman, Zygmunt (2002) *Society Under Siege*, Cambridge: Polity Press.
Bell, Colleen and Brad Evans (2010) 'Terrorism to Insurgency: Mapping the Post-Intervention Security Terrain', *Journal of Intervention and State Building*, 4:4, pp. 9–28.
Blair, Tony (2007) 'A Battle for Global Values', *Foreign Affairs*, January–February.
Booth, K. (1991) 'Security and Emancipation', *Review of International Studies*, 17:4, pp. 313–26.
Booth, K. (ed.) (2005) *Critical Security Studies and World Politics*, London, Lynne Rienner.
Braidotti, Rosi, Clare Colebrook and Patrick Hanafin (eds.) (2009) *Deleuze and Law: Forensic Futures*, Basingstoke: Palgrave.
Buchanan, Ian and Adrian Parr (eds.) (2006) *Deleuze and the Contemporary World*, Edinburgh: Edinburgh University Press.
Burguete Cal y Mayor, Araceli (2003) 'The De Facto Autonomous Process: New Jurisdictions and Parallel Governments in Rebellion', in Jan Rus, Rosalva Aída Hernández Castillo and Shannan L. Mattiace (eds.), *Mayan Lives, Mayan Utopias: The Indigenous Peoples of Chiapas and the Zapatista Rebellion*, Lanham, MD: Rowman and Littlefield.
Buzan, B. (1991) *People, States and Fear: An Agenda for International Security Studies in the Post Cold War Era*, Boulder: Lynne Rienner.
Buzan, B., O. Waever and J. de Wilde (1998) *Security a New Framework for Analysis*, Boulder, Lynne Rienner: 1998.
Dillon, Michael (2007) 'Governing Terror: The State of Emergency of Bio-Political Emergence', *International Political Sociology*, 1:1, pp. 7–28.
Dillon, Michael and Julian Reid (2009) *The Liberal Way of War: Killing to Make Life Live*, London: Routledge.
Deleuze, Gilles (1988) *Bergsonism*, trans. H. Tomlinson, New York: Zone.
Deleuze, Gilles (1990) *Negotiations: 1972–1990*, trans. M. Joughin, New York: Columbia University Press.
Deleuze, Gilles (1999) *Foucault*, trans. S. Hand, London: Continuum.
Deleuze, Gilles (2004) *Desert Islands and Other Texts: 1953–1974*, trans. M. Taormina, New York: Semiotext(e)
Deleuze, Gilles (2006) *Nietzsche and Philosophy*, trans. H. Tomlinson, London: Continuum.
Deleuze, Gilles and Félix Guattari (1994) *What is Philosophy?* trans. G. Burchell and H. Tomlinson, London: Verso.
Deleuze, Gilles and Félix Guattari (2002) *A Thousand Plateaus*, trans. B. Massumi, London: Continuum.
Derrida, Jacques (1984) 'Deconstruction and the Other', in R. Kearney (ed.), *Dialogues With Contemporary Continental Thinkers*, Manchester: Manchester University Press.
Duffield, Mark (2007) *Development, Security and Unending War: Governing the World of Peoples*, Cambridge: Polity Press.
Duran de Huerta, Marta and Nicholas Higgins (1999) 'An Interview with Subcomandante Insurgente Marcos', *International Affairs*, 75:2, pp. 269–79.
Earle, Duncan and Jean Simonelli (2005) *Uprising of Hope: Sharing the Zapatista Journey to Alternative Development*, Oxford: Alta Mira Press.
El Kilombo (2007) *Beyond Resistance: Everything. An Interview with Subcomandante Insurgente Marcos*, Durham, NC: Paperboat Press.

Evans, Brad (2008) 'The Zapatista Insurgency: Bringing the Political Back into Conflict Analysis', *New Political Science*, 30:4, pp. 497–520.

Evans, Brad (2009) 'Revolution Without Violence', *Peace Review*, 21:1, pp. 85–94.

Evans, Brad (2010) 'Terror in All Eventuality', Special Symposium on Deleuze and War, *Theory and Event*, 13:3.

Evans, Brad and Michael Hardt (2010) 'Barbarians to Savages: Liberal War Inside and Out', Special Symposium on Deleuze and War, *Theory and Event*, 13:3.

Falk, Richard (1995) *On Humane Governance: Towards a New Global Politics*, Cambridge: Polity Press.

Habermas, Jürgen (1987) *The Philosophical Discourse of Modernity*, trans. F. Lawrence, Cambridge: Polity.

Hardt, Michael and Antonio Negri (1994) *Labor of Dionysus: A Critique of the State Form*, Minnesota: University of Minnesota Press.

Hardt, Michael and Antonio Negri (2000) *Empire*, Cambridge, MA: Harvard University Press.

Hardt, Michael and Antonio Negri (2004) *Multitude*, London: Hamish Hamilton.

Hardt, Michael and Antonio Negri (2010) *Commonwealth*, Cambridge, MA: Harvard University Press.

Higgins, Nicholas (2004) *Understanding the Chiapas Rebellion: Modernist Visions and the Invisible Indian*, Austin: University of Texas Press.

Holloway, John (2002) *Change the World Without Taking Power*, London: Pluto Press.

Ignatieff, Michael (2003) *Empire Lite: Nation-building in Bosnia, Kosovo and Afghanistan*, London: Vintage.

Kilcullen, David (2009) *The Accidental Guerrilla: Fighting Small Wars in the Midst of a Big One*, Oxford: Oxford University Press.

Lambert, Gregg (2008) 'Deleuze and the Political Ontology of "The Friend" (philos)', in Ian Buchanan and Nicholas Thoburn (eds.), *Deleuze and Politics*, Edinburgh: Edinburgh University Press.

Marcos, Subcomandante (1994) *In Our Dreams We Have Seen Another World*, Zapatista Communiqué: March.

Marcos, Subcomandante (1999a) *Under Siege*, Zapatista Communiqué: August.

Marcos, Subcomandante (1999b) *The Zapatistas and Newton's Apple*, Zapatista Communiqué: May.

Marcos, Subcomandante (1999c) *From the Underground Culture to the Culture of Resistance*, Zapatista Communiqué: October.

Marcos, Subcomandante (2001) 'Interview Between Julio Garcia and Subcomandante Marcos', *Proceso*, 11 March, pp. 10–16.

Marcos, Subcomandante (2002) 'The Fourth World War Has Begun', in T. Hayden (ed.), *The Zapatista Reader*, New York: Nation Books, pp. 270–85.

Marcos, Subcomandante (2003a) *The Thirteenth Stele: Part Two*, Zapatista Communiqué: July.

Marcos, Subcomandante (2003b) 'The World: Seven Thoughts in May', *Rebeldia*.

Marcos, Subcomandante (2006a) *The Other Campaign*, San Francisco: City Lights.

Marcos, Subcomandante (2006b) *An Other Theory?* Zapatista Communiqué: March.

Mattiace, Shannon (2003) 'Maya Utopias: Rethinking the State', in Jan Rus, Rosalva Aída Hernández Castillo and Shannan L. Mattiace (eds.), *Mayan Lives, Mayan Utopias: The Indigenous Peoples of Chiapas and the Zapatista Rebellion*, Lanham, MD: Rowman and Littlefield.

May, Todd (2005) *Gilles Deleuze: An Introduction*, Cambridge: Cambridge University Press.

Olesen, Thomas (2000) 'Globalising the Zapatistas: from Third World Solidarity to Global Solidarity', *Third World Quarterly*, 25:1, pp. 255–67.

Olesen, Thomas (2005) *International Zapatismo: The Construction of Solidarity in the Age of Globalization*, London: Zed Books.

Patton, Paul (2008) 'Becoming-Democratic', in Ian Buchannan and Nicholas Thoburn (eds.), *Deleuze and Politics*, Edinburgh: Edinburgh University Press.

Ross, John (2005) 'Celebrating the Caracoles: Step by Step, the Zapatistas Advance On the Horizon', *Humboldt Journal of Social Relations*, 29:1, pp. 39–46.

Ross, John (2006) *Zapatistas: Making Another World Possible*, New York: Nation Books.

Schmitt, Carl (1996) *The Concept of the Political*, trans. G. Schwab, Chicago: University of Chicago Press.

Schmitt, Carl (2006) *Political Theology: Four Chapters on the Concept of Sovereignty*, trans. M. Hoelzl and G. Ward, Chicago: University of Chicago Press.

Sierra-Sierra, Maria (1995) 'Indian Rights and Customary Law in Mexico: A Study of the Nahuas in the Sierra de Puebla', *Law and Society Review*, 29:2, pp. 227–54.

Smith, Rupert (2006) *The Utility of Force: The Art of War in the Modern World*, London: Penguin.

Stivale, Charles (2008) *Gilles Deleuze's ABC's: The Folds of Friendship*, Baltimore: John Hopkins University Press.

Virilio, Paul (2003) *Ground Zero*, trans. C. Turner, London: Verso.

Wyn-Jones, R. (1999) *Security, Strategy, and Critical Theory*, Boulder: Lynne Rienner.

Žižek, Slavoj (2004) *Organs Without Bodies: Deleuze and Consequences*, London: Routledge.

Defining Activism

Marcelo Svirsky   Cardiff University

Abstract

Activism is defined in this paper as involving local instigations of new series of elements intersecting the actual, generating new collective enunciations, experimentations and investigations, which erode good and common sense and cause structures to swing away from their sedimented identities. By appealing to Spinozism, the paper describes the microphysics of the activist encounter with stable structures and the ways in which activism imposes new regimes of succession of ideas and affective variations in the power of action. Rather than understanding activism as supporting or leading social struggles, the definition of activism pursued here conceives it as an open-ended process and stresses the role of investigation in relation to practices within the social situations to which activism addresses itself.

Keywords: activism, revolution, intervention, encounter, ideas, affects

> O Romeo, Romeo, wherefore art thou Romeo?
> Deny thy father and refuse thy name, . . .
> 'Tis but thy name that is my enemy.
> Thou art thyself, though not a Montague.
> What's Montague? It is nor hand, nor foot,
> Nor arm, nor face, nor any other part
> Belonging to a man. O, be some other name!
> What's in a name? . . .
> So Romeo would, were he not Romeo call'd,
> Retain that dear perfection which he owes
> Without that title. Romeo, doff thy name . . .
> (*Romeo and Juliet*, 2, 2, 33–47)

Deleuze Studies Volume 4: 2010 supplement: 163–182
DOI: 10.3366/E1750224110001182
© Edinburgh University Press
www.eupjournals.com/dls

The proper name, functioning as a colour-line in this dramatic work, creates a dividing gulf – an obstacle that impedes a love – which, for Juliet, can only be fulfilled in the after-life of the name, beyond the violence of the couple's actual subjectivities. Here, Juliet's plea is not a lament, nor a banal cry of grief. It is far more significant; it is a discovery, or better, a rebellion in itself. Two moments are simultaneously involved in it. First, Juliet reproaches the organising function of the name in relation to the pre-personal body – 'Tis but thy name that is my enemy: Thou art thyself, though not a Montague.' And second, in order for this reproach to become an active challenge, Juliet urges Romeo to dissent, to 'doff thy name' – to abandon it – demanding that he transcend his own organisation and alter the logic imposed by his name, for the sake of a bastard love. Her affect already recognises that the possibility of a prohibition 'would require *both persons and names*' (Deleuze and Guattari 1983: 161).

Juliet thus asks Romeo to detach his body from the subjective territory of the Montague – 'Deny thy father...' (Reynolds 2009: 50). The two moments expressed here – the discovery of an organisation taking place and the call for action – are united in a critical attitude towards that which suffocates love, which, for the twosome, is really that which suffocates life. However, we must notice that what turns this attitude into an inflective relation to life lies in the relation between these two moments. Juliet's rejection of the organising function of the name in relation to the body – 'What's Montague? It is nor hand, nor foot, nor arm, nor face, nor any other part' – is an invitation to each body part to reclaim its autonomy, and to enter into the transversality of love. Her inquiry makes clear that the opposition to, or negation of, the state of things in the actual ('Tis but thy name that is my enemy') is to be subordinated to an affirmation of life through the potentiality of new assemblages to come, assemblages that halo the actual and are associated with a particular state of things ('without that title...'). What comes first, anyway, if we may speculate, is the positivity of the love running between Juliet and Romeo throughout their encounter.

This is their first affective discovery, which draws them into a search for alternatives. The negation is secondary due to the character of the inquiry: it has the power to make the reader wonder the unthinkable for the sake of performing the impossible love: does an arm, or a face, have a name? What does it mean to change a name? Juliet's inquiry thus creates the idea of another rhythm in which the love might be consummated. In this way her intervention joyfully affects the play, shifting the reader from one degree of reality to another. Here Juliet is, in a Deleuzian sense, fabulating, hallucinating 'a couple to come' (Deleuze 1995: 174). She incites Romeo to depart from the protective world of his own familial fabulations, this time in the Bergsonian sense (cf. Bogue 2006: 202–23).[1] Another idea of love starts to condense throughout the scene, one indicative of an alternative image of the encounter of Juliet and Romeo.

There are three interconnected practical qualities present in Juliet's radicalism:[2] a confrontation with a stratifying organisation (the name and its filiative association); a situational engagement (Juliet's demand for Romeo to engage actively and intervene in his circumstances to produce another sociability, that is, another encounter which might enable their love); and, lastly, an inquiring attitude towards the actual – a militant investigation which eludes the pincers of royal science and its representations (the place of the family in the city of Verona, the tribal prohibitions, and so on). As a necessary step in the creation of new conditions, Juliet interrogates the conditions she wishes to leave. It is from the perspective of the third quality that we should read her enigmatic call at the beginning of the scene, intended to shake Romeo from his familial knot: 'Wherefore art thou Romeo?' – a genealogical call asking for reasons, interrogating the processes by which Romeo has come to own and still retains his name. Juliet directs her question towards Romeo's positioning in the world, interrogating his commitment and obedience to the attachments and stratifications now trapping him in immobility. From this perspective, 'Wherefore art thou?' means: 'What are your reasons for clinging to, in what ways are you committed to, your particular name and your way of life?' Or, as Deleuze and Guattari might put it: 'What are your microfascisms, Romeo?' In other words, Juliet's speech suggests that we should abandon the organised and patriarchal sense of the state of things (the name) by way of problematising *our relations* with other bodies, ideas and things in their actual state, not in general, but in an encounter within the situation in which they dwell. This calls for a reconsideration of the present composition of such relations. Indeed, ultimately, it is *a call to arms*, a call for new and better encounters – an approach I shall call the activist problematic.

I. Introduction

This brief detour through Shakespeare introduces us to the main focus of this article: to try to develop a conceptualisation of activism, working towards a definition. As we shall see, this will involve a return to the practical qualities we have just discerned in Juliet's speech. The concept of activism I envisage here is intended to open up what is analysed, making possible further connections and intersections, and bolstering activism itself. Only when we manage to create a productive relationship between the material aspect of the assemblage ('the intermingling of bodies reacting to one another' [Deleuze and Guattari 1987: 88]), on the one hand, and its discursive aspect, on the other, is representation eluded, allowing us to open the actual up to a more transparent relation with the virtual. In other words, activism has to be also present *in* the concept, stirring both thought and action. From this, we can see why there is little interest here either in the investigation of individual motives or in a normative framework. For instance, the psychological and social mechanisms used in political psychology to explain activism in terms of the structure of causality between the individual psyche and the action itself – such as parental inculcation, principled education, political morality, universal moral duty, social altruism, and so on (see, for example, Gross 1997) – in fact explain very little concerning the empirical relationships between bodies and things. Such mechanisms do not account for the body of the activist, the field of action, the assemblages involved, and the multitude affecting and being affected. The tendency of such psychology to search for the origins of political actions in terms of the theorisation of psycho-social motives appears misplaced when we think of the world in terms of fluxes of incessant creation.

Spinozism, as Deleuze contends, 'confers on finite beings a power of existence' that is never exhausted, and which 'bears with it a corresponding and inseparable capacity to be affected, [which is] *always exercised*', in an infinity of ways (Deleuze 1992: 91, 93; emphasis added). In other words, the power of acting is not something to be found in a personality of this or that type, nor necessarily in one specific environment rather than another. More simply,

> We can know by reasoning that the power of action is the sole expression of our essence, the sole affirmation of our power of being affected. But this knowledge remains abstract. We don't know what this power is, nor how we may acquire or discover it. *And we will certainly never know this, if we do not concretely try to become active.* (Deleuze 1992: 226; emphasis added)

Instead of theorising incentives, it is better to explore by experimentation that which is already actively varying. Western normative ethics have tried to impose a democratic framework that limits and contains nomadic forms of resistance (the concept and practice of civil society bear the hallmark of all forms of that containment). But merely by creating distinctions between moral worlds, such normative ethics do nothing to further the exploration and intensification of present activist potentialities.

It is crucial for what follows that we examine the relationship between activism and the concept of revolution. Deleuze and Guattari clarify what revolution means: 'schizophrenising the existing power structure, making it vibrate to a new rhythm, making it change from within, without at the same time becoming a schizophrenic' (Buchanan 2008: 10; Deleuze and Guattari 1983). Therefore, revolution is given in the passage of a structure from rhythm A to rhythm B (the structure changing in the passage), where the structure can that of a social, political or economic system, a system of friendship, an educational system, a household, an individual person, a specific human-animal system (for example bovine slaughter regulations, or practices of species preservation), a field of art, or of any other stable natural or social environment. However, it is important to stress that we are not advocating here a sequential model of revolution, one determined by a telos adopted in advance. As revolutionaries, we always exist in many dimensions, in the midst of that from which we try to escape and struggle against, interwoven with the material we start to experiment with. It is the passage that is revolutionary, not the final arrival at a new rhythm. And yet, activism is not itself that passage of rhythms; rather, it is a temporary sub-rhythm of denunciation, wounding the first rhythm, from which it carves out a becoming into new territories. As Raunig explains, drawing on Holloway's works on the Zapatista movement: 'it is more the first steps into seemingly new terrain, posited on the old terrain, fighting against this old terrain and using it at the same time to transform it into something different' (Raunig 2007: 41–2).

Always starting as a wound of alterity within the habitual, activism refers to that fleeting fraction of encounters and connections still not engaged in the organisation of the second rhythm. If, following Guattari, we conceive the machine as being in opposition to structure (Guattari 1984: 111–20), then we may conceive activism as machinic, that is to say, plugging a movement of deterritorialisation into a territorial assemblage, and thereby activating the territory for further connections (Deleuze and Guattari 1987: 333). This causes the assemblage to swing 'between a territorial closure that tends to restratify [it] and a deterritorialising movement that, on the contrary, connects [it] with the Cosmos' (337). When activism connects itself to a system, an established relation of forces is distracted, and to some extent diverted into a far-from-equilibrium state. In other words, we learn from Deleuze that the revolutionary passage occurs when a system is pushed beyond a critical threshold, moving from a state of equilibrium into a state far from equilibrium (see Bonta and Protevi 2004). As an assemblage of encounters pushing the system towards new states, activism is one of the causes bringing about evolution and re-creation within the system. Nothing concerning the success or betrayal of the revolutionary passage is relevant to us here; rather, the focus is on the assemblages of affects agitating stable systems in order to tip them in non-linear directions. As a sign of denunciation, activist practices trace out and map the lines of a society at specific zones – its intensities and boundaries – with a view to grafting an outside onto them. In this way, they become indicative of those zones' new potentialities. By installing themselves in official territories, activist practices thus become the harbingers of a new openness.

There is, however, no dissociative distinction between activism and revolution; rather, activism infuses the concept and practice of revolution with an incessant discomforting movement that helps to protect new revolutionary forms of organisation from the dangers of stratification and its oppressive side effects. In this perspective, activism nurtures revolution, keeping it alive. Here, Raunig's treatment of the concept of the revolutionary machine, used to explore missed concatenations between art and revolution during the nineteenth and twentieth centuries, might help clarify the relationship between the two concepts. Following Negri's works from the 1970s, and Hardt and Negri's *Empire* (2000), Raunig adopts the 'triad model of the revolutionary machine' as comprised simultaneously of insurrection, resistance and constituent power (see Raunig 2007: 25–66). For Raunig, insurrection is the mediating component that concatenates the revolutionary screams of horror – the expression of resistance, and hope – and the expression of constituent power (see 41–8). Immanently, the three components are all present in activism, but the irruptive character of insurrection – its 'temporary flare' (56), compared with the more laborious character of resistance and constituent power – make it a better basis for exploring the relationship between activism and revolution. Contra Raunig, the division he proposes between a time of duration of the permanent molecular revolution (expressed by resistance and constituent power) and a time of rupture (expressed by the event of insurrection) runs the risk of dispensing with the latter when the former is actualised through processes that deepen the fascistic tendencies in the new organisation. Incessant activist ruptures are vital to maintaining a rhythm of infinite movement in a revolutionary machine. Activism, we might say, is revolution's *conatus*, its tendency or instinct to persevere in its revolutionary power; thus we have a series of activist ruptures within revolutionary processes – the power of creation as constituent power remains faithful to the eternal return of difference, and draws itself away from the entrapments of constituted power. Deleuze and Guattari pointed to the coupling of resistance and constituent power in their treatment of the war machine; opposition, resistance, can engage in revolutionary action '*only on the condition that they simultaneously create something else*' (Deleuze and Guattari 1987: 423).

Although Raunig, as did Hardt and Negri before him, portrays insurrection as essentially spectacular (think the Paris Commune of 1871, the Russian Kolkhozes, or the Zapatistas), it is possible to understand insurrection as a perceptible act of opposition to a ruling power or habit, without tying it to a Hollywood-style image. For instance, a Bartlebyan moment of refusal is an act of opposition which might infect a state of affairs and develop into an activism,[3] whether it occurs in a scrivener's office, in a call for a love, or at home through the forces exerted by a change in posture of a woman's body when a patriarchal tradition is challenged. It is in the insolence and intensity of the challenge posed against constituted power (whatever its form or mode), and its associated way of life, that activism is located, and not necessarily on the barricades or protest marches.

Activism's logic is thus interventionist and operationally hyper-active. First, it latches onto certain zones and injects external forces, causing a differential change in the system. Second, it involves an emphatic attention to life, similar to Bergson's attentive recognition; that is to say, it evaluates each object by causing it to pass through different planes in order to gain a critical appreciation of it; at the same time it frees itself from the distractions of habitual recognition that social systems impose upon us (cf. Deleuze 1989: 44–68).

II. A Second Distinction

For Deleuze, life has an ever-changing problematic structure. Every multiplicity changes its virtual structure by way of actualisations, that is, by passing into temporary solutions (the virtual differentiates itself and becomes different from itself in the process). This brings forth new conditions for the creation of the new in the real (see Smith 2007). Aided by various representational and mystifying machines, patterns and forms hide these processes; further, stratified patterns have the power to create interests, which in turn force neurotic and paranoiac functions onto desire (see Deleuze and Guattari 1983). As a result, there is a backwash of narrowing our belief in the potentiality of virtual structures. With little belief in the virtuality of life, always interwoven with social obedience, a peaceful and wide zone of sedated individuals is secured. Balibar's Spinozism explains how this passivity is engendered:

> When an individual is passive, it is because his soul has been subjugated by the circulation of the affects and by the 'general ideas' that inhabit the collective imagination... His body too will have been simultaneously subjugated by the unrestrained influence of all the surrounding bodies. (Balibar 1998: 94–5)

From this passage it becomes clear why activist practices take it to be part of their responsibility to recirculate affects away from the 'general ideas' of a society (or of smaller multiplicities). In so far as, collectively, we vehemently stick to the dominant forms of life (practices and discourses) without any critical intake, we deepen our complicity with the burial of the virtual, as well as with the betrayal of the infinity of life. Activism finds here its most basic function: the unfolding of a Julietian critical engagement with dominant forms of life and their self-reproductive representations – the 'general ideas'. In this sense, activism is that which diverts life from its tendency to eternalise and deepen itself in its actual forms, that which pledges to 'connect the roots or trees back up with a rhizome' (Deleuze and Guattari 1987: 14).

A critical engagement can be deployed at least in two ways, following a distinction between two conceptions of how to revolutionise the world (Colectivo Situaciones 2001: 31). The first is characteristic of traditional leftist politics, which base their political struggles on a yearning to change the world. Here, activism is expressed in the encounter of forces, bodies and things which furthers direct struggles against multiplicities, and in which singularities are perceptibly isolated by agglomerations of the ordinary. In this version, strategically, activism collides with the stable structure, producing a sort of dialectical relation. Theatrically, the subject in this drama is the resulting antagonism. Operationally, it aims at a transformation of the state of things that may amount to a combinatorial view of novelty: 'only little more than the rearrangement of matter in the universe into ever new forms' (Smith 2007: 2).

In contrast, some contemporary forms of escape – those proliferating alternative life-experiences – are not concerned with changing the world, but rather would like 'to produce it anew' (Colectivo Situaciones 2001: 31). These activisms problematise the structure of the existence of the actual form by contemplating and experimenting with the changing conditions of the new – 'testing... alternative forms of social organisation' (Raunig 2007: 60) – bringing about change not in a combinatorial fashion, but in the nature of particular areas of life. By embracing the whole of the real and not only the actual, new singular points are created by changing the multiplicity in question. What is most significant in these sorts of activisms is that resistance is thought and operated not in a dialectical contraposition to constituted power (*potestas*) in a reactive mode; rather, though an unavoidable relation of conflict with constituted power comes into being, resistance here unfolds as immanent difference which draws on the natural force of creation (*potentia*).[4] From this perspective, Raunig's distinction between resistance and constituent power appears redundant; the two are not just linked but mutually implicated.

This version of activism multiplies new practices, and in doing so bypasses existent stable practices and their manifestations of oppression.[5] The first mode of activism assumes that solidifications and closures can be challenged. The second mode leans on the assumption that oppression cannot take on everything; this mode always opens up a reflexive distance that is absent in the first mode. As praxis, the first mode of political activism is reactive, polemical, litigious, and engaged in incessant argumentation. As examples we can think of pressure groups for legislation change, High Court petitions, protests, persuasion campaigns, and so on. The second mode is more quiet but ontologically invasive. Examples include alternative modes of education, promoting new ways of life, rethinking narratives, investigating the conditions of oppression, and so on. Comparing the two versions, we should keep in mind that there is a 'feedback' aspect in confrontational activism: challenging a practice or an idea has a nurturing effect.

III. The Functions of Activism

Activism is not a secluded or hidden phenomenon. It is extroverted, involved in the generation of public events. Most activisms I know of take very seriously the repercussions of their actions within the broader society, both locally or/and globally. Many activists publish reports on their practices and experiences, have internet sites, or, more traditionally, distribute printed material to the general public; indeed, it is well known that they are anxious to encourage the public to participate in and attend their discursive dramas.

Ill-advisedly, some forms of activism develop into missionary activity, and sometimes wind-up as messianic. This carries the risk of destroying the very becoming characteristic of activism. Any presumption on the part of activists to define life in moral terms – instead of understanding their activity as promoting potentialities – functions to homogenise activism and fill the plane of consistency with energy of just one type. This excess then becomes equivalent to a drastic reduction in the potential of bodies, hence the indices of heterogeneity and of transversality are reduced as well. This version of activism, which is unfortunately always present to some extent, generally takes the form of a paranoid reaction to the world on the part of well-defined and determined subjects – 'the Stalins of the little groups' (Deleuze and Parnet 2002: 139). The terror they impose, like that of the majoritarian society, is one of reterritorialisation.

What is it that activism brings about? What occurs in the encounter between activist practices (body A) and its spectators (body B)? What can be said of that encounter? We are going to need to anchor off Spinozist shores (*Ethics*, Books II and III). First we need to add to the drama a necessary third body, C, which is that body of stable relations (social, political, educational, cultural, and so on) into which activism taps. We already know that, for most of us and for most parts of our lives, a relation of commitment and obedience is what characterises our relationship to C (B–C).

What activism does, when it acts, is introduce an initial movement of deterritorialisation into the internal relations of body C, forcing a variation in the latter's relations to the spectators (body B), and in the interim creating a new relation between activism and the spectators. Let us take a simple example to see how the three main bodies may encounter one another in a concrete situation. In Israel, a segregationist educational system (body C) complements a broader structure of social segregation between Jews and Palestinians, citizens of Israel. In 1998, a group of parents (body A) set up an initiative to establish a bilingual, Arabic–Hebrew School in the northern region of the Galilee. Sufficient numbers within the local communities (body B) were enthusiastic enough to join in, and, ultimately, the school named *Galilee* was established and has operated ever since (see Svirsky et al. 2007; Svirsky 2010). In this example, reaching new operational rhythms was bound up with the repressive operations of older rhythms (mainly rooted in an obsession with collective identity).[6]

As the encounter begins to express itself, effects on the different bodies start to circulate, caused by the intermingling of affections between them (affections might include: one's route home changes because of a demonstration; police repress demonstrators; a class is cancelled by the student union; humanitarian relief reaches a population under siege; an alternative school building is found; and so on). Following Spinoza's epistemological parallelism, we may say that to every object or thing there corresponds an idea (Deleuze 1992: 113–4). Following the activist encounter then, at least two sorts of ideas are being affirmed on the bodies: ideas that have friction, itself caused by activism as their object, and ideas that have as their objects different aspects of the system of relationships A–B–C. The affections caused by the activist encounter arouse different spiritual and bodily sympathies and antipathies, which are tantamount to the ideas of these affections (attesting to different degrees of compossibility between the bodies in the encounter and their different capacities for being affected). Correspondingly, the power of acting of the bodies involved in the encounter either increases or decreases. Whichever is the case, we are, according to the definition of Spinozist affects, in the presence of a regime of the succession of ideas, which is followed by a variation in the power of action or in the force of existing. Deleuze explains that 'this kind of melodic line of continuous variation' is defined by Spinoza as affect (Deleuze 1978: 3–4). It is not unlikely that the circulation of new passions will be one of the effects of an activist initiative. When faced with the eruption of a new activism, spectators may react with either enthusiasm or anger, or some permutation of the two. But activism makes clear that there is no linear correspondence between such passions and the variation in the power of acting (increase or decrease), since the displeasure or rage triggered by a certain activism may lead ultimately to counter-activism.

The key point here concerns the slide or passage between two different states of ideas in the bodies involved, and, especially, the attitudes of the bodies in respect of the ways they come to perceive the functioning of the stable body C under the activist attack. These perceptions will depend on the ways we understand the activist encounter in its relations both with the social stable body under attack and with us, the spectators; they depend on the kind of ideas we have of these relationships and effects. Though 'our ideas of affections do of course "involve" their own cause, that is, the objective essence of the external body', it is also true that 'as long as I remain in the perception of affection, I know nothing of the [action]'. Thus, my idea of a particular demonstration, of a new school, of a humanitarian aid project, and so on, is only partial, and of the lowest kind in Spinoza's terms, since they only '*indicate* a state of our body' (Deleuze 1992: 146–7; 1978: 6).

What this kind of knowledge creates is an image that only expresses the objects (the activist encounter and the relationships between the bodies) by their effects on us. How bad are these inadequate ideas for our analysis of activism? Practically speaking, what would it mean for us, as spectators, to have a higher knowledge of causes – that is, to have 'notion-ideas' of the activist encounter and to become the cause of our own affects, rather than having merely 'affection-ideas' of it? And how might activism help us to move away, at least partially, from the passions that the accidental pattern of the encounter affirms in us? All these questions are important in so far as they contribute to the more general question of how activism approximates the threshold of becoming a project of alternative collective action.

A notion-idea, says Deleuze, 'no longer concerns the effect of another body on mine, it's an idea which concerns and which has for its object the agreement or disagreement of the characteristic relations between two bodies' (Deleuze 1978: 10).[7] This notion of agreement (and disagreement) between the encountering bodies needs to be seen in light of Deleuze's account of the Spinozist idea of 'what a body is capable of': its significance depends on our efforts to know which affections we and others are capable of, given our society, our culture, our specific historical life, and so on. From the point of view of the notion-idea, drawing up an ethological chart of the compositions of relations seems to be essential for activism. Put simply, this means developing a reasonable knowledge of 'what a people can bear' when they are confronted with practices such as those introduced by activism (contrary to what critics may think, this is not necessarily equivalent to developing practices which are in harmony with the actual). What we can bear politically is seen here as linked to what our bodies can do in relation to a specific political issue. Reasonable knowledge leans on the assumption that affecting others joyfully should not be considered a sin for activists. For Spinoza, reason is, after all, a problem of becoming, and self-righteous 'anti-becoming' attitudes abound among activists. This question of reasonable knowledge takes us back to Juliet's investigation of the conditions for a new, more agreeable encounter with Romeo. And the idea of investigation being part of activist practice leads us on to what has been implemented lately by activists and researchers as *militant research* (see Biddle et al. 2007; Malo de Molina 2004; Benasayag and Sztulwark 2000). As defined in 2009 by the Collective 'Precarias a la Deriva' (Madrid), militant research is a process of re-appropriating our own capacity for *world*-making, which questions, problematises and pushes the real through a series of concrete procedures. More forcefully, for the Argentinean 'Colectivo Situaciones', activism is not about leading or supporting struggles but about dwelling actively in the situation – investigating it – with a view to the emergence of an alternative sociability (Colectivo Situaciones 2001: 37). The first premise of activist militant research is that there is no global knowledge on how things should be; rather, activism entails an engagement in the production of situational or local knowledge. This is why the activist-machine is a paradigmatic case of learning in Deleuze's sense – a constant experimentation of the discordant exercise of the faculties disconnected from every form of identity (cf. Deleuze 1994: 164–7).

In terms of how this might be done, organising protests on behalf of the rights of weakened groups, or filming their experiences to gain sympathy (or prizes), is not enough. What is needed is the combination of activist research with populations experiencing alternative sociabilities (Colectivo Situaciones 2001: 38).[8] Here resides one of the major differences between investigation-based activists and classical civil society NGOs, which tend to adopt an a priori agenda for change. It is not that regular acts of protest lack any significance; rather, the claim here is that they cannot be seen as the focus of revolutionary action. The situational production of knowledge should be seen in direct relation to the difference between changing the world and creating it anew, with revolutionary activism being committed to the latter.

It is true that the activist-machine 'kills the joy' (Ahmed 2009) of those fearing the effects of the activists' revolutionary horizon on their peaceful life and privileges. In so doing, activism necessarily undermines solidarity. But producing unhappiness cannot be activism's goal or sense. Although sadness inevitably accompanies every activism – even those supporting the action may feel 'local sadness' (Deleuze 1978: 9) – it is hard to see the point to causing sad affects in others. We already know one of the activist's bad habits: to induce in us sadness and resentment as the necessary preparation for forming a critical attitude which will make us politically active.[9] But there is no good reason to look for such bad encounters as a matter of strategy (tactical bad encounters might be considered circumstantially, assuming an awareness of their destructive effect on all bodies involved). '[N]othing in sadness ... can induce you from within sadness to form a notion common to something which would be common to the bodies which affect you with sadness and to your own' (11). At times, as activists, we feel the urge 'to make things clear' to help people to understand a particular issue by engaging in radical action, as if they are in need of a brighter light in their life. But pure intensity does not necessarily lead to a good encounter: 'a blue that is too intense for my eyes will not make me say it's beautiful' (14).

From a Spinozist ethical perspective then, working towards a level of strategic knowledge concerning the ways bodies A, B and C can be mutually affected goes hand in hand with the need to 'organise encounters' as 'the effort to form an association of men in relations that can be combined' (Deleuze 1992: 261). The incredible amount of time activists spend on articulating ideologies will count for little if their practices are separated from a strategy that includes, at least partially, entering into joyous participation with others – meaning, pursuing compossible relations with them. Activism's role is not to secure that compossibility, but to open up and remain open to its potentiality.

Let us move on to another of activism's functions. The inadequate idea brought forth by the affections between the bodies involved in the activist encounter has two sides: 'they "involve privation" of the knowledge of their cause, but are at the same time effects that in some way "involve" that cause' (Deleuze 1992: 149). The second aspect, explains Deleuze, contains something positive, indispensable for the passage into adequate ideas, which is, in fact, the power of thinking, or what is enabled in the first instance by the faculty of imagination (149–50). This natural condition not only leads to the conceptualisation of the passage into common notions, but also means that we might have a multiplicity of several and different affection-ideas – inadequate ideas. Reacting to an activist action, we might form a specifically fearful image of a particular intervention as the result of becoming affected with anger. But, in addition, the intermingling of affections in the activist encounter also actualises the formal idea of the revolution. Whichever of the affects it arouses, the variation of affection-ideas caused by the activist encounter involve a sort of 'background noise' – a singular range of frequencies of perceptions – involving an idea (inadequate as it might be) of a 'people to come' hovering above and intersecting with activist practices. In other words, given that 'the ideas we have are signs, indicative images impressed in us' (147), we are claiming that the disrupting action of activism imprints in us a hallucinating sign which indicates the formal presence of a revolution. This is why we said before that activism is not itself the revolutionary passage of rhythms in a structure, but only announces that passage's potential existence. It is apparently to this feature of activism that Appadurai directs his words:

> The imagination has become an organised field of social practices, a form of work... and a form of negotiation between sites of agency... and globally defined fields of possibility... The imagination is now central to all forms of agency, is itself a social fact... [it] is today a staging ground for action, and not only for escape. (Appadurai 1996: 31)

This function of activism stands in relation with the other, that of striving for the formation of common notions. Though causing bad encounters for many, for the 'background noise' not to become dead noise and activism not to be washed away, activism needs to avoid creating an excess of the unhappiness it inevitably causes. For example, when activists clash with the institutional forces responsible for raising separation walls (the Berlin Wall, the West Bank wall, and so on), they still need not to overlook the idea or possibility of more agreeable encounters taking place between the segregated bodies.

IV. Method

The life of an activist is marked by a sense of urgency, anxiety and alertness to a life under attack. It involves both a type of discomfort with the world, and a life-force seeking out the new; activism is therefore in and of itself turbulent and restless. It threatens our neat and secure life. It is the pure form of terror. This is perhaps why the drama of activism can be so annoying for spectators, and so dangerous for activists.

To describe activism's machinations I turn to Deleuze's theory of the series, as formulated in *The Logic of Sense* (1990). The claim here is that every activist-machine working in a particular zone of social, cultural or political action comes into being through the creation of a new series of interconnected elements as a result of alternative connections with (a) given registers of the actualised world, and (b) new imaginations. The new series engendered by the activist-machine never isolates itself, but rather aims at producing a communication of divergence with a specific official series within a particular zone of thought and action. This is analogous to a situation in which, suddenly and without warning, we introduce a new set of actors from among the audience or the street, to become an integral part of a performance on stage – or, if you prefer, we add an entirely new deck into the middle of a card game, or bring on a third team during a football game. In all of these instances a new game is created; by dissolving the former rules we bring new connections to bear upon the large conjunctions to which subjects and objects are currently in thrall, thereby changing the structure of the game. Once such a connection between the series has been established, a disjunctive and productive movement of distancing between the old and the new series appears, certain modes of excess start to circulate, and, finally, new products and flows come into play.

For example, when the State of Israel, its governments and its Jewish majority insist upon referring to Israel as 'The Jewish State', they are appealing to a certain associated series of elements in order to affix a certain symbolic meaning to a structure that is 'haunted by a desire for eternity' (Guattari 1995: 37): Jewish-State-the-Biblical-Land, Jewish-State-Holocaust-European-debt, Jewish-State-the-few-against-the-many, Jewish-State-agricultural-revolution,   Jewish-State-stretching-out-its-hand-in-peace,   Jewish-State-the-only-democracy-in-the-Middle-East, and so on. Conversely, when activist groups in Israel/Palestine articulate the name of Israel with other elements that are 'shaped by a desire for abolition' (37) – such as Israel-Nakba, Israel-segregation-apartheid, Israel-Gaza-strip-blockade,   Israel-the-West-Bank-the-Wall,   Israel-discrimination-Arab-minority, Israel-militarism, and so forth – they are in fact appealing to an alternative series of real relations implicating the state's name. This second series attaches itself to the first series by implanting a differential correspondence between the respective elements of the series, thereby creating disequilibrium. As José Gil has pointed out, the true machine of innovation in Deleuze's thinking of the event is the disjunction as the synthetic movement of divergent terms (Gil 2008: 18). There is an excess of one series over the other through their common interface, in this case with the name of Israel functioning as the Empty Square, and enabling 'indirect interactions between elements devoid of so-called natural affinity' (Deleuze and Guattari 1987: 348).

Through the activist interlacement of a new series, a paradox is introduced: 'Paradox is initially that which destroys good sense as the only direction, but it is also that which destroys common sense as the assignation of fixed identities' (Deleuze 1990: 3). This being the case, we can understand why, today, both Zionists and their critics sense a certain discomfort when appealing to the name of the Jewish state. This forced encounter between the two series, instigated by activism, redefines the trajectory of the name of Israel – approximating this name to its problematic actualisations. From the activist-machine perspective, a straightforward proposition such as: 'It is the Jewish state that is oppressing, segregating and committing war-crimes' changes something in the way the struggle is expanded upon, since new, real connections and relations are being claimed.

The question, in the case of Israel and its name, becomes not whether Israel must be recognised as a Jewish state, but what this name expresses in terms of actual experiences and virtual potentials. In this respect, Derrida's treatment of the name of apartheid might be worth quoting, interspersed with references to the Middle-Eastern analogy:

> Those in power in South Africa [Israel] have not managed to convince the world, and first of all because, still today, they have refused to change the real, effective, fundamental meaning of their watchword: apartheid [the Jewish state]. A watchword is not just a name... is also a concept and a reality... [They]... wanted to keep the concept and the reality, while effacing the word, an evil word, *their* word. They have managed to do so in *their* official discourse, but that's all. Everywhere else in the world... people have continued to think that the word was indissolubly – and legitimately – welded to the concept and to the reality. (Derrida 1986: 163)

In the past, Derrida urged the world to call a thing by its name with regard to South African apartheid. In contrast with Juliet's plea, calling Israel by its preferred name 'will remain the "unique appellation" of this monstrous, unique, and unambiguous thing' (Derrida 1986: 159). By calling the thing by its name, while imposing a contretemps upon it, this part of the actual loses its grip on recent identifications. This is where we face the polyphony of the naming-function. On the one hand, in *Romeo and Juliet*, 'the proper name, when assigned to people, functions to consolidate... the subjective territories of individuals within a given society, that is, within an official culture' (Reynolds 2009: 48). On the other hand – as in the case of the names of the apartheid and the Jewish state: 'the naming-function provides a counter-tactic by which to undermine societies' mechanisms of control and surveillance' (280).

The connection between the two series of elements instigated by activism forges a new space of relations and a new structure in which a problematisation of social and political issues is brought to the fore. The connection – or *ligaçao* in Gil's terms – is what creates 'a critical distance between members of the same species' by introducing variation (Deleuze and Guattari 1987: 322). We are now in a position to dare to offer an alternative reading to the famous 'Lodge yourself' passage in *A Thousand Plateaus* (161): investigate; create an alternative series of elements having new visual, audible and material elements; investigate-experiment. Then, by making connections, this series should intersect the dominant series at different points; investigate-experiment. You will be overwhelmed by the apparition of new images and affections, and, as a result, a reconsideration of life becomes inevitable.

Notes

1. As Bogue explains, for Bergson, fabulation is a protective shield (against social dissolution) which 'goes hand in hand with religion in creating the myths of forces, myths, and deities that foster social cohesion and individual contentment' (Bogue 2006: 205). In Shakespeare's play, familialism takes the place of religion.
2. I follow here the way the Argentinean Colectivo Situaciones (2001) explain their perspective on *Contrapoder* ('counter-power'). For Benasayag and Sztulwark (2000), the contemporary *Contrapoder* is expressed by creative and constructionist struggles that are not derived from sadness and do not rely on models or seek central power. Rather, they produce an anti-systemic subjectivity and are situational in their operation.
3. To appropriate Bartleby beyond this point will be futile, since Bartleby, as Deleuze explains, 'is too smooth for anyone to be able to hang any particularity on him' (Deleuze 1997: 74). As such, Žižek's (2006) Bartlebyan politics – premised upon an essential movement of subtraction from the hegemonic system which both guarantees an outside and allows one to criticise contemporary forms of what he defines as pseudo-resistance – as well as Hardt and Negri's (2000) take on Bartleby as the iconic anti-Empire work-refusnik – are both excesses of interpretation (cf. Beverungen and Dunne 2007), desperate formalisations of Bartleby.
4. As Raunig explains, in *Foucault* (2006), 'Deleuze makes the point that a social field offers resistance before it is organised according to strategies' (Raunig 2007: 53). In Hardt and Negri's register, 'resistance is prior to power'.
5. Oppression here is understood as the oppression of creative processes. Aiming at the ontological conditions of creation, oppression is infinite stratification, i.e. the accumulative spatialisation, homogenisation and quantification of duration. Oppression is a natural tendency, the twin of creative processes. In its social register, oppression mystifies stratification using the logic of representation. It occurs everywhere, including throughout activist initiatives.
6. This means that the idea that a revolutionary initiative can construct itself in isolation from the 'general society' in a separate territory is a short-term illusion. I have explained elsewhere how *Galilee*, as an intercultural assemblage, is being thrown back into the dichotomies of ethnicity just because it doesn't confront properly the fact that *potestas* can't be ignored (see Svirsky 2010).
7. To clarify: the affection-idea is associated with the effects of the mixing of bodies in the encounter, whereas the notion-idea is associated with the degree of agreement or disagreement of the characteristic relations of the bodies.
8. Since their appearance in the late 1990s, Colectivo Situaciones have made several interventions-investigations with different groups, such as with 'escraches-groups' (actions aimed at unmasking mainly individuals involved in the last Argentinean dictatorship), with Tupamaros (a revolutionary movement that emerged in Uruguay during the 1960s), and with the 'Movimiento de Trabajadores Desocuapdos de Solano' (a movement of the unemployed in the locality of Solano). For an extensive list of their activities and their published literature see: http://www.situaciones.org
9. Sometimes activists are not that different from Spinoza's priest or despot, who needs the sadness of his audience and their feelings of guilt in order to influence them. But sadness can only diminish our power of acting.

References

Ahmed, Sara (2009) 'Killing Joy', lecture given at Cardiff University, 22 October 2009.

Appadurai, Arjun (1996) *Modernity at Large: Cultural Dimensions of Globalisation*, Massachusetts: University of Minnesota Press.

Arnott, Stephen J. (2001) 'Solipsism and the Possibility of Community in Deleuze's Ethics', *Contretemps*, 2, pp. 109–23.

Balibar, Etienne (1998) *Spinoza and Politics*, trans. Peter Snowdon, London: Verso.

Benasayag, Miguel and Diego Sztulwark (2000) *De La Potencia al Contrapoder*, Buenos Aires: De Mano a Mano.

Beverungen, Armin and Stephen Dunne (2007) 'I(d) Prefer Not To: Bartleby and the Excess of Interpretation', *Culture and Organization*, 13:2, pp. 171–83.

Biddle, Erika, S. Shukaitis and D. Graeber (eds.) (2007) *Constituent Imagination: Militant Investigations, Collective Theorization*, Edinburgh: AK Press.

Bogue, Ronald (2006) 'Fabulation, Narration and the People to Come', in Constantin V. Boundas (ed.) *Deleuze and Philosophy*, Edinburgh: Edinburgh University Press, pp. 202–25.

Bonta, M. and Protevi, J. (2004) *Deleuze and Geophilosophy: A Guide and Glossary*, Edinburgh: Edinburgh University Press.

Buchanan, Ian (2008) *Deleuze and Guattari's Anti-Oedipus: A Readers Guide*, London: Continuum.

Colectivo Situaciones (2001) *Contrapoder*, Buenos Aires: mano a mano.

Colectivo Situaciones (2005) 'Something More on Research Militancy: Footnotes on Procedures and (In)decisions', *Ephemera*, 5:4, pp. 602–14.

Colectivo Situaciones (2009) *Inquietudes en el Impasse: Dilemas Politicos del Presente*, Buenos Aires: Tinta Limon.

Deleuze, Gilles (1978) *Les Courses de Gilles Deleuze*, trans. Timothy S. Murphy, www.webdeleuze.com, 24/01/1978.

Deleuze, Gilles (1989) *Cinema 2: The Time-Image*, trans. Hugh Tomlinson and Robert Galeta, London: Athlone Press.

Deleuze, Gilles (1990) *The Logic of Sense*, trans. Mark Lester with Charles Stivale, ed. Constantin Boundas, New York: Columbia University Press.

Deleuze, Gilles (1992) *Expressionism in Philosophy: Spinoza*, trans. Martin Joughin, New York: Zone Books.

Deleuze, Gilles (1994) *Difference and Repetition*, trans. Paul Patton, New York: Columbia University Press.

Deleuze, Gilles (1995) 'Control and Becoming', in *Negotiations 1972–1990*, trans. Martin Joughin, New York: Columbia University Press, pp. 169–76.

Deleuze, Gilles (1997) 'Bartleby or, The Formula', in *Essays: Critical and Clinical*, trans. D. Smith and M. Greco, Minneapolis and London: University of Minnesota Press, pp. 68–90.

Deleuze, Gilles and Félix Guattari (1983) *Anti-Oedipus*, trans. Robert Hurley, Mark Seem and Helen R. Lane., Minneapolis: University of Minnesota Press.

Deleuze, Gilles and Félix Guattari (1987) *A Thousand Plateaus*, trans. Brian Massumi, Minneapolis: University of Minnesota Press.

Deleuze, Gilles and Claire Parnet (2002) *Dialogues II*, trans. Hugh Tomlinson and Barbara Habberjam, New York: Columbia University Press, pp. 124–147.

Deleuze, Gilles (2006) *Foucault*, trans. and ed. Sean Hand, London: Continuum.

Derrida, Jacques (1985) 'Racism's Last Word', trans. Peggy Kamuf, *Critical Inquiry*, 12, pp. 290–9.

Derrida, Jacques (1986) 'But, Beyond. . . (Open letter to Anne McClintock and Rob Nixon)', trans. Peggy Kamuf, *Critical Inquiry*, 13, pp. 155–70.

Gil, José (2008) *O Imperceptível Devir da Imanência – Sobre a Filosofia de Deleuze*, Lisbon: Relógio D'Água.

Gross, Michael (1997) *Ethics and Activism: The Theory and Practice of Political Morality*, Cambridge: Cambridge University Press.

Guattari, Félix (1984) *Molecular Revolution: Psychiatry and Politics*, trans. Rosemarie Sheed, Harmondsworth: Peregrine.

Hardt, Michael and Antonio Negri (2000) *Empire*, London: Harvard University Press.

Holloway, John (2002) *Change the World Without Taking Power: The Meaning of Revolution Today*, London and Ann Arbor, MI: Pluto Press.

Malo de Molina, Marta (2004) *Common Notions*; http://transform.eipcp.net/transversal/0406/malo/en#redir#redir

Melville, Herman (1986) 'Bartleby the Scrivener: A Tale of Wall Street', in H. Melville, *Billy Budd and Other Stories*, New York: Penguin.

Raunig, Gerald (2007) *Art and Revolution: Transversal Activism in the Long Twentieth Century*, trans. Aileen Derieg, Los Angeles: Semiotext(e).

Reynolds, Bryan (2009) *Transversal Subjects: from Montaigne to Deleuze after Derrida*, London: Palgrave.

Shakespeare, William (1980) *Romeo and Juliet*, ed. Brian Gibbons, London: Arden.

Smith, Daniel (2007) 'The Conditions of the New', *Deleuze Studies*, 1:1, pp. 1–22.

Svirsky, Marcelo (2009) 'A Stirring Alphabet of Thought', *Deleuze Studies*, 3:3, pp. 311–24.

Svirsky, Marcelo (2010) 'Captives of Identity: The Betrayal of Intercultural Cooperation', *Subjectivity*, forthcoming.

Svirsky, Marcelo, A. Mor-Sommerfeld, F. Azaiza and R. Hertz-Lazarowitz (2007) 'Bilingual Education and Practical Interculturalism in Israel: The Case of the Galilee', *The Discourse of Sociological Practice*, 8:1, pp. 55–81.

Žižek, Slavoj (2006) *The Parallax View*, Cambridge, MA: MIT Press.

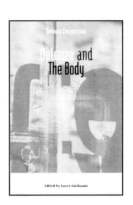

Edinburgh
University Press

Deleuze Studies Special Issue
Deleuze and Marx
by Dhruv Jain
January 2010 • 96 pp Pb
978 0 7486 3893 2 • £16.99

▶ Offers new perspectives on Deleuze's early work

▶ Illuminates new connections between Deleuze's and Marx's work

▶ Includes a critical re-reading of Deleuze's work

▶ Foregrounds a critique of Capitalism in Deleuze's work

▶ Contributors include: Bruno Bosteels, Alberto Toscano, Jason Read, Jeremy Gilbert, Simon Choat and Aidan Tynan

www.euppublishing.com/book/978-0-7486-3893-2

EUP JOURNALS ONLINE
Paragraph

ISSN   0264-8334

eISSN   1750-0176

Three issues per year

Find *Paragraph* at
www.eupjournals.com/PARA

Founded in 1983, *Paragraph* is a leading journal in modern critical theory. It publishes essays and review articles in English which explore critical theory in general and its application to literature, other arts and society.

Regular special issues by guest editors highlight important themes and figures in modern critical theory. *Paragraph* publishes regular special issues by guest editors that highlight important themes and key figures in modern critical theory. A selection of recent titles include:
- Rhythm in Literature after the Crisis in Verse
- Walter Benjamin between the Disciplines
- Extending Hospitality
- Cinema and the Senses
- Roland Barthes Retroactively
- Blanchot's Epoch
- Deleuze and Science
- Idea of the LIterary
- Jacques Rancière
- Men's Bodies
- Gender and Sexuality

Edinburgh University Press

**Register for
Table of Contents Alerts at
www.eupjournals.com**

The Warwick Journal of Philosophy
Volume 18 (2007)

Superior Empiricism

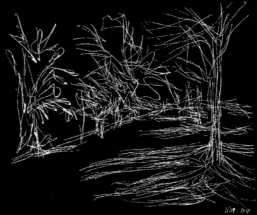

'If we had a choice between empiricism and the all-oppressing necessity of
thought of a rationalism which had been driven to the highest point, no free spirit
would be able to object to deciding in favour of empiricism.'

-F.W.J. von Schelling, *On the History of Modern Philosophy*

Pli is a journal of philosophy edited and produced by members of the Graduate School of the Department of Philosophy at the University of Warwick. *Pli* has no specific set of philosophical concerns but previous issues have tended to focus upon European philosophical traditions, reflecting the interests of the graduate community at Warwick. In particular, Pli has published translations of works otherwise unavailable in English by philosophers including Éric Alliez, Gilles Deleuze, Jacques Derrida, Michel Foucault, François Laruelle, Jean-François Lyotard, Jean-Luc Nancy, and Friedrich Nietzsche.

Volume 18 of *Pli* is a collection of papers dealing with the question of empiricism as it occurs in Dewey, Deleuze, Althusser, Levinas, Dilthey, James, Duns Scotus, Husserl, Schelling, Spinoza, Matisse, Bergson and Sartre, as well as a number of reviews of recent publications in continental philosophy.

http://www.warwick.ac.uk/philosophy/pli_journal/
Plijournal@googlemail.com